Jewish Fundamentalism
and the Temple Mount

D1613419

Jewish Fundamentalism and the Temple Mount

Who Will Build the Third Temple?

By
Motti Inbari

Translated by
Shaul Vardi

Published by State University of New York Press, Albany

For information, contact State University of New York Press, Albany, NY
www.sunypress.edu

Production by Kelli W. LeRoux
Marketing by Fran Keneston

Library of Congress Cataloging-in-Publication Data
Inbari, Motti.
    [Fundamentalizm Yehudi ve-Har ha-bayit. English]
    Jewish fundamentalism and the Temple Mount : who will build the Third
Temple? / Motti Inbari.
        p. cm. — (Suny series in Israeli studies)
    Includes bibliographical references and index.
    ISBN 978-1-4384-2623-5 (hardcover : alk. paper)
    ISBN 978-1-4384-2624-2 (pbk. : alk. paper)   1. Temple Mount (Jerusalem)
2. Religious Zionism—Israel.   3. Jewish fundamentalism—Political aspects—
Israel.   4. Israel—Politics and government—21st century.   5. Messianic era
(Judaism)   6. Judaism—Relations—Christianity.   7. Christianity and other
religions—Judaism.   I. Title.
    DS109.28.I5313 2009
    296.4'82—dc22

                                                                    2008036209

10 9 8 7 6 5 4 3 2 1

Contents

Acknowledgments

For the past ten years I have been studying active messianic movements in modern-day Israel. I joined End of Days cults, I interviewed "prophets," and I demonstrated at the gates of the Temple Mount. I witnessed the strength of millennial expectations, followed by the failure of prophecies and the subsequent decline of messianic faith.

So, why is a secular Jew who comes from a leftist, almost antireligious, family involving himself with people so enchanted by religious dreams and aspirations? Truthfully, I was drawn to this study by accident.

In 1994, as a junior freelance journalist, I was assigned by my editor, along with my wife who was also a reporter, to explore the story of a strange new phenomenon. A rabbi named Uzi Meshulam, who lived in a small town near Tel-Aviv, had organized a violent demonstration with his followers that started when they barricaded themselves inside Meshulam's home. The police eventually broke into the house after they had had it under siege for forty-seven days. As journalists, we came to the conclusion that this group was fueled by acute messianic expectations that encouraged them in their violent behavior; they believed that the messiah would come to rescue them.

During this time, I had started graduate studies at the Institute for Contemporary Jewry at the Hebrew University of Jerusalem. The incident so interested me that I wanted to investigate it further, so I decided to take a course on messianism. I enrolled in a seminar with Jonathan Frankel and I wrote a paper based on what I had witnessed during the unfortunate affair. That seminar paper later became my master's thesis.

In 2001 I began doctoral studies at the Hebrew University of Jerusalem. Under the supervision of Jonathan Frankel and Menachem Feidman, I started a new project that became my doctoral dissertation. The book you are holding now is a revised version of that study.

I wish to express my gratitude to many people who have taught me and assisted me in the years in which I prepared this work.

I consider it a great honor to be the student of the late Professor Jonathan Frankel, who has guided my academic studies for more than ten years. With his help I learned how to conduct research and produce academic papers.

I am also grateful to have Menachem Friedman as an adviser for this study. It is an honor for me to thank Eliyahu Schliffer for reading the draft manuscript. His advice was essential to the success of the work. I am also fortunate to have the support of generous colleagues including Yaakov Ariel, who shared his expertise, critical insights, and friendship, and Kenneth Wald, who offered dedication and devotion to my research. The same goes for Israel Bartal. I wish to express my gratitude to Dov Schwartz, Yoram Bilu, Maria Leppakari, Ted Sasson and Gerald Murray. Their insights and collegiality were of major importance.

I would like to express my thanks to the following institutions for their generous grants: the Cherrick Center for the Study of Zionism at the Hebrew University; the Tami Schtinemitz Center for Peace Studies at Tel-Aviv University; the Francis Gunter Prize in the Study of Jerusalem and its Environs; the Ben-Shemen Best Dissertation Award for the Study of Zionism and the State of Israel; and the Dorot Fellowship from the Jerusalem campus of the Hebrew Union College. I send special thanks to Dr. Mitchell G. Bard and the American-Israeli Cooperative Enterprise and the Schusterman Family Foundation for supporting my postgraduate studies and granting me the best publication award in Israel Studies.

This research was conducted with the support of several of the activists studied in this book. I would like to thank Rabbi Yossef Elboim, Baruch Ben-Yossef, Gershon Salomon, Yehuda Etzion, Yoel Lerner, and Hillel Weiss.

It is a pleasure to thank the Institute for Contemporary Jewry at the Hebrew University of Jerusalem. It was, and still is, my intellectual home. I am grateful for the support of the Center for Jewish Studies at the University of Florida that granted me the Schusterman Visiting Assistant Professorship that allowed me to translate and revise this research. I wish also to thank the Schusterman Center for Israel Studies at Brandeis University, headed by a dear colleague and friend, Dr. Ilan Troen, for granting me a postdoctoral fellowship that allowed me to finish preparing this book.

I am pleased to have the State University of New York Press as my publisher. I especially appreciate Russel Stone, editor for the series in Israel Studies.

Finally, I owe thanks to my wife Aliza for her patience and support over the long haul. Without her encouragement, advice, and gentle prodding, this work would not have reached publication. To her and to our children, Shani and Shir, I dedicate this book.

Portions of the first chapter are reprinted by the permission of Indiana University Press. Originally published as "Religious Zionism and the Temple Mount Dilemma," *Israel Studies* 12, no. 1 (2007): 29–47.

Portions of the fifth chapter are reprinted by the permission of the *Hebrew Union College Annual.* Originally published as "The Oslo Accords and the Temple Mount: A Case Study—the Movement for the Establishment of the Temple," *Hebrew Union College Annual* 74 (2003): 279–323.

Introduction

The Temple Mount is the most sacred site of Judaism and the third most sacred site of Islam, after Mecca and Medina in Saudi Arabia. The sacred nature of the site has made it one of the main foci of tension and friction in the context of the Israeli-Arab conflict.[1]

The year 1996 marked an important milestone in the world of Religious Zionism. The Committee of Yesha Rabbis (a group of Orthodox rabbis from the settlements in Judea, Samaria, and the Gaza Strip) ruled that Jews are permitted and even encouraged to enter the Temple Mount. The committee imposed restrictions regarding specific areas where entry is permitted, and urged visitors to undertake special ritual purification before doing so. Nevertheless, every rabbi was encouraged "to go up [to the Temple Mount] himself, and to guide his congregants on how to do so in accordance with all the constrictions of Halacha (Jewish religious law)."[2] Since 2003, when the Temple Mount was reopened to Jewish visitors after a three-year closure due to the Al-Aqsa Intifada, this ruling has been put into practice. Every day, dozens, if not hundreds, of Jews, mainly students from the nationalist yeshivas, visit the Temple Mount and engage in solitary prayer.[3] According to Israel Police records, some seventy thousand Jews visited the site between November 2003 and October 2004[4]—an average of six thousand visitors a month.

The ruling by the Committee of Yesha Rabbis is contrary to longstanding religious edicts, to the position of the leaders of the Mercaz Harav yeshiva, to the position of the Chief Rabbinate, and to the opinion of the majority of Haredi rabbis. All these authorities argue that it is a grave religious transgression for Jews to enter the Temple Mount. According to Halacha, all Jews are considered impure because they have been in contact with the dead, either directly or with others who have been in such

1

contact. During the Temple Period (536 BCE–70 CE) Jews were cleansed of this impurity by virtue of the "sin water"—the ashes of the red heifer mixed in water. Since the destruction of the Second Temple, red heifers have not been available. Moreover, the precise dimensions of the Temple have been lost, including the location of the Kodesh Kodashim—the most sacred site—identified as the dwelling place of the Shechina, the Divine Presence. Entry into this section was absolutely prohibited, with the exception of the High Priest (who was cleansed with the sin water before performing his sacred duties) on the Day of Atonement. Since the location of the Temple is no longer known, and since red heifers are unavailable, it was ruled that Jews are prohibited from entering the entire Temple Mount area, even though this area is known to be bigger than that of the Temple itself. Accordingly, a person who enters the Temple Mount area incurs the (theoretical) penalty of *Karet* (the divinely imposed death penalty). This position that prohibits Jews from entering the Temple Mount has been supported in numerous Halachic rulings.[5]

While the rabbinic prohibition defused the interreligious tension on the Temple Mount, the declared purpose of the ruling issued by the Yesha Council was to change the status quo on the site. This was manifested in a dramatic manner after the opening of the Mount in 2003, as thousands of students from the nationalist yeshivot flooded to the site. An explanation must be provided regarding this development in the Orthodox Jewish world.

This book discusses the changes that have occurred in Israeli religious society regarding the question of the Temple Mount and the vision of rebuilding the Temple, as part of an idea of establishing a theocracy over the secular state. The book ends with the examination of the theological responses to the implementation of the Disengagement Plan (2005). These changes are partly the result of an ongoing campaign that has been waged by several institutions in the Orthodox world that advocate the construction of the Third Temple. The study presents those movements, identifies their historical and ideological roots, and describes the nature of their public activities. This examination relates to the following movements and organizations: the Temple Institute, headed by Rabbi Israel Ariel; Yehuda Etzion and the "Chai Vekayam" movement; the Temple Mount Faithful, led by Gershon Salomon; the Movement for the Establishment of the Temple, headed by Rabbi Yosef Elboim; and Rabbi Yitzhak Ginzburg and his students from the "Od Yosef Chai" yeshiva.

The Temple Mount: Historical Background

The Temple Mount is the holiest site for Judaism. The Jewish Temple in Jerusalem stood there: the First Temple (built circa 967 BCE, destroyed circa

586 BCE by the Babylonians), and the Second Temple (rebuilt circa 516 BCE, destroyed in the siege of Jerusalem by the Romans in 70 CE). According to a commonly held belief in Judaism, it is to be the site of the final Third Temple to be rebuilt with the coming of the Jewish Messiah. Known to Muslims as the Noble Sanctuary, it is also the site of two major Muslim religious shrines: the Dome of the Rock (built circa 690 BCE) and Al-Aqsa Mosque (built circa 710 BCE).

According to an *Aggadah* (legend) in the Talmud, the world was created from the Foundation Stone on the Temple Mount (Babylonian Talmud Yoma 54b). And in the Bible, it is written that upon the cessation of a plague King David purchased a threshing floor owned by Aravnah the Jebusite on which to erect an altar. He wanted to construct a permanent temple there, but as his hands were "bloodied," he was forbidden to do so himself, so this task was left to his son Solomon, who completed the task (2 Sam. 24:18–25).

Around 19 BCE, Herod the Great expanded the Temple Mount and rebuilt the Temple. In the course of the First Jewish-Roman War, it was destroyed by Titus in 70 CE. The Romans did not topple the Western Wall (also known as the Kotel). The Western Wall is holy because of its proximity to the location on the Temple Mount of the Holy of Holies of the Temple, the most holy place in Judaism. Due to Jewish religious restrictions on entering the most sacred areas of the Temple Mount, the Western Wall has become, for practical purposes, the holiest generally accessible site for Jews to pray. Upon the destruction of the Temple, the Rabbis revised prayers, and introduced new ones to request the speedy rebuilding of the Temple and the city of Jerusalem.[6]

The primary reason for the importance of the Temple Mount is the Muslim belief that in 621 BCE Muhammad arrived there after a miraculous nocturnal journey aboard the winged steed named Buraq to take a brief tour of heaven with the Archangel Gabriel. This happened during Muhammad's time in Mecca, years before Muslims conquered Jerusalem (638 BCE).

After the Muslim conquest of this region, the Temple Mount became known to Muslims as al-Haram al-Sharif (the Noble Sanctuary). In 690 BCE an octagonal Muslim building topped by a dome was built around the rock, which became known as the Dome of the Rock.

In 715 BCE the Umayyads built the al-Masjid al-Aqsa, the Al-Aqsa Mosque or the "furthest mosque," corresponding to the Muslim belief of Muhammad's miraculous nocturnal journey as recounted in the Qur'an and hadith.[7]

Until the Six-Day War (June 1967), when Israel conquered the site, the question of Jews entering the Temple Mount was purely theoretical. Since the thirteenth century, Jews had not, on the whole, entered the Temple Mount because of rabbinical prohibition and because those controlling the site (particularly the Muslim authorities) did not permit Jews to enter. In the thirteenth century the Muslim authorities ruled that non-Muslims were not allowed to enter the site, and a death penalty was sentenced for disobeying the rule.[8]

During the nineteenth century a number of Jews visited the Temple Mount, but the traditional Jewish community in Palestine sought to prevent such visits because of the religious prohibition. After Israel's War of Independence (1948), the Temple Mount was left under Jordanian control, and Jews were not allowed to enter the old city of Jerusalem. The status of the site changed only after it was taken by the Israeli Defense Forces (IDF) in June 1967.

Since the 1967 war, Israeli governments have always sought to mitigate the tension raised by this subject, allowing the Muslim Waqf to maintain its control of the Temple Mount. The status quo arrangement that was introduced by Moshe Dayan (Israel's minister of security at the time), following the occupation of the holy sites stated that the Temple Mount would continue to serve as a Muslim place of prayer, while the Western Wall would be a Jewish place of prayer. Under this arrangement Jews and Christians are permitted to visit the site. As a security measure the Israeli government has agreed to enforce a ban on non-Muslim prayer on the site. In 1968, the Israel Supreme Court decided not to intervene in the question of Jewish prayer on the Mount, ruling that this was a political issue rather than a judicial one. The court permitted the Israel Police to establish procedures for entry into the Temple Mount on the basis of security considerations.[9]

Since the occupation of the Temple Mount by IDF forces in the Six-Day War, however, a number of groups within Israeli society have demanded a change in the passive approach of the Jewish religious establishment and the Israeli government on the question of the site. These groups advocate action to end Muslim control of the site and to start a process what will lead into the establishment of the Third Temple. This book describes those groups.

Orthodoxy and the Temple Mount: Historical and Sociological Background

Since around the middle of the nineteenth century, a new discourse began to emerge among a number of Jewish religious authorities that anticipated the renewal of the religious rites on the Temple Mount. This narrative was a result of the perception that modern times carry a divine sign of the ultimate redemption. Thus, Tzevi Hirsch Kalischer (1796–1874) was the first to suggest the renewal of the Passover Sacrifice on the Temple Mount because this ceremony can be preformed by a layman and does not require the appointment of priests.[10]

At the beginning of the twentieth century, several Orthodox leaders advocated the resumption of study of the Talmudic tractates relating to the sacrifices. Israel Meir Hacohen of Radin—the Hafetz Haim—ordered his followers to start studying the Kodashim order to prepare for the immanent redemption. In 1921, Rabbi Avraham Yitzhak Hacohen Kook established Torat Cohanim yeshiva in the Muslim Quarter of the Old City of Jerusalem. Members of the traditional priestly caste studied those tractates in the yeshiva as part of their anticipation of the arrival of the Messiah (this topic is discussed at length in chapter 1).

A different approach may be found in the teachings of Rabbi Hayyim Hirschensohn (1857–1935), a unique philosopher who attempted to combine Jewish religious law with the values of democracy. Hirschensohn emigrated from Palestine to Hoboken, New Jersey, where he was hired as a chief rabbi.[11] The Balfour Declaration (1917) supporting the Zionist goal of establishing a Jewish "national home" in Palestine created a vast wave of enthusiasm among many Jews. In 1919, Hirschensohn published his book *Malki Ba-Kodesh*, presenting the idea that a House of Peace be established on the Temple Mount to function as a "Court of Nations." This institution was not perceived as a Temple or a synagogue in the traditional sense, but would serve as a house of prayer for all the nations (in keeping with Isa. 56:7). The institution was to enjoy supreme authority over the Court of Peace in The Hague and the League of Nations. It would represent a universal vision of peace, where all nations would live next to each other in harmony, as prophesized in the Bible.[12]

In addition to the religious statements summarized earlier, a secular approach also developed. During the second half of the twentieth century, the adherents of the Lechi movement (known also as the Stern Gang) an armed underground Zionist faction in the Palestine Mandate, discussed the construction of the Third Temple as part of their nationalist ideology. However, they viewed the Temple as a national symbol rather than a center for religious practice. In the Principles for Revival (1940, 1941), the manifesto of the movement, this last principle was articulated as follows: "The building of the Third House as a symbol of the new area of total redemption." According to Zeev Ivinsky, it should not be assumed that Yair Stern, the leader of Lechi, took a traditionalist position on this issue. Rather, he perceived the Third Temple as a manifestation of admiration for Hebrew religion and culture, as part of the future Kingdom of Israel. Ivinsky also stated that Lechi leaders such as Eliyaho Lankin and Shlomo Ben-Shlomo were opposed to the inclusion of this chapter in the manifesto in view of the secular nature of the movement.[13]

Another approach, which was a synthesis of religiosity and nationalism, was embodied by the Brith HaChashmonaim youth movement. This movement was established in 1937; its followers volunteered in the Lechi underground movement. The movement advocated the establishment of a Jewish theocracy. They argued that the exile of Jews from their homeland had distorted true religious practice; accordingly, the return of the Jews to their land requires the repair of their faith. This can only be achieved by observing all of the commandments of the Halacha. Thus, the establishment of the Temple was perceived as part of the organic observance of Jewish law. After the establishment of the State of Israel this movement was dismantled and its followers were integrated in the Mizrachi movement, the Religious Zionist organization. The unique feature of the movement was its combination of a radical nationalistic vision and zealous adherence to the Halacha.[14]

All the different approaches to the Temple Mount were dramatically changed after the site was conquered by IDF soldiers during the Six-Day War. During the postwar period we can detect two major developments in the religious approaches. The first contains several key trends: a demand to pray on the mount, a demand to make the Mount the center of Jewish nationhood, and several operational plans to blow up the mosques on the Temple Mount to facilitate full redemption. The second development focused on education, seeking to change opinions in the Religious Zionist public regarding the question of building the Third Temple.

This book focuses on the second development, although it also contains a short discussion of the prestate period and the impact of the Six-Day War. The focus on the past two decades enables an examination of the growing public interest in this phenomenon and the intensification of related activities—processes that in turn permit the location of sources for the study.

Orthodoxy and Zionism

Before discussing the issue of the Temple Mount and the demand to change its status, it is important to review the enormous changes that have occurred within Orthodox Judaism on the broader subject of messianism and Zionism. This theoretical discussion is important in order to understand the demand to build the Temple and to appreciate the unique nature of the phenomenon examined by this study.

The central foundation of classical Orthodoxy was the principle of passivity. According to Jacob Katz, all three types of Orthodoxy that emerged in the late nineteenth century in Germany, Russia, and Hungary shared this principle, which was a hallmark of Jewish society in the premodern era: "This was far reaching passivity with respect to long range planning for the future of the Jewish community." With the exile from their homeland, the Jewish people lost faith in their capacity to engineer their redemption. This change could come only as the result of Divine and miraculous intervention.

The modern era brought new opportunities for Jews: emancipation, emigration, and in 1948 the establishment of a Jewish state. However, Orthodoxy—or more exactly, Haredim (ultra-Orthodoxy)—seemed reluctant to free itself from its premodern mentality, and refrained from taking a leading role in any of these enterprises. In the case of the Jewish national movement, the Haredi leadership found theological justifications for its opposition. It is true that other voices could be heard, most notably those of Rabbi Avraham Yitzhak Hacohen Kook, but his support of Zionism was rejected by most of the Haredi leadership.[15]

The dominant Haredi theological position continued the tradition of passivity and refused to consider the Zionist enterprise as connected to the process of redemption. For the most part, rabbinic literature did not envisage an interim state between exile and redemption, and in this sense Zionism constituted an illegitimate deviation from the course of history. Moreover, the theological interpretation adopted by some of the most extreme Haredi elements, such as the Eda Haredit and Neturei Karta, views Zionism as no less than the work of the devil, aimed at confusing the Jews and diverting them from their path to redemption. Drawing on mystical and Kabbalistic perceptions, the dramatic historical events undergone by the Jewish people—the Holocaust, the establishment of the State of Israel, and the subsequent dazzling victory in the Six-Day War—were interpreted through the prism of a cosmic struggle between God and the diabolical forces of the Other Side, and all these events were seen as a manifestation of the growing force of evil. Those who took this approach argued that Jewish people would be returned to their homeland and to sovereignty not by their own hand, but only by the Divine hand. Any attempt to "hasten the End" would actually delay the coming of the Messiah and the ultimate redemption. Accordingly, they were fiercely opposed to the Zionist entity, and refused to recognize it or to participate in its institutions. Aviezer Ravitzky has argued that while this group is considered to represent a small minority of the Haredim, its moral influence extends far beyond its inner circle.[16]

Orthodox Zionism (commonly referred to as Religious Zionism) continued the ideological approach of Rabbi Kook, coloring the development of the Zionist enterprise with a messianic dimension through its definition as the "the first stage of our redemption," and attaching innate religious significance to secular and even heretical actions. According to this approach, the time would come when secularity would give way to sanctity, and the final process of redemption would then be possible.[17] In 1974 the Gush Emunim (Bloc of the Faithful) movement was established. Comprised of Orthodox youth and the graduates of Orthodox Zionist yeshivot, Gush Emunim presented a much sharper version of this position, claiming that they knew God's will, and that by settling all the parts of the biblical Land of Israel conquered in the 1967 war, they could expedite the end and bring redemption nearer.[18]

Thus, within the reality of the State of Israel, Orthodoxy, which had begun as a passive doctrine, became an active and aggressive force, at least among some of its exponents. Manifestations of this change can be found not only within Religious Zionism, such as in Gush Emunim, but also in other sectors, such as the developments within the Chabad Hassidic movement since the early 1990s. The Chabad movement has become a key advocate of the Greater Land of Israel, and has also been swept into a radical messianic approach that identifies its late leader, Menachem-Mendel Schneerson, as the King Messiah. Many members of Chabad fervently anticipate his return from death and his ultimate coronation as Messiah. David Berger has even argued that the majority of Chabad shares this position despite the fact that in theological terms it is closer to Christianity than to Judaism, recalling the Christian doctrine that Jesus the Messiah was crucified, died, and resurrected, and will return at the end of history.[19] Additional manifestations of Orthodox extremism may be found in the increasing support among Haredi circles for fundamentalist and theocratic ideologies such as that of the Kach movement, a far-right political party in Israel founded by Rabbi Meir Kahane. Neri Horwitz argues that the connection between Religious Zionist activism and Haredi radicalism creates the potential for fundamentalism. He believes that the processes of fragmentation already at work within the Haredi society may provide a fertile breeding ground for the "fanatical potion," which blends the activism of Religious Zionism—without the restraint that comes from the identification of Israel as "absolute sanctity" and hence without the commitment to the State of Israel and its laws—with Haredi radicalism, without the restraint of its former passivity.[20] A study of voting patterns among the Haredi public in the Knesset elections suggests that this trend is expanding, leading to the systematic loss of votes for the Haredi parties in favor of other parties. For example, the elections for the Sixteenth Knesset (2003) produced a high level of support among the Haredi party for a political list identified with the Kach movement, who developed a fiercely nationalistic religious theology.[21]

These extremist tendencies created the space within which the movements for the Third Temple could function. Since their followers come mostly from Religious Zionist circles, it is important to explain briefly the changes that have occurred among this population.

From its establishment, Religious Zionism stood between two hostile camps: secular Zionism and non-Zionist or anti-Zionist Orthodoxy. Religious Zionism sought to bridge the gap between them while presenting a model of Orthodox religiosity in the framework of Zionist commitment. Its position between the other two groups put Religious Zionism in a weak position; on the one hand, the political leadership of the Zionist movement largely ignored the demands and needs of the religious camp.[22] On the other hand, their religious institutions did not manage to develop significant religious scholarly works, and it was difficult for them to find teachers for the religious studies. Many of the young adults left the camp—either to Haredim or to secularism.[23]

The younger generation of the National Religious camp sought to free themselves from what they considered the inferiority complex of their parents' generation and to assume a leading role in Israeli society. Their opportunity came after the Six-Day War.

The Israeli victory in the war led to the strengthening of the activist wing of Religious Zionism, which was dominated mainly by the younger generation of the National Religious Party.[24] In the course of the war, areas of the biblical homeland were occupied by the IDF, and Motte Gur, the commander of the Paratrooper Division, made the famous declaration that "the Temple Mount is in our hands." These dramatic events created a groundswell of opinion that would later fuel the establishment of the Gush Emunim settlement movement. Although the movement was only established in 1974, it quickly became the dominant stream within Religious Zionism.[25]

Support for the settlement drive in the Territories united the Religious Zionist camp, which tended henceforth to focus on this issue. Many Religious Zionists viewed their pioneering acts in the settlements as tools of leadership for the entire state. Beginning in the 1990s, however, those channels were blocked as the result of the political process starting from the Madrid talks (1991), and later the Oslo Process (1993) and the establishment of the Palestinian Authority. Above all, Israel's Disengagement Plan (2005) led to the uprooting of all the Israeli settlements in the Gaza Strip, as well as four settlements in northern Samaria. Therefore, the energies of leadership were forced to be channeled to other directions.

These challenges have resulted in a number of conflicting developments within the religious camp. One trend is increased liberalism in religious practice. During the past two decades there has been a gradual improvement in the status of women within the religious institutions. More women pursue religious studies and women have also entered the rabbinical courts as rabbinic pleaders and have served on religious councils.[26]

Conversely, signs of increased extremism can also be seen, particularly in terms of the abandonment of the perception of the State of Israel as a holy institution; this trend in public discourse has been particularly prominent since the Disengagement Plan. A further example is the emergence of the phenomenon of the Youth of the Hills.

The basic argument of the Merkaz Harav yeshiva, a leading religious institution within this community established by Rabbi Kook (the father), is that the ingathering of Jews in the State of Israel is a manifestation of God's will to redeem His people. Israel's victories are considered revelations of the divine plan. Accordingly, the followers of Merkaz Harav have emphasized two key concepts: the holiness of the Land of Israel and the holiness of the State of Israel. According to Rabbi Zvi Yehuda Hacohen Kook (the son) (1891–1982), the leader of this institution, the Land of Israel is one unity, a complete organic entity imbued with its own will and holiness. This entity is connected and united with the entire Jewish people— present, past and future—so that the people and the land are in a complete oneness. Therefore, no one has a right to give away any parts of the land because it does not belong any more to one group than to another.[27]

This unity came as a result of the actions of the Zionist movement. Therefore, if the tool to implement God's will can be found in Jewish nationality, then the Israeli state should be sanctified as part of the messianic process, even if it is secular.[28]

According to the Merkaz Harav philosophy, these two sanctities are expected to complement and complete each other. This has not always been reflected in Israeli reality, however. After the peace process between Israel and Egypt (1978) and the Israeli withdrawal from Sinai (1982), many Gush Emunim supporters were forced to confront the increasing erosion of their basic beliefs regarding the character and destiny of the State of Israel. The Israeli withdrawal from Sinai, and the subsequent Madrid talks and Oslo Process, which led to an Israeli withdrawal from parts of Judea and Samaria, provoked a profound theological crisis that was intensified by the demolition of Jewish settlements during the Disengagement. The fundamentalist religious dilemma is of a profound character: how can a state that uproots settlements and hands over parts of the biblical Land of Israel to Arab rule be considered "absolutely sacred?" What sublime religious meaning can be attributed to the actions of a secular state unaware of its purpose of serving as "the foundation for God's throne in the world," which threatens to destroy by its own hands the chance of realizing the messianic hope?

These sentiments led many rabbinical authorities of Gush Emunim to reconsider their attitude regarding the sanctity of the State of Israel and the nature of the actions required to expedite the redemption process. This aspect is elaborated on in the concluding chapter.

One of the manifestations of these ongoing ideological crises can be found in the development of a new phenomenon among the young generation of the Religious Zionist camp—the Youth of the Hills. This group is estimated to number a few hundred activists. They represent the second generation of settlers in Judea and Samaria, but their behavior and ideology differ dramatically from those of the parent generation that founded Gush Emunim. These young people are leaving their educational institutions and isolating themselves in the hills of Judea and Samaria. According to Shlomo

Kaniel, this group reflects a crisis in the Religious Zionist education that is the result of the dissonance between modernity and self-fulfillment and the religious way of life that demands commitment to the halachic world. This group is well known for its lack of regard for authority and its radical ideology (this subject will be discussed in chapter 6).[29]

These trends of change in the Orthodox world have fueled the emergence of the movements for the Temple Mount, and this is the background against which they should be considered. First, however, a brief definition of the main terms used in the book is called for.

Definitions

Over the past two decades or so, there has been substantial growth in the strength of religious movements that are commonly termed "fundamentalist" and that seek to manifest their religious faith in the political arena. This process is often characterized as a counterreaction to broader processes of modernization and globalization.

A comparative study on fundamentalism by the American Academy of Arts and Sciences founded several components that have "family resemblance." Fundamentalism was defined as a spiritual phenomenon that was created as a counterreaction to secularism, which threatened the very existence of religion. Thus, this reaction is not just a conventional response, but it holds characteristics of a cosmic battle of good and evil. The fundamentalists are afraid to lose their struggle, and they therefore tend to retreat from society and form their own enclaves. Their retreat is not escapism, but an attempt to strengthen their position in preparation for an assault on secular society. This assault will employ modern tools; while they may reject modern philosophy, they use modernity to disseminate their message. Fundamentalist movements will also tend to become messianic; since they claim to know the ways of God, they also claim to know the path for redemption.[30]

Another term that needs to be explained is "messianism." Our discussion will adopt the definitions proposed by Dov Schwartz, which distinguish between apocalyptic and naturalistic Jewish messianisms.

Apocalyptic messianism is not merely "miraculous" or "supernatural," but refers to a profound and basic transformation in the cosmos, amounting to its very demolition and reconstruction. Divine providence plays a crucial role in a dazzling messianic sequence with strong mythological overtones. Naturalistic messianism challenges the assumption that the end of the world is a requirement for redemption. According to this approach, hope should not be abandoned that this present world can be repaired, and accordingly it is wrong to seek to establish a new world out of the ruins of the present one. This approach lessens, and sometimes completely removes, direct Divine intervention as a force in the process of redemption.

The visions in the biblical, Talmudic, and Midrashic sources prophesized a day of vengeance and reprisal, and anticipated a totally transformed world for those who fear God (and, in most cases, only for the Jews among them). A popular perception anticipated a great and terrible Day of the Lord on which He would wreak vengeance on the Gentiles for the suffering they had caused to His Chosen People. Intellectual Judaism struggled to counter this dramatic approach through authorities (such as Maimonides, the Rashba, and others) who confronted the apocalyptic stream. An effort was made to soften the messianic descriptions and to give them a universal and enlightened quality. The apocalyptic approach despaired of the potential of this world to bring redemption, and instead established an imaginary new world. By contrast, the naturalistic approach believes that the messianic era will occur within history, and not on its collapse. The world will continue to function normally, and the essence of redemption will lie in the establishment of a just authority and society—a future world that will devote its energy and resources to cultural development and to spiritual and intellectual productivity.[31]

Fundamentalist movements that hold a messianic belief and view themselves as leading toward the End of Days could adopt apocalyptic or naturalistic perceptions. For example, American fundamentalists follow the Dispensational theory. They believe that this earthly reality is at the point of collapse. The events of the End of Days are about to begin, even if it is still not known exactly when they will occur, and the world we currently know will be destroyed, paving way for the Second Coming. The only way to survive the horrors of the apocalypse is by accepting Jesus as a personal messiah. Only the true believers can escape the Great Tribulations and remain intact. Therefore, the activities of American Christian fundamentalists are driven from a sense of urgency to save humanity by accepting the Christian faith.[32]

Contrary to these apocalyptic approaches, other fundamentalist movements adhere to the naturalistic approach. An example can be found in the school that developed from the Merkaz Harav yeshiva and the Gush Emunim movement. Driven by the Kook family philosophy, the followers of this movement claimed that the creation of secular Zionism is a divine sign of full redemption. Full redemption itself, however, can come only after secular Jews acknowledge the errors of their ways and repent. Only then can redemption be fulfilled by establishing a Torah state and adopting religious law. The way to expedite redemption, according to the Gush Emunim movement, is by promoting the settlement enterprise in the West Bank and the Gaza Strip and by strengthening a repentance movement among the seculars.[33]

Another term I employ in this study is "cognitive dissonance." When applied to messianic movements, this familiar sociological theory argues that a crisis caused by prophetic failure may paradoxically reinforce, rather than weaken, religious faith. The failure of the prophecy, which might in logical terms be expected to have led to a weakening of confidence in its accuracy, sometimes creates the completely opposite phenomenon, with a strengthening of religious belief and practice, in an effort to set the messianic process back on course. This theory is founded in the assertion that an individual will attempt to maintain his or her faith. When someone who believes wholeheartedly in something—is committed to this belief and has even taken irreversible actions on the basis of this belief—is confronted with ostensibly irrefutable evidence contradicting the erroneous belief, the individual may strengthen his or her faith, and invest renewed efforts in convincing others that his or her worldview is accurate.[34]

This theory, developed over half a century ago, has been the subject of lively academic debate. Criticism focuses on the argument that the major tool for coping with failed prophecy is to convert others to the faith. Subsequent research has shown that not all movements cope with failure by proselytizing to others.[35] However, none of the studies in the field have challenged the basic claim that millenarian movements have to find logical explanations for their failed prophecies that reaffirm their faith; this is the only way for them to maintain their belief system.[36]

In this study, I examine the question of whether a failure of faith can lead to strengthening of messianic belief. The preconditions, however, are different from all those who studied it before. The cognitive dissonance theory emphasizes that to get into that situation, a messianic movement must accept fully its miscalculations. Also the following research examined the situation in which it was absolutely proven that the calculations were wrong. Therefore, what happens when failed prophecy is not yet proven? Can we still also detect a cognitive dissonance in a place where there is a fear of failure, but in which it was not absolutely proven? Can a messianic movement that holds a naturalistic vision without end dates come into a dissonance?

In this book, I raise an assumption that messianic radicalization can be a counterreaction. The facts on the ground that prove a gap between faith and reality create a process of radicalization, to impose the faith on the reality. The fear of losing creates a dissonance that leads into messianic radicalization.

Other Publications Written on the Subject

Over the past two decades there have been dramatic changes in the attitude of the Religious Zionist population over the question of entering the Temple Mount and promoting the ideal of reestablishing the Third

Temple. Those changes became more visible during the last decade, after the emergence of the Oslo Process.

However, when I started my research, I was surprised to find out how limited the scholarly work is on the subject. Moreover, much of it was not up-to-date. Even the semiacademic literature, written in the journalistic jargon, did not study the last decade.

To date, no comprehensive academic study has been published relating to the Temple Mount groups and including attention to the events of the 1990s and the first years of the new millennium. The present book aims to fill this gap.

Two important journalistic works about the Temple Mount have appeared, however. In 1995, journalist Nadav Shragai published his book *Mount of Dispute* in Hebrew.[37] Shragai's work was published a decade ago; the present study includes attention to an extensive and highly significant period in activities relating to the Temple Mount and the Third Temple, including discussion of the ramifications of the Oslo Process. Another work is *The End of Days*, by journalist Gershom Gornberg.[38] This work focuses on the connection between fundamentalist and premillenarian Christianity and the idea of rebuilding the Temple, and pays less attention to the Jewish groups that have demanded the rebuilding of the Temple. Gornberg reports on the latter groupings in a more factual and journalistic manner, without the systematic and analytical approach I attempt to bring to the present study.

Accordingly, this book exposes movements, individuals, and opinions that have received little research attention to date, and provides an additional strand in professional knowledge relating to contemporary religious society in Israel, and extreme right-wing circles in particular. It also delineates the different attitudes toward the Temple Mount, showing the connections between the different trends and revealing the inherent potential for subversion and violence.

This book places the subject of the Temple Mount at the center of discussion relating to contemporary Orthodox Judaism and it presents an examination of a political process underway that is contributing to changing religious law and to overcoming the grave prohibition against Jews entering the Temple Mount area. It also reveals the growing penetration of the Temple Mount issue among diverse population groups, and the manner in which the question of Jews entering and worshipping on the Temple Mount has become an issue of utmost importance.

The research will also make a contribution to the study of the place of the Temple Mount in Zionist ideology, an issue that has been largely ignored. This issue will be raised in the context of the fundamentalist and messianic right-wing.

How I Conducted the Research

Locating sources for this study—which relates to small, extremist, and semiclandestine groups—was one of the main problems I faced during the research stage. Regrettably, the publications of the groups examined are rarely to be found in libraries and archives; accordingly, I was obliged to locate them independently.

I gathered much of the reference material through active participation in the groups that formed the subject of the research. During the course of my work, I participated in religious classes, demonstrations, visits to the Temple Mount, ceremonies held by the gates to the Mount, political conventions, seminars and study days, working meetings of the Temple Admirers and the Committee of Yesha Rabbis, prayer services, and fund-raising evenings. During and after these events, I held extensive conversations with other participants in a relaxed and noncommittal atmosphere. I also held formal interviews with various individuals, including current members of the organizations and others who had since left these groups.

Above all, however, the study is based on the written materials produced by the various groups, to which I gained access thanks to the contacts I developed with activists in the Temple movements.

The Structure of This Book

Chapter 1 offers an introduction to the question of Jews entering the Temple Mount among Religious Zionist circles, in general. It describes the positions of the Mercaz Harav yeshiva and examines the debate on the question of entering the Temple Mount within the Israeli Chief Rabbinate. This is followed by a discussion of the decision by the Yesha Council. The chapter's conclusions form the foundation for our subsequent inquiries.

Chapter 2 describes the activities of the Temple Institute, a central and leading body in Temple Mount circles. It examines the circumstances that led to the establishment of this institution, the activities it undertakes, and the ways in which the Religious Zionist mainstream views the institute.

Chapter 3 presents the political establishment of the Temple Mount builders. It begins by examining the work of Yehuda Etzion, best known for his involvement in a plot to blow up the mosques on the Temple Mount. Etzion based his ideology on the writings of Shabbtai Ben Dov (1924–1979), a largely forgotten member of the Lechi underground movement who elaborated a practical plan for transforming Israel from a parliamentary democracy into a religious theocracy. This chapter also includes a discussion of Ben Dov's ideology.

The following chapters focus on movements situated on the periphery of Religious Zionism. Chapter 4 examines the Temple Mount Faithful movement, established by Gershon Salomon in the late 1960s. This movement differs from the others examined here in its institutional, religious, and political behavior.

Chapter 5 discusses the Movement for the Establishment of the Temple, which was established by a Belzer Chasid by the name of Yosef Elboim in 1988. Its activists come from the Haredi neighborhoods of Jerusalem, and are joined by a number of Kach activists. The main significance of this movement has been the development of a worldview that combines messianic activism with strict adherence to the Haredi way of life.

Chapter 6 discusses in depth the worldview of Rabbi Yitzhak Ginsburg and his students from the "Od Yosef Chai" yeshiva in Yizhar. Ginsburg is considered the leading religious authority of the extreme right. His actions reflect a sense of messianic urgency.

The conclusion considers the influence of the Temple Mount movements within the broader public. The reactions to the Disengagement Plan are taken as a case study for examining the penetration of their theocratic narrative.

At first glance, the subject of my research may seem esoteric, restricted to marginal groups within Israeli society. From a broader perspective, however, it should be noted that this subject is not confined to the esoteric sectarianism of small groups, but extends far beyond. While these groups are indeed considered to represent a small minority of Zionist Orthodoxy, their moral influence extends far beyond its inner circles.

Moreover, the question of the Temple Mount is highly sensitive, with far-reaching political and strategic ramifications that could influence the world peace order. Avi Dichter, until recently the head of the Israeli General Security Service, has commented that the possibility of Jewish extremists launching an attack on the Temple Mount constitutes a key strategic threat to the State of Israel, and that it is right to be extremely concerned about such an eventuality.[39]

Accordingly, the book will examine extremist groups, expanding knowledge of their ideological sources and patterns of behavior. This will contribute to a more precise evaluation of their social and political power. The comparative dimension may also contribute to research into messianism as a general phenomenon that remains powerful in modern times. The study will also offer a further angle for examining the wave of fundamentalism that has swept the Middle East—a phenomenon whose ramifications extend beyond the confines of the Israeli-Arab dispute, impacting on the entire Western world.

1

Religious Zionism and the Temple Mount Dilemma
Key Trends

Since the latter half of the 1990s, a shift can be observed in the Religious Zionist approach to the question of praying on the Temple Mount. The reopening of the Mount to Jewish visitors in 2003, after it was closed for three years, made this change very clear. In May 2007, for example, forty leading rabbis from the National Religious camp visited the Mount, as a declaration of their attachment to the site.[1]

To understand the dynamics of the transformation on this subject, it is worth examining in greater depth the common perceptions among Religious Zionist circles relating to the question of entry into the Temple Mount and the reinstatement of religious worship on the site. To that end, in this chapter I review the key trends among Religious Zionist rabbis on the subject. I begin with a discussion of the approach of the leaders of the Mercaz Harav yeshiva school: Rabbi Avraham Yitzhak Hacohen Kook and his son Zvi Yehuda. Their philosophy has shaped the approach of the majority of rabbinical leaders in contemporary Religious Zionist circles. After the death in 1981 of Zvi Yehuda Kook, leading representatives of this approach include Rabbi Shlomo Aviner and Rabbi Zvi Tau. I then examine the position taken by the Israeli Chief Rabbinate, the supreme Jewish religious governing body in the State of Israel and the Halakhic authority for the state. This historical discussion provides the background for our discussion of contemporary developments, informing our analysis of the changes that have taken place among the approaches of the settler rabbis.

Rabbi Avraham Yitzhak Hacohen Kook
and Merkaz Harav Yeshiva

The activist messianic approach of Religious Zionism, which was fueled
by the vision of Rabbi Avraham Yitzhak Hacohen Kook (1865–1935),
mandated the goal of the reestablishment of the Temple as a key Zionist
objective. Secular reality was perceived as temporary and transient—an
external shell that would later be replaced by a messianic future, whose
overt purpose was the reinstatement of the religious ritual on Mount Moriah.[2] This dialectic was also manifested in the positions of Rabbi Kook on
entering the Temple Mount in the present period and on the construction of the Third Temple.

According to Rabbi Kook, the process of national revival of the Jewish
people was perceived as a Revealed End, and was ultimately due to lead to
the full redemption of Israel, namely, the establishment of the religious kingdom and the renewal of the rites on the Temple Mount. To this end, he established the Torat Cohanim yeshiva in 1921. This institute of religious
higher learning was intended, as its declared intentions stated, to study the
"Talmudic order of Kodashim, the regulation of worship in the Temple, the
commandments that relate to the Land of Israel and the religious laws relating to the state."[3] The yeshiva was founded on the basis of the expectation
that the movement of national revival led by Zionism, which was characterized by a disconnection from religion, would rapidly return to the fold of
sanctity, the completion of ultimate redemption, and the building of the
Temple. As is clear from his pamphlet *Sefatei Cohen* (Lips of a Priest) in which
he described the goals of the new yeshiva, Kook believed that the revival of
the Hebrew nation, despite the fact that it constituted primarily a secular initiative by Jews who rejected religious authority, was nevertheless intended to
secure a sublime spiritual purpose. It would ultimately emerge that the final
purpose of this revival was to bring religious redemption to the Jewish people, the zenith of which is the building of the Temple:

> The anticipation of seeing the priests at their worship and the
> Levites on their stand and Israel in their presence—this is the
> foundation that bears this entire revival.[4]

According to Rabbi Kook, this day was steadily emerging, and preparations must therefore be made. Torat Cohanim yeshiva was thus intended
to attend to the practical preparation of priests and Levites for their worship in the Temple, based on the acute messianic expectation that the
Temple would indeed be built "speedily and in our days." Rabbi Kook may
well have found a precedent for this approach—which demanded that
priests and Levites be prepared for the Temple worship on the basis of

the expectation that redemption was near—in the spiritual heritage of an important Orthodox leader, Israel Meir Hacohen (1838–1933), the author of the *Chafetz Chaim*, who was considered one of the architects of the Orthodox position.[5]

Hacohen's position on the issue was articulated in "The Anticipation of Redemption," which was composed in Radin, Russia, where he lived. The Chafetz Chaim attempted to address the question of the secularization of the Jewish people, and to withstand the powerful attraction of the Hovevei Zion and Zionist movements among the Jewish masses. In his article, which was dominated by a pessimistic sense that Jewish religious values and tradition were being abandoned, the rabbi offered a dialectic interpretation of the phenomenon of secularization, seeing the very weakness of religion as a positive sign. He believed that the period in which he found himself was consonant with the "birth pangs of Messiah"—the period that preceded the ultimate redemption, which is characterized by a serious decline in both spiritual and material terms.[6]

In the face of the Orthodox vulnerability when challenged by the changes of the period and by the pseudomessianic fervor aroused by Theodor Herzl and his Zionist message,[7] the Chafetz Chaim proposed a different messianic program: In previous generations, when affairs were running smoothly, there was no great need to accelerate the process of redemption, since the Torah passed from father to son in an orderly and uninterrupted manner. In the present generation, however, there was a real danger that no one would remain to whom the Torah could be transferred, and traditional Judaism would be obliterated from memory. Accordingly, God must open the eyes of the people through the miracles of redemption. This call seems to have been formulated, in part, as a response to the sense among observant circles that the Jewish masses had abandoned religion and embraced sin to the point that it was no longer worthy of redemption.[8]

The Chafetz Chaim did not confine himself to messianic rhetoric, and sought to show his audience that Torah study also leads to action. To this end, he established a special yeshiva for priests, teaching the Talmudic tractate of Kodashim, which includes sections discussing the Temple worship that had been largely neglected over the long period of exile. The Chafetz Chaim also demanded that every Jew (and not only every priest) familiarize himself with the Temple worship and the sacrifices. He explained that this was necessary because if the Messiah were to appear suddenly and the people did not know how to worship the Lord, "this would be a disgrace to him [the Messiah]."[9]

Rabbi Kook taught the tractate of Kodashim in the context of this hope that the sacrifices would be reinstated, and this seems to have formed the background for the establishment of Torat Cohanim yeshiva.

A correspondent with the London newspaper *The Christian* visited the yeshiva, which was situated in the Muslim Quarter of the Old City of Jerusalem. He informed his readers that Rabbi Kook had established the yeshiva because of his sense of extreme urgency regarding the establishment of the Temple. The Zionist executive in London demanded an explanation following this report, and Rabbi Kook replied that the requirement to study the Temple worship was now more pressing than ever:

> Our faith is firm that days are coming when all the nations shall recognize that this place, which the Lord has chosen for all eternity as the site of our Temple, must return to its true owners, and the great and holy House must be built thereon . . . An official British committee some time ago asked for my opinion regarding the location of the Temple according to our estimation. I told them that just as you see that we have the right to the entire Land [following the Balfour Declaration of 1917], even though the entire world was distant from this . . . so days shall come when all the nations shall recognize our rights to the site of the Temple.[10]

This position reflects the characteristic dynamics of Rabbi Kook's work. His messianic activism, which led him to prepare priests and Levites for their worship, stopped at the gates of the Temple Mount. He argued that the building of the Temple was conditioned on the recognition by the gentiles of the Jewish people's right to the Temple Mount. The preparation of the priests was intended to take place outside the area of the Temple Mount, and the establishment of the yeshiva did not imply that he actually intended to enter the site with his students, let alone commence the sacrificial rituals.

In support of my argument, I would note an additional source from the period, found in a rabbinical responsum published by Rabbi Avraham Yitzhak Hacohen Kook in his book *Mishpat Cohen*, published in 5681 (1921). In the responsum, Rabbi Kook issues a strong warning against entering the Temple Mount area.[11] It seems that this responsum was issued in reaction to the proposal by Rabbi Chaim Hirschenson, mentioned in the book *Malki Ba-Kodesh*, to construct a house of prayer on the Temple Mount.[12] In his responsum, Rabbi Kook gives the explanation of *mora hamikdash* (Awe of the Temple), according to which, given the sanctity with which this holy place is to be treated (and since its holiness has not been lost[13]), the public must stay away from the Temple Mount and refrain from entering the area. The dialectical explanation he offered for this was that distancing oneself from the site of the Temple would lead to a deeper spirituality, and hence to a profound sense of attachment: "The power of the memory of honor and the awe of sanctity is all the greater when it comes through denying proximity and through distancing." The rabbi ended his responsum with the following comments:

> And when, through God's infinite mercy, a fragment of the light of the emergence of salvation has begun to shine, the Rock of Israel will, with God's help, add the light of his mercy and truth, and will reveal to us the light of his full redemption, and bring us speedily our true redeemer, the redeemer of justice, our just Messiah, and will speedily fulfill all the words of his servants the prophets, and will build the Temple, speedily in our days. . . . And, until then, all Israel shall as friends associate in a single union to steer their hearts toward their Father in heaven, without bursting out and without departure, *without any demolition of the fence and without any hint of transgressing against the prohibition of profanity and impurity of the Temple and its holinesses.* (emphasis added)[14]

The Six-Day War created a new reality in the Middle East. In the course of the war, Israel occupied the West Bank, the Gaza Strip, the Golan Heights, and the Sinai Peninsula. The Israeli victory created fervent hope among the younger generation of Religious Zionists. The dominant school within this population, the graduates of Mercaz Harav yeshiva in Jerusalem, headed by Rabbi Zvi Yehuda Hacohen Kook, propagated the perception that the Israeli victory in this war reflected God's will to redeem His people. The postwar era therefore represented a higher stage in the process of redemption. The Gush Emunim mass settlement movement, established in 1974 and led by the graduates of the yeshiva, aimed to settle the territories occupied by the IDF to establish facts on the ground, and to settle the biblical Land of Israel with Jews. They saw settlement as a manifestation of God's will to redeem His people.

On the issue of the Temple Mount, however, Rabbi Zvi Yehuda Hacohen Kook did not diverge from his father. Although Zvi Yehuda is considered the spiritual guide of the Gush Emunim movement, which acted out of a strong sense of messianic urgency, he continued to view the Temple Mount as out of bounds. Zvi Yehuda signed the declaration issued by the Chief Rabbinate immediately after the occupation of the site, prohibiting Jews from entering the Temple Mount.

Indeed, Zvi Yehuda sharply criticized Shlomo Goren, the Chief Rabbi of the Israel Defense Forces, and later a Chief Rabbi of the State of Israel, who advocated Jewish prayer on the Mount, as discussed in the following section. Zvi Yehuda felt compelled to oppose in the fiercest possible terms the idea of Jews entering the Temple Mount area in order to pray.[15] Indeed, both of the Kooks ruled that the sanctity of the Temple Mount was so great that it was prohibited even to place one's fingers inside the cracks in the Western Wall. Zvi Yehuda fiercely opposed the demand to undertake archaeological excavations on the Temple Mount, since it "is surrounded by a wall. We do not pass this wall and we have no need for [the site] to be studied."[16]

It should be emphasized that the principled position of Zvi Yehuda against Jews entering the Temple Mount was not intended to weaken the demand for Israel to demonstrate its sovereignty on the site. He argued that the Jewish people enjoyed "property ownership" of the area of the Temple Mount. However, he explained that the State of Israel had not yet attained a spiritual level permitting Jews to enter the area of Mt. Moriah. Only after the state had been built in the spirit of the Torah, in both the practical and spiritual realms, would it be possible to enter the holy site.

The Chief Rabbinate and the Temple Mount Issue

After the Six-Day War, and the reestablishment of Jewish sovereignty over the Temple Mount, the Chief Rabbinate decided to continue the passive tradition on the question of the Temple Mount. In other words, Jews were to confine themselves to the reintroduction of prayers at the Western Wall.

Just a few hours after the Temple Mount came under the control of the Israeli forces on June 8, Israel Radio issued the warning by the Chief Rabbinate not to enter the site. At the first convention of the Council of the Chief Rabbinate after the war, Chief Rabbis Yitzhak Nissim and Isser Yehuda Unterman continued to argue that Jews must not be permitted to enter the site.

The Rabbinate's announcement was drafted by Rabbi Bezalel Jolti, who was invited to the meeting even though he was not a member of the Council of the Chief Rabbinate. He wrote, "Since the sanctity of the site has never ended, it is forbidden to enter the Temple Mount until the Temple is built."[17]

The minority position in the meeting was represented by Rabbi Chaim David Halevy, then rabbi of Rishon Lezion, who proposed that the question of entering the Temple Mount be left to the local rabbis, who would issue their edict to those following their authority. Shaul Israeli (a prominent teacher at Mercaz Harav yeshiva) sought to prepare a map identifying the permitted areas on the Temple Mount. Despite the minority position, the Council of the Chief Rabbinate ruled that the entire Temple Mount area was off limits. Yitzhak Abuhatzeira, rabbi of Ramle, was the first rabbi to demand that warning signs be placed at the entrance to the site forbidding Jews to enter.[18]

Despite the firm ruling of the assembly of the Chief Rabbinate prohibiting entry to the Temple Mount, two Chief Rabbis—Shlomo Goren and Mordechai Eliyahu—have, in a personal capacity, permitted Jews to enter. In addition, former Chief Rabbi Avraham Shapira's opposition to entering the site has weakened in recent years.

Shlomo Goren was the Chief Rabbi of the IDF at the time of the Six-Day War. This biographical fact constitutes a key point in the development of his personal approach and his vigorous campaign to open up the Temple Mount. After the war, he initiated the mapping of the site by soldiers from the Engineering Corps to identify areas prohibited to Jews, since the Temple Mount site of today is considerably and indisputably larger than the original dimensions of the First and Second Temples. When he realized that his initial expectation that the Islamic presence would be removed was not going to materialize, and that the mosques were to remain, Goren sent a confidential memorandum to Prime Minister Levi Eshkol demanding that entry to the Temple Mount be closed to both Jews and gentiles; but this was rejected. After the war, Goren established his office on the Temple Mount. On Tisha B'Av (a day of mourning to commemorate the destruction of the First and Second Temples,) the rabbi and a group of his supporters brought a Torah scroll, ark, and prayer benches to the Temple Mount, where they prayed Mincha (the afternoon service). After the prayer, Goren announced that he would also hold Yom Kippur (Day of Atonement) prayers on the site. His plans were thwarted by the intervention of Minister of Defense Moshe Dayan and Chief of Staff Yitzhak Rabin.[19]

In 1972, Goren was appointed Ashkenazi Chief Rabbi of Israel. In this capacity, he attempted to change the position of the Chief Rabbinate on the subject of Jewish prayer on the Temple Mount. He initiated a discussion in the plenum of the Rabbinate, and at two sessions in March 1976 lectured at length on his research. Despite his vigorous demand, the council refrained from making any changes to its original decision, while nonetheless urging Goren to publish his studies. They later added that when his recommendations were presented in writing, it would be possible to convene a broader forum than that of the Council of the Chief Rabbinate. This served as a pretext for removing the issue from the agenda.[20] At the same time, Goren's efforts in the political arena to persuade Prime Minister Menachem Begin to ease the government position regarding Jewish prayer on the Temple Mount also failed.[21]

In the absence of political and rabbinical support, Goren was unable to issue an official and public permit allowing entry to the Temple Mount. Moreover, the question of the entry of women was one of the aspects that deterred him from issuing an independent declaration opening the Temple Mount to all Jews. Goren believed that women must not be permitted to enter the Temple Mount area due to the question of ritual impurity, and was afraid that a sweeping permit for Jews to enter would also result in women entering the site.[22]

Goren found a faithful supporter in Mordechai Eliyahu, Israel's Sephardi Chief Rabbi from 1983 to 1993. Eliyahu adopted an innovative and creative Halachic approach when he proposed that a synagogue be built on the Temple Mount, within the permitted areas. The wall facing the Mount would be constructed of glass, so that the worshippers would look through the clear wall toward the square occupied by the Dome of the Rock. He proposed that entry into the synagogue would be directly from the entrance to the Temple Mount, and that the building would not have an exit point on to the Mount, thus avoiding any danger of Jews entering forbidden areas. Eliyahu proposed that the synagogue be higher than the Al-Aqsa and Dome of the Rock mosques to manifest its superiority over the Muslim houses of worship, whose presence he saw as a reminder of the destruction. This idea also failed to materialize.[23]

Among other proposals, Eliyahu advocated the formation of a sub-committee within the Council of the Chief Rabbinate o define the permitted areas on the Mount. He initiated a discussion in the council, and permitted Gershon Solomon, the leader of the Temple Mount Faithful movement, to speak at the session. Ultimately, however, the Council of the Chief Rabbinate decided not to alter the existing prohibition against entering the Temple Mount as it had determined in 1967. Eliyahu's colleague, Ashkenazi Chief Rabbi Avraham Shapira, was opposed at that time to permitting Jews to enter the Temple Mount, following the approach of Avraham Yitzhak Hacohen Kook. After the 1995 Israeli-Jordanian peace treaty, which granted Jordan preferential status in the future management of the Temple Mount, Shapira softened his opposition to entering the site, as noted earlier, commenting that "those who wish to rely on Rabbi Goren should do so."[24]

In conclusion, although the position of the Chief Rabbinate continues to prohibit entry to the Temple Mount, the first cracks in this position have begun to emerge among several leading figures. It should be noted, however, that while they were in office, Rabbis Goren and Eliyahu did not publicly express their position permitting Jews to enter the Temple Mount in the current era. They seem to have taken pains to avoid expressing this opinion out of deference to their official status as Chief Rabbis, although their opinions were well known among the general public.

The Committee of Yesha Rabbis

After the disclosure of the Oslo Process , which was based on an attempt to secure a compromise between Israel and the Palestinians regarding the territories of Judea, Samaria, and Gaza within the framework of a political process, and which was expected to culminate in a further compromise on the Temple Mount, positions and attitudes among the messianic school of Religious Zionism were profoundly shaken. While the followers of the approach of Mercaz Harav yeshiva believe wholeheartedly in a determinism that is leading the Jewish people and the State of Israel toward complete redemption, the emerging reality showed precisely the opposite position: the State of Israel seemed, in some respects at least, to be growing more secular, and its governments were leading a political process founded on painful concessions of parts of the Land of Israel in return for a partial peace agreement. The establishment of the Palestinian Authority and Israel's recognition of this body inevitably challenged the vision of the Greater Land of Israel. In the background, there was also concern that the Temple Mount would be lost and handed over to Palestinian control. Thus, the zenith of messianic expectation—the anticipated establishment of the Temple as the peak of the messianic process—now faced a grave danger due to the gradual surrender of sovereign territory.

This alarming situation led some of the rabbis most concerned about the issue of the Temple Mount into a dissonant paradox, whereby their concern at the possible failure of messianic faith led to a strengthening of religious practice and intensified messianic expectation. The risk that the vision of redemption might collapse led some members of the Committee of Yesha Rabbis to believe that they were facing the ultimate test, in which they were required to demonstrate supreme spiritual elevation.

I shall briefly mention some of the reactions to the challenge of faith faced in the wake of the Oslo Accords. Rabbis, such as Shlomo Aviner and Eliezer Melamed, felt that the way to withstand this test was to advocate the intensification of the settlement enterprise, which would foil the implementation of the accords.[25] A further way to cope with this tension was to issue Halachic rulings prohibiting the relinquishing of sections of the Land of Israel and prohibiting the removal of settlements and of IDF bases.[26] In 1995, Shaul Israeli, head of the Mercaz Harav yeshiva, went further still, urging people to stop reciting the prayer for the welfare of the state, which includes a blessing for "its leaders, ministers and counsels."[27]

In this situation, an increasing number of religious authorities, including leaders of the settlement movement, began to express positions that interpreted the Israeli withdrawal from territories in Judea and Samaria as divine punishment for the lack of Jewish attention to the Temple Mount, due to the rabbinical prohibition against entering the site. For example, Dov Lior, rabbi of Kiryat Arba and one of the leading spiritual leaders of contemporary Religious Zionism, stated:

> We, who believe in reward and punishment and in Divine providence, must know that one of the main reasons why we are suffering torment is the profound apathy among large sections of

our people concerning the Temple Mount in general and the construction of the Temple, in particular.[28]

The fear of further concessions led to practical measures designed to thwart any such developments. In 1996, during the high point of the opposition to the Oslo Process among the settlers, the Committee of Yesha Rabbis issued a bold ruling urging all rabbis who held the position that it was permissible to enter the Temple Mount to "ascend the Mount themselves, and to guide their congregants in ascending the Mount within all the limitations of the Halacha." Effectively, the committee thus adopted the original minority position as presented by Rabbi Chaim David Halevy at the meeting of the Chief Rabbinate Council in 1967. The ruling of the Yesha Rabbis stated that their position had been adopted in response to "the facts that are being established on the ground by the Arabs." The argument behind the ruling was that the lack of a Jewish presence on the Temple Mount, due to the Halachic prohibition against entering the site, had led the Israeli governments to see the site as one that could easily be relinquished. Accordingly, if masses of Jews began to enter the Mount to pray, it would be harder for the Israeli government to transfer sovereignty over the site to the Palestinian Authority.[29] This decision also constituted an expression of defiance vis-à-vis the Israeli Chief Rabbinate, challenging its repeated rulings. It should be noted that the change of line was preceded by an unsuccessful request to the Chief Rabbinate to change its position on the matter.[30] The decision of the Yesha Rabbis also challenged the traditional position of the Mercaz Harav yeshiva, which prohibits Jews from entering the Temple Mount "for the present time," despite the fact that most of the members of the Committee of Yesha Rabbis are graduates of this institution.

I should add that this position on the part of the Yesha Rabbis has been a source of controversy within Gush Emunim. Those opposing this approach are led by Rabbis Shlomo Aviner and Zvi Tau, among the leading figures of the Mercaz Harav school. Their principal thesis is that the current generation is not yet ready for the reconstruction of the Temple. They argue that first the nation must be further prepared. The Temple is perceived as the tip of a pyramid, while the people are currently merely constructing its first foundations. Moreover, the Third Temple cannot be a temporary and imperfect structure along the lines of the First and Second Temples, which were destroyed as a consequence of their imperfection. The Third Temple should be built only after the spiritual foundations have been established in the form of the ideal Kingdom of Israel acting in accordance with the laws of the Torah. The Temple must stand for eternity, and accordingly must be built on flawless foundations. Thus, until that time, entrance to the Temple Mount is prohibited.[31]

The Opening of the Temple Mount

As already noted, the three-year period following the outbreak of the second Intifada (2001), when the Temple Mount was closed to Jews, provoked public and rabbinical discussion in Religious Zionist circles. Just before the Temple Mount reopened to Jewish visitors in September 2003 this intense awakening was challenged in a fierce written debate that appeared over a period of more than a month in the weekend supplements of *Hatzofe*, the journal of the National Religious Party and the representative of Religious Zionist interests in the Knesset. Various articles appeared examining the question of the Temple Mount. Rabbi Shlomo Aviner provided the focus of the discussion, presenting the traditional position prohibiting Jews from entering the Temple Mount. In the first of three articles, he noted that he had received numerous requests from young people informing him of their intention to enter the Temple Mount area to pray. Aviner responded that his reply to those who asked him was that, on this matter, they should follow the ruling of the Israeli Chief Rabbinate, which had weighed the issue and prohibited Jews unequivocally from entering the site.[32] He emphasized that most of the leading rabbis had signed the statement by the Chief Rabbinate, as had Rabbi Zvi Yehuda Hacohen Kook, who even claimed that the mere discussion of the issue reflected a grave weakness in observing the commandment to "hold the Temple in awe."[33] He added that it was his belief that Maimonides did not enter the Temple Mount and pray on the site during his sojourn in the Holy Land.[34]

Each of Aviner's columns was answered by two articles opposing his position. Haggai Huberman, a leading correspondent for the newspaper, replied that Shlomo Goren had prayed on the Temple Mount as part of a religious quorum, as he had himself.[35] Yisrael Meidad claimed that the Chief Rabbinate's position was of a political rather than a religious character. Meidad urged rabbis to issue a new ruling on the question, given the changes that had occurred in the status of the Temple Mount, and the destruction of ancient remains on the site by the Waqf.[36] Rabbi Israel Rosen forcefully and rhetorically wondered why the obligation to obey the rabbinate was "wedged like a sword" into the foot of the Temple Mount. Rabbi Daniel Shilo, the spokesperson for the Committee of Yesha Rabbis, wrote that were Rabbi Zvi Yehuda Hacohen Kook alive today, he would surely permit Jews to enter the Temple Mount. On the question of "awe for the Temple," Shilo responded that Shlomo Goren was surely not among those who did not share this sentiment.[37]

The stand taken by Rabbi Shlomo Aviner may be seen as a rearguard battle. As soon as the Temple Mount reopened, dramatic changes could be observed regarding visits to the site. During the first three months after the site reopened for Jewish visitors, some four thousand Jews entered the site.[38] This trend has continued, and almost every day Jewish religious communities, sometimes numbering hundreds of people, come to pray on the Mount. As of October 2004, some seventy thousand people had visited the site.[39] This outburst of enthusiasm has been led by important religious and political leaders from within the Religious Zionist camp, and not necessarily from its more extreme wings. Thus, for example, those visiting the site have included not only such highly nationalistic rabbis as Dov Lior, Nachum Rabinowitz, Zefaniya Drori, Israel Rosen, and Shabtai Rappoport, but also more moderate figures such as Rabbis Yuval Sherlo and Shlomo Riskin.

The demand to enter the Temple Mount, which has been led by students from the national-religious yeshivot, now seems to have swept through the more moderate leadership, even those opposed to entering the site. For example, in July 2004, Rabbi Shlomo Aviner participated in a convention whose title speaks for itself: "Drawing Near to the Sacrifices." He even attended the "Circling of the Gates," which took place after the convention. This was an event in which the participants circled the walls of the Temple Mount reciting dirges mourning the destruction of the Temple. Aviner conditioned his participation in the conference when his reservations regarding entry to the Temple Mount were published.[40] My assessment is that Aviner was pressured to participate in activities he did not support, and which in the past he would have avoided, because of the dynamics created on the Temple Mount issue. The fact that the conference and the march around the gates took place outside the Temple Mount allowed him to participate in the events, responding to public pressure. Activities held apart from the Temple Mount pose a dilemma for the moderate religious leadership of the settlers. As Orthodox Jews, they cannot negate or deny the anticipation of the reinstatement of the sacrifices, and accordingly, they cannot oppose the substance of such informational activities, as long as these do not take place on the Mount itself.

Conclusion

The general rabbinical approach to the question of entering the Temple Mount may be divided into four main schools. The first rejects such a possibility, which is left to messianic times. This position is shared by the majority of members of the plenum of the Israeli Chief Rabbinate.

The second seeks to prepare actively for redemption, but within the legitimate religious frameworks, through theoretical study of the laws relating to the sacrificial worship. This approach does not include actual entry into the Temple Mount site, and remains within the accepted framework of Torah study. The approach of Avraham Yitzhak Hacohen Kook reflects this position.

The third school argues that the construction of the Temple is indeed a public commandment, but before this takes place, spiritual elevation is needed, through settlement across the entire Holy Land and the dissemination of the light of faith, which constitute the foundation on which the Temple may be constructed. Thus, until that time, entering the Mount is prohibited. This approach is the most common among the Mercaz Harav yeshiva school.

The fourth and most activist school permits Jews to enter the Temple Mount, with certain restrictions. To this end, much effort is devoted to identifying the borders of the Temple area to avoid problems of ritual impurity that arise in entering the prohibited areas. This fourth school is becoming more dominant among the Religious Zionist leadership, both political and rabbinical.

The study also discusses the clear phenomenon of the erosion and weakening of the prohibition against Jews entering the Temple Mount. It is difficult to ignore the growing support for this approach among ever wider circles. The research also discusses the manner in which a political process—the Oslo Accords—led to a series of counter reactions, influencing religious approaches that had previously been considered immutable. We see that strict Orthodox circles have changed their religious behavior as the result of changing times. The fear that the Temple Mount will be lost and transferred to Arab control legitimized far-reaching changes in a long-standing religious ruling.

The yearning of the religious population for the Temple Mount and for the ideal of reestablishing the Temple grew stronger because of the threat to Israeli sovereignty over the site. As long as Israel controlled the site and the idea of handing the Mount over to Palestinian sovereignty as part of a peace agreement was not raised, even activist circles among the Religious Zionist community did not, for the most part, seek to change the reality on the Temple Mount. Although the desire to build the Temple is a central theme among these circles, it was postponed until a later stage of the process of redemption, as they see it. By contrast, since the emergence of the Oslo Accords and discussion of the division of sovereignty in the Holy Basin (the Western Wall and the Temple Mount), there has been an increasingly strong counterreaction demanding that Jews enter the site and create facts on the ground. The proof of this is the large number of people who have entered the Mount over the years since the Mount was reopened in September 2003, despite the Halachic prohibition. It is reasonable to suggest that it will be difficult to continue to ignore this growing support for action on this question among ever-widening circles.

It is still too early to determine what will become of these trends. It is also possible that the further developments would be a result of the changing political reality. It may be, on one hand, that the question of

Jews entering the Temple Mount will become a routine. On the other hand, if the crisis and violent situation continues, there could be found those who would desire to attack the mosques on the site to promote the messianic process.

Based on these conclusions we shall enter our discussion on the Temple Mount activists. Chapter 3 examines the activities of the Temple Institute headed by Rabbi Israel Ariel. This institute is the leading force among the Temple Mount advocates.

2

Messianic Naturalism as the Product of Dissonance

The Activities of the Temple Institute

The Temple Institute is an educational institution that runs various Jewish religious enterprises, including a college preparatory school curricula, a museum, a publishing house, a yeshiva for young adults, a yeshiva for youths, and a project that seeks to produce and recreate the objects used in the Temple Mount. The institute was established in 1984 by Israel Ariel; over the past two decades, its activities have become an influential force. The institute is recognized as an official institution by the Ministry of Education, which sends thousands of students from state-religious schools to its programs; IDF soldiers visit the institute in a large number of organized groups; dozens of young religious women performing national service volunteer in its programs; and, on occasion, the institute has even secured the support of the Israeli Chief Rabbinate (e.g., a religious conference on subjects relating to the Temple was organized under the auspices of the rabbinate). Thousands of Christian evangelists also visit the institute each year.

This successful and officially recognized body appears to have managed to position itself within the public consensus. Accordingly, its activities to promote the building of the Temple are not seen as exceptional. In this approach, the institute has straddled the boundary between "legitimate" academic study of the Temple (theoretical studies and folkloristic replications) and actual actions intended to promote the construction of the Third Temple—something that is considered taboo in religious terms. Since the institute does not advocate actions on the Temple Mount itself, and its main activities take place away from the site, it has managed to secure legitimacy and even support from religious institutions.

Indeed, the institute claims, at least officially, that it is involved solely in propagating knowledge regarding the history and practices of the Temple. This may be construed as a "nod" in the direction of the Halachic world, since in principle there is no Halachic objection to such activities. Despite this, many observers assume that the institute actually promotes the idea of building the Temple—indeed, it is considered one of the main bodies involved in such efforts. Its directors and activists, led by Israel Ariel, are among the leading members of the various Temple Mount movements, and they regularly visit the Temple Mount and pray on the site. Moreover, Israel Ariel is widely known to hold radical theocratic views that negate the existence of Israeli democracy.[1] Despite this, state institutions and bodies support his activities and finance the institution. In the period 2000–2003, the total level of support provided by various government ministries for the Temple Knowledge College, which operates under the auspices of the institute, exceeded one million shekels (more than US $200,000).[2]

As noted, the central figure and moving spirit behind the institute is Israel Ariel. Ariel is the youngest son of a respected Religious Zionist family. His elder brother Yaacov Ariel is considered one of the leading Halachic teachers to have been trained by the Mercaz Harav yeshiva, and he currently serves as the Ashkenazi Chief Rabbi of Ramat Gan. In 2003, Yaacov Ariel was even considered for the post of Chief Rabbi of Israel. All the sons of the Ariel family were educated at the prestigious Mercaz Harav yeshiva. However, in many respects Israel Ariel has moved beyond the boundaries set by the yeshiva. In political terms he may be described as a supporter of Kach, a far-right political party in Israel founded by Rabbi Meir Kahane; in 1981 he was second on the party's list for the Knesset elections. Ariel was one of the leaders of the Movement to Stop the Withdrawal from Sinai, and took part in confrontations with the security forces. During the riots that accompanied the eviction of Yamit in Sinai, he urged IDF soldiers to refuse to obey the order to demolish the Jewish communities (1982).

The attitude of the Religious Zionist establishment toward the Temple Institute is an example of the "messianic dilemma" facing Religious Zionism, which traps the leadership and makes it difficult for it to combat extremist elements who demand religious perfection. Accordingly, it is apparent that the prevailing approach is one of tacit acceptance of the institute's activities, combined with generous support. This approach is possible since the institute is careful to avoid excessive external manifestations of its ambivalent position, and concentrates on activities outside the Temple Mount site.

This chapter discusses the motivations that led Ariel to establish the Temple Institute, the basic philosophy of the institute, and the activities the institute has initiated.

The Origins of the Crisis

The formative moment and turning point in the life of Israel Ariel came with the conquest of the Temple Mount in 1967. Ariel has repeatedly described his memories of that day; they are documented at length in the publications of the Temple Institute, in interviews with the religious press, and in the *Lekhatchilah* newsletters. Ariel relives his experience of taking part in the battle for Jerusalem when he was a paratrooper in the standing army. On the first night after IDF troops entered the Old City, Ariel was posted as a guard by the Al-Aqsa Mosque.

Many of the journalists who have interviewed Ariel have tended to regard this description as no more than a picturesque anecdote that can add color to their article. I argue that Ariel's description of these memories positions them as a critical peak experience in his life, offering an opportunity to understand the inner drives that have motivated his practical and political development. In my opinion, Ariel's personal experiences during the Six-Day War, and the interpretation he has since given them, constitute a classic case of an encounter with crisis, suggesting that he underwent a process of radicalization in reaction to the fear of the failure of faith. Ariel's wartime experiences can also offer an explanation for his decision to abandon the approach of the Mercaz Harav yeshiva.

Regrettably, Ariel refused my request for an interview for the purposes of this chapter. I was informed that this is in line with an in-principle decision by the leaders of the institute to stop granting interviews. Accordingly, I am obliged to rely on written materials from the institute, on journalistic studies that have included references to Ariel's work, and on additional information gathered from various sources.

An interview in the *Or Chozer*, a journal of the Hesder yeshiva students, offers a particularly frank and detailed description of these experiences, and provides an appropriate starting point for our discussion. Before examining Ariel's comments in this interview, it is worth emphasizing that these constitute a personal testimony given for a specific purpose; they should be examined accordingly. The experiences I will describe are not necessarily identical with the actual historical facts relating to the day on which the Temple Mount was occupied. This testimony is, however, extremely important as a source of insight into the motivations that led Ariel to initiate the establishment of the Temple Institute.

During the period of tension preceding the Six-Day War, Ariel was performing his military service in the paratroopers division. His unit was expected to engage in combat with the Egyptian army in the Straits of Tiran, but the mission was changed and his company was sent to the Old City of Jerusalem.

Ariel found himself among the forces that led the Israeli advance toward the Western Wall, and the experience of running excitedly toward the holiest sites of Judaism—the Western Wall and the Temple Mount—aroused profound messianic fervor in him. Overcome with emotion as he was entering the area in front of the Western Wall on his way to the Temple Mount, he heard some soldiers who had reached the site before him comment that they met "two old men" while they were bursting into the area:

> I thought to myself: The Messiah and the Prophet Elijah must have arrived. Who else would appear here during the battle for the Temple Mount after two thousand years? That was what seemed natural at the time.[3]

At this point in time, as the Israeli army secured a stunning victory over the Jordanian Legion and entered the Temple Mount, Ariel indeed felt that the messianic era was arriving. His inner feeling was that the Messiah would arrive on the very same day and build the Temple. This elation was the product of a critical combination of the education he had received at the Mercaz Harav yeshiva, which perceived the State of Israel as the "beginning of Redemption," and the powerful experience of his personal presence at the moment when the Temple Mount returned to Jewish control.

> No one who was privileged enough to witness this moment, and whose feet stood on the Lord's mountain after thousands of years of Jewish absence, could fail to be elated by the great moment for the Jewish people. These are the Days of Messiah—there is no other expression for it. These are the Days of Messiah!
>
> Naturally, the two old men who should appear at this time are the Messiah and the Prophet Elijah. So I went off to meet the Messiah and the Prophet Elijah. I asked myself where I would find them. Surely on the Temple Mount—they must have come to build the Temple. But I saw everyone running toward the Western Wall. For some reason people were more moved by the wall than by the Temple Mount. Awareness of the Western Wall is much greater among the people than awareness of the Temple . . .
>
> I arrived at the Western Wall, and below me I saw two old men—none other than my two rabbis and teachers from the yeshiva, Rabbi Zvi Yehuda Kook ZTS"L ["may the memory of righteous be blessed"] and the "Reclusive Rabbi" ZTS"L [David Hacohen]. We embraced and stood with tears running down our cheeks, in complete silence, sensing that Messiah was still on the way—it would just take another hour or two.[4]

The previous day, during preparations for the military offensive in the Old City, Ariel met Shlomo Goren, the Chief Rabbi of the IDF, at the Rockefeller Museum outside the walls of the Old City. Ariel asked the rabbi what Halachic steps should be taken if Israel took the Old City. Should entry to the Temple Mount be confined to Cohanim (preists)? Would ritual bathing be required before entering? Should the priestly garbs be prepared? Although he was a graduate of the Mercaz Harav yeshiva, Ariel had not studied the laws relating to the Temple Mount and the Temple, and had no idea how he should act. Ariel later related that Goren's response was that these questions should not be examined, since there was no certainty that the IDF would indeed conquer the Temple Mount. For Ariel, this response reflects the alienation of the rabbinical authorities from discussion relating to the Temple, and their lack of faith in the possibility of securing the objectives of Redemption.

The next evening, when the Temple Mount was already under Israeli control, Ariel was stationed as a guard at the entrance to the Dome of the Rock:

> They placed me—of all spots—at the western entrance to the Dome. According to my calculations and my limited knowledge at the time, I realized that this was more or less the location of the *Kodesh Kodashim* (Holy of Holiest) . . .
>
> It was at this point that I realized the dimensions of the victory. . . . This was not just a peak of conquests, but a peak of the manifestation of Divine love for the people of Israel. The Song of Songs found its true place in that hour—the song of the Assembly of Israel to its Father in heaven, and the parallel Divine song. This was not poetry—it was reality. At a Divine moment of mercy, all nature surrendered before us, and after thousands of years of suffering, all was erased from the board. Indeed, now "The Lord has made you superior over all the peoples of the earth." All the blessings of the Torah, all came true in that hour. Where? *At the Place*! At the Place of Divine revelation. I was privileged to be a partner in this, and no expression I could find could illustrate this matter. (emphasis in the original)[5]

Even twenty-three years after the event, during his interview with the journal *Or Hachozer*, Ariel was still awestruck as he described the special day on which he experienced this sense of miracle and destiny. As he guarded the site of the Temple by night, his feet on the very spot (he believed) where the Kodesh Kodashim stood, he had no doubt that at any moment he might meet the Messiah in person and in the flesh. For Ariel, these hours were spent on the brink, in fervent expectation of a miracle that would realize the biblical prophecies of Redemption. He felt privileged to have been stationed as guard on that fateful night, and that he would experience the appearance of Divinity in all its force, transcendental yet utterly real, as the Temple descended from heaven, complete and ready, directly to its rightful place on the Temple Mount. "It is so very difficult to describe the feeling that filled us during that extraordinary time in the life of the nation—the liberation of Jerusalem and of the Temple on 25 Iyar 5728 (1967). The phrase 'ringing the bells of the Messiah' expresses in a limited way what was being felt in the heart."[6]

In his description of the events of that portentous day, Ariel recalls that even at this early stage he found it irritating that the Western Wall, rather than the Temple Mount, was the focus of attention. He spoke of seeing commanders and soldiers holding secret conversations, with Shlomo Goren among them. Ariel fully expected that "[w]e would soon see soldiers appear from somewhere carrying crates with the vessels of the Temple. In my mind's eye I saw the Cohanim signing as they lit the Temple candelabrum, as in the days of the Hasmoneans." But nothing happened. Shlomo Goren blew the shofar in the area in front of the Western Wall. Ariel's teachers from the Mercaz Harav yeshiva also passed through the Temple Mount, but they were heading for the Western Wall. "It was evident from their eyes that the tremendous achievement of the people's return to the site of the Temple was greater and more serious than anything they could have imagined. This is presumably why they did not stay on the Mount, but descended down to the Western Wall."[7]

The return to the site of the Temple required Halachic preparations, something for which the rabbinical authorities were unprepared. "There was an expectation of more to come, of a Divine event, of a miracle that would remove any question marks that had appeared." Ariel, too, anticipated a miracle, waiting for the Messiah to bring with him the Temple, complete and ready.

The day passed. Weeks and months followed, and the Messiah failed to appear. Ariel was filled with messianic disappointment. The spiritual reckoning sparked by his disappointment led him to new conclusions. Evidence of his disappointment, and of the conclusions he drew from it, may be found in a poem he wrote that was published in his *Prayerbook for the Temple*:

> I shall approach the Western Wall, these giant stones/Can man find any words here?!/To pray, to speak to such a mighty God?/ To sing a song of joy and blood.
>
> The prayer emerges crushed and broken/For the unique people of the world/For the dispersed that shall gather in imminent Redemption/Pains of the individual and the salvation of the nation.

I turn to the left, I turn to the right/Where is our just
Messiah?/Where is the messenger of the end of days . . .

I wonder: where is Ben Yishai? Where is his pleasant violin?/
Why is the sound of the news delayed?/And a heavenly voice
replies: How can I come when the Temple is in ruins?/Hew the
rock and build a house of glory!

The day is near! The sun rises and shines/Over a mountain
and an eternal home/Here are the young priests!/Building the
altar!/The poets are on the podium—and the Levites shout
and cheer.

All the dispersed of Israel shall gather then and come/
To Jerusalem and to the Temple/All the nations and all dwellers
of Earth shall recognize/That a new light has shone in Jerusalem![8]

Ariel describes in colorful terms how a "heavenly voice" made itself heard
to him, explaining his error: Messiah can come only when the Temple is
standing. Accordingly the miraculous belief that Messiah would build the
Temple is mistaken. The construction of the Temple is thus a task incumbent on the public as a whole, as a precursor to the coming of the Messiah.[9]

It would take almost twenty years for Ariel to translate his personal realization into action. In the interim, he experienced the traumatic Israeli
withdrawal from Sinai, with the disappointment and ideological crisis this
event brought. As noted earlier, Ariel was among the leading opponents
of the withdrawal from Sinai under the terms of the peace treaty with
Egypt. These events left him scarred, adding to the questions he had been
asking himself since the Six-Day War. Indeed, there is a direct connection between that war and the endeavor he established through the Temple Institute, despite the time gap. The establishment of the Temple
Institute constituted a delayed reaction to the crisis caused by the non-
realization of the messianic vision in 1967, which was further exacerbated
by the withdrawal from Sinai.

The manner in which Ariel describes the details of the day on which
the Old City and the Temple Mount were occupied also reflects his disappointment with his teachers, the heads of the Mercaz Harav yeshiva.
While he had cast them in the role of the Prophet Elijah and the Davidic
Messiah, and expected them to be partners in the dramatic process of
the establishment of the Temple, they actually shied away from any discussion of such issues. Moreover, their entry onto the Temple Mount immediately after the end of the fighting, riding in an IDF jeep, was not a
"messianic entrance," but a fatal mistake that they later regretted, since
they had been taken to the Western Wall by army drivers without even
knowing where they were heading. The contrast between the dramatic
expectations of that day and the partial and volatile reality that emerged

would later lead to a somber awakening. Ariel's disillusionment with miraculous perceptions of Redemption joined his disappointment with the two heads of the Mercaz Harav yeshiva and with Shlomo Goren, on whom he had cloaked his messianic vision and whom he expected to lead the people toward the ultimate realization of Redemption. This awakening led him to the activist direction and to the establishment of the Temple Institute.

In the psychological and spiritual behavior of Ariel, it is possible to identify the characteristics of the cognitive dissonance that threatens the fervent adherents of messianic expectations. The fact that the Messiah failed to appear immediately after the war, despite the tremendous expectations Ariel held during those early days, did not lead him to weaken his resolve. On the contrary, his demand for Redemption was only strengthened. Ariel identified a tactical solution for the messianic crisis that mandated a different course of action to realize redemption. His spiritual reckoning led him to identify his error in apocalyptic theological approaches that anticipate Divine revelation and supernatural occurrences. The inevitable conclusion he reached was that this religious structure must be replaced by naturalistic messianic activism. Accordingly, this is the emotional and personal background to the establishment of the Temple Institute. In this action, Ariel took the Religious Zionist principle of commitment to human activism to its ultimate conclusion.

After the war, Ariel remained in the army through 1975. He served in the Chief Rabbinate, constituting a unique model of a rabbi and combat fighter. After his release from the army, he urged his brother, Yaacov Ariel, who was serving at the time as the rabbi of Kfar Maimon, to establish a yeshiva in Kfar Darom in the Gaza Strip. The yeshiva was later relocated to Yamit in Sinai. In 1977, Prime Minister Menachem Begin attended the dedication ceremony of the yeshiva, which was directed jointly by both brothers. Israel Ariel also served in the capacity of rabbi of Yamit.

After learning that the government intended to vacate the city, a disagreement erupted between the two brothers. Israel, the more militant of the two, advocated a physical struggle against eviction. For example, in a demonstration against the withdrawal two months before its implementation, he shouted at IDF soldiers, urging them to disobey the eviction order.[10] Yaacov was opposed to any confrontation with IDF soldiers. The two brothers did not oppose each other's positions within the yeshiva, but in practice Israel left the institution, which was thereafter managed solely by Yaacov.

During the eviction, Israel Ariel was one of the most extreme activists in the Movement to Stop the Withdrawal from Sinai. As noted, he did not negate the possibility of a physical confrontation with the soldiers who came to evict the settlement. Ariel believed that a determined struggle was the only way to leave the town intact, and he was not opposed to the use of any means that could secure this goal. In the final analysis, however, he did not realize his extreme threats, after he realized that the vast majority was opposed to acts of violence, and there was no practical benefit in isolated individuals waging a private campaign.[11]

In 1981, after the withdrawal from Sinai, Ariel joined the Kach list for the Knesset, reflecting his disillusionment with the leadership of Gush Emunim. He moved to the Jewish Quarter in the Old City of Jerusalem, and taught at the Haidra yeshiva, which was established by Shlomo Goren and overlooks the Temple Mount. When the "Jewish Underground" movement —a group that committed revenge attacks on Arabs and planned to blow up the mosques on the Temple Mount—was uncovered in 1984, Ariel was among the lone voices that supported its actions. He even founded a journal called *Zefiyah* that was devoted to justifying the actions of those convicted and to encouraging the expectation of the construction of the Temple.[12]

Observing the Commandments
Means Building the Temple

"The goal facing the members and founders of the Temple Institute is to observe the positive commandment in the Torah—to build a Temple to the Lord. Maimonides defines this commandment as one that is imposed on the public." This statement appears in the preamble to the constitution of the Temple Institute association, which is registered with the Registry of Associations.[13] The constitution defines the Temple Institute as an operational instrument for realizing the commandment of the construction of the Temple.

During the latter half of the 1980s, the institute began to develop its presence, guided by the requirement to observe all 613 commandments in the Torah, and by the perspective that the entire Torah is to be regarded as a single entity. Many of the commandments in the Torah relate to the order of sacrifices and the Temple. It thus follows that to realize the Torah in full, it is imperative to reconstruct the Temple. The explanatory notes to the constitution emphasize that the return of the Jewish people to the Land of Israel imposed an obligation on the public to observe all the commandments that relate specifically to the Land and to the Temple. Performing these commandments is not optional, but a Halachic obligation. As long as the Temple remains unbuilt, some two hundred commandments from the Torah cannot be observed:

A healthy and complete perception of Jewish life knows one thing only: the observance of the commandments of the Torah in their entirety. . . . If the Creator of the world commanded us in

His Torah to observe 613 commandments, we cannot declare
ourselves "God-fearing and complete" while observing only a
small portion thereof.[14]

The constitution of the Temple Institute challenges the apocalyptic theological position, which anticipates the construction of the Temple as a
supernatural and miraculous act. To prove that this expectation is mistaken, the constitution includes a form of "historical evidence" that it sees
as constituting conclusive evidence: the Jews who returned from exile in
Babylon devoted themselves to the task of building the Second Temple
despite the difficult situation they faced in material, political, social, and
economic terms. "What was right for forty thousand immigrants from
Exile is also right for over three million Jews who now live in Israel
(almost one hundred times as many)," the constitution challenged.

Moreover, the public is required to resolve by itself the unresolved
Halachic issues relating to the Temple, such as the precise location of the
tabernacle and the altar; the absence of prophecy, and so on. The constitution quoted rulings by Maimonides in his Halachic essays that the
construction of the Temple is a commandment from Torah, as well as the
ruling of Nachmanides, stating that it is not permissible to rely on miracles. According to the constitution, Halacha and Jewish faith reject an approach that makes the performance of the commandments dependent
on transcendental powers. "Thus the construction of the Temple and the
commandments performed there are also not a matter of legend and
faith, but are commandments."[15]

Ariel argued that the situation of the Jewish people in the State of Israel required a revision of the Halacha. The starting point was a recognition that the period of "subjugation by the nations," as he put it, had come
to an end. The achievement of independence and liberty, combined with
the "God-given gift" of the location of the Temple, demanded Halachic
recognition. As long as the Jewish people had been under "subjugation
by the nations," and faced the threat of annihilation, it had been exempt
from commandments that it could not possibly observe. This was no
longer the case once "through God's mercy, the people of Israel [had] regained its strength." Since Israel's Declaration of Independence in 1948,
the situation had changed in a manner that could no longer be ignored.
Israel's independence in its own land had created a new Halachic reality.

Ariel attaches profound religious significance to the comment by
Motte Gur: "The Temple Mount is in our hands." This statement is compared to the declaration by Cyrus: "Whosoever there is among you of all
His people—his God be with him—let him go up to Jerusalem . . . and
build the house of the Lord" (Ezra 1:3). This required the Jews to leave
the exile of Babylon and build the Temple. "This declaration ['The Tem-

ple Mount is in our hands'] did not merely change the Jewish history of two thousands years' exile. The declaration put an end to the period of the 'subjugation by the nations' and opened the period of the Third Temple." Once the feet of an Israeli soldier had trodden on the Temple Mount, the people were required to build the Temple and worship God there, according to the example set by the Babylonian exiles.[16]

Ariel argued that two thousand years of exile had led many Jews who adhered to the Torah to develop a fear of responsibility, as reflected in their tendency to ignore the commandments relating to the building of the Land of Israel and the Temple. However, "the reality of the resurrection of the state is a Halachic fact that cannot be evaded." He believed that political independence required the full observance of all 613 commandments, and the reinstatement of the sacrifices on the Temple Mount. The Halachic revision this demanded was nothing less than a fundamentalist and all-embracing revolution with the objective of establishing a theocracy.

Ariel developed the concept of "the firm hand of Israel," which he interpreted as meaning a Divine instruction to Israel manifested through exceptional human successes that reflect God's will. He interpreted the Israeli victory in the Six-Day War as a Divine call to reinstate the worship of the Temple. This commandment must be observed even if it entails dangers, and even if it would lead to an uprising among the surrounding nations. "It is a commandment to trust God and observe His commandments, even if this involves danger,"[17] he stated categorically. For Ariel, the process of redemption of the Jewish people in its current phase demands neither caution nor moderation, but dynamic, forceful, and unbridled action. He argues that distilled truth, as established in the Halacha, must be the sole guide and yardstick for deciding on actions. There is no place for relying on securing authorization and permits from the authorities, or on convincing public opinion.

According to Ariel, the Torah teaches that whenever the Jews neglected the commandment to establish the tabernacle and the Temple they were struck by disaster. He notes that God brought a plague on the Jews during the reign of King David because of their neglect in establishing the tabernacle; seventy thousand people paid with their lives. Similarly, during the period of the Prophet Samuel, when the Jews failed to bring the tabernacle of Shilo back after it was captured by the Philistines, the result was famine; only after they built the Temple was prosperity restored. Accordingly, the modern leaders of the nation bear a grave responsibility lest a further disaster ensue as the result of their prevarication. Israel Ariel even hinted that the large number of Israeli casualties in the Yom Kippur War (October 1973), some six years after the 1967 war, were the result of the delays in the building of the Temple.[18]

Preparations for the
Building of the Temple

Ariel argues that preparations are required for the construction of the Temple. He fears that even if the Israeli government were to permit religious worship on the Temple Mount, it is doubtful whether Halachic figures could be found who could execute the ritual actions relating to the Temple, since their studies of this field have been neglected:

> In the existing conditions, it would emerge that the Halachic figures are lost when it comes to the Temple and its worship, such as how to build the altar. Where should it be located? What is the order of service? Who are the Cohanim? What are the priestly clothes and how are they made? How does one inspect the animal for blemishes? What is the order of actions for the proper performance of the commandment? What of impurity and purification? And so forth.[19]

To prepare for the realization of these sublime goals, training must be provided for worthy individuals from various Halachic fields, and appropriate frameworks for study must be opened. Accordingly, Ariel established the Temple Institute as an academic research base—a form of "Halachic technical college" equipped with laboratories, lecture halls, and research programs.[20]

In addition, the Temple Institute committed itself to preparing the groundwork in terms of general public opinion. To this end, curricula on the Temple were prepared for use in schools; a museum was opened that presented information and exhibits relating to the history of the Temple and the various types of worship; opulent prayer books for daily and festival use were prepared and included aspects relating to the temple; and books and other types of written media were published that discussed the relevance of the Temple to modern life and the question of permission to enter the Temple Mount.

Ariel was well aware that his activities lay within the confines of Halachic legitimacy, since there is nothing improper about studying and engaging in preparatory activities relating to the laws concerning the Temple, or in preparing its ritual vessels. Accordingly, the constitution of the institute emphasizes that it will not address the question of the specific location of the Temple—an issue that Ariel defined as "political."[21] He argues that as Halachic solutions are developed and practical preparations continue, and as the circles of those involved in the preparations widen, this political question will disappear, "to be replaced by the natural need of the Jewish people in its homeland to renew its days as of old."[22]

Strict attention to this boundary in the institute's activities enabled it to secure widespread rabbinical support. While most of the support came from Religious Zionist circles, it is interesting to note that several Haredi rabbinical authorities also visited the institute. In 1994, the institute reported that the chairman of the Council of Torah Elders of Agudat Israel, the Sadigura Rebbe, visited the institution, "during which visit he made many extremely instructional comments." The Boston Rebbe also visited the Temple Institute.[23]

In effect, Ariel extracted the underlying rationale of the position of the Mercaz Harav yeshiva and drew it to its logical conclusion. If the State of Israel is a manifestation of the "beginning of redemption," then the conclusion of this process is the construction of the Temple and the installment of a religious dominion. Ariel's naturalistic messianic perspective thus led him to pursue this course, guided by the ultimate purpose of building the Temple.

The Activities of the Temple Institute

Even though the Temple Institute was established in 1984, actual activities were only begun in 1987. The early years were devoted to organizational developments. From its inception, the institute sought support from official sources, including government ministries, the Jerusalem municipality, and the Chief Rabbinate, recognizing that without such assistance it would find it difficult to realize its goals. The presentation of the institute as a center of educational- and folklore-related activities, innocently seeking to inform people of the past and without making any explicit demand for the construction of the Third Temple, meant that such support was forthcoming, and generously so.

The first project the Temple Institute undertook was to recreate the ritual vessels of the Temple—a considerable task including ninety-three different objects. Some aspects of the restoration project were relatively simple, while others required extremely intricate and expensive work. Over the years, dozens of items were added to the exhibition at the institute, including the showbread table, the golden altar, the basin, the ephod of the High Priest, including the sardonyx stones, the *mizrakim*, the incense chalice, the harps and trumpets, and so forth.

The restoration work has been undertaken by a number of craftsmen, some of whom are new immigrants from the former Soviet Union, recruited for the various artistic projects. The most notable craftsman is Chaim Odem, who came to Israel from the Soviet Union in the mid-1980s and has become the leading artist in the restoration effort. Odem is also active in the Chai Vekayam movement, founded by Yehuda Etzion.

Since the late 1980s, the institute has held an annual conference on Temple research. The conference examines Halachic questions relating to the Temple, as well as historical aspects. Over the years, the Chief Rabbinate has begun to support the conference, joined later by the Jerusalem municipality and the Ministry of Religious Affairs. Participants have included respected religious figures, and the speakers have not been confined to marginal characters or Temple Mount activists. By way of example, Israel Meir Lau, prior to his appointment as the Ashkenazi Chief Rabbi of Israel, gave a lecture at one conference entitled "The Commandment of Pilgrimage in Modern Times."[24] Sephardi Chief Rabbi Eliyahu Bakshi-Doron gave a lecture on "The Sardonyx and the Ephod in the Garments of the High Priest."[25]

In 1992, the Temple Institute moved into larger and more comfortable premises in the Jewish Quarter of the Old City of Jerusalem. In the institute newsletter, Ariel thanked "those in various government ministries" who had helped greatly to reduce the institute's debts incurred by the move. In the same year, the institute began to market "Temple products" to the public on a commercial basis, including posters, calendars, miniature models of the Temple, and so on. The economic strategy of the institute included direct appeals to investors to provide substantial funds for the various projects that operated as commercial endeavors.

Over the course of the same year, the institute intensified its educational activities. The Midrasha (college), established under the auspices of the institute, initiated projects in cooperation with state-religious schools, featuring a daylong tour of Jerusalem and including a visit to the institute. Contacts were developed with educational institutions, and these have since been elaborated further. Within a few years, the Temple Institute began to hold seminars for inspectors, school principals, teachers, and students from all educational sectors. To attend to such a large number of visitors, volunteers acted as guides and instructors.[26]

In 1994, educational demand for the institute's services grew after the subject of the tabernacle and the sacred vessels was included in the matriculation examinations in Bible studies. Following requests from educational institutions, the institute began to provide lessons in schools to help students prepare for their examinations. A video was also produced to this end.[27] In 1995, the institute reported that thirty-five thousand students had visited the establishment over the course of the year. The institute improved its school teaching programs and introduced modern curricula in the field.[28] Educational programs for schools constitute one of the main fields of activity at the institute, and the Midrasha is recognized and funded by the Ministry of Education.

An additional sector that took an interest in the institute was evangelical Christian pilgrims. The institute worked hard to develop strong connections with this sector, and Rabbi Chaim Richman was appointed to coordinate this aspect of its work. In 1999, the institute informed Gershom Gornberg that this target audience provided 60 percent of the income from the sale of entrance tickets and products in the museum shop.[29] In their newsletter, the institute staff noted: "We have recently seen a growing level of interest among many peoples who hold the Bible, Jerusalem, and the Temple close to their hearts. Thousands of them visit the exhibition, and, after returning home, serve as excellent ambassadors for the Temple Institute."[30] This interest led the Ministry of Tourism to examine various possibilities for cooperating with the institute. In 1997, a commercial company was established to bring foreign tourists to the establishment.[31]

During the 1990s, the Temple Institute began to publish books, including prayer books for daily use and for the festivals. These publications include a description of the order of worship in the Temple, as well as colored illustrations prepared by the institute's artists. The institute also began to produce products for marketing in several languages.[32]

Under the auspices of the institute, a group of young violinists took on the task of recreating the tunes used by the Levites in Temple. Thus, the institute embarked on an additional endeavor to renew the musical aspects of the Temple, including the harp, violin, flute, and cymbals.[33]

In 1994, the institute received unusual support from the Dead Sea Works. Israel Ariel contacted this powerful economic corporation with the goal of learning about various types of salts, since the ritual actions of the High Priest included the use of salt. The director of the Dead Sea Works responded enthusiastically, donating a scaled model of the altar, two meters high, based on plans prepared by the institute architect Shmuel Balzam. A model sheep was also provided to illustrate the process of sacrifices. Both items are on display in the institute museum.[34] In 1996, the Dead Sea Works agreed to provide a full-scale model of the altar (thirty-two meters high) so that the institute staff could gain practical experience in the rituals relating to the sacrifices.[35] This model was housed at the Dead Sea Works and attracted numerous visitors; however, a new director at the plant ordered that the model be disassembled.

In 1994, the institute's newsletter reported on the efforts to locate and raise a red heifer in Israel.[36] In Judaism, the red heifer (Hebrew: *parah adumah*) is a heifer that is sacrificed and whose ashes are used for the ritual purification of people who came into contact with a corpse. A heifer is a young cow before she has had her first calf. Ashes of a red heifer are a necessary prerequisite for participating in any Temple service.

Although the institute has not yet managed to raise a red heifer that meets the Halachic requirements for use in the sacrifices, significant progress has been achieved. Two red heifers have been born in Israel, but these did not meet the strict laws on the issue.[37] It is reasonable to assume that the enormous efforts being made by the institute to breed a kosher red cow will eventually be successful.

During the course of 1994, the institute began to engage in political activities, initiating a proposed law (through Member of Knesset Esther Salomonovitch of the Tzomet Party) to secure the rights of the Jewish people to the Temple Mount. The institute also published a declaration signed by Rabbis Avraham Shapira and Dov Solvaytchik regarding the exclusive Jewish ownership of the site. Efforts by the institute resulted in a discussion in the office of the Chief Rabbis regarding its position on the question of visits to the Temple Mount by Jews, in light of the political changes caused by the Oslo Process. The discussion did not have any practical outcomes.[38]

The improvement in the economic position of the institute led it to launch more extravagant and far-reaching initiatives, such as the creation of a model of the Temple made from marble and gold. The flagship project, however, was the construction of a model of the Temple candelabra coated in pure gold. One of the first projects of the institute was to produce a model of the candelabrum used in the Second Temple, made from plastic and wax. The model was made by the artist Chaim Odem, based on a combination of diagrams provided by Maimonides and the form of the candelabrum that appears on Titus's Gate in Rome.[39] At Passover in 1997, the institute announced the inception of a new project: to produce a gold-plated candelabrum, while adding that the third stage of this endeavor—the casting of a candelabrum made from solid gold—could not yet be begun due to financial reasons. In 1999, the institute completed the casting of a bronze candelabrum coated in gold (42.5 kg) in a single unit. The project was funded by the businessman Vadim Rabinovitch, chairman of the Jewish Congress of the Ukraine, whose support was recruited by the local Lubavitch emissary. The estimated cost of the project is US $1,000,000.[40] Additional significant projects implemented by the institute include the preparation of a model of the altar and of the showbread table, both gold-plated. These items formed the basis for an exhibition by the institute staged in France in 2003.[41]

In 2000, the Women for the Temple movement began to operate on a formal basis. The "movement" consists of six women who are active with the support of the institute, and who organize an annual religious conference for women only. The issues examined by the conference include "the role of women in Redemption in general, and in the Temple in particular," as well as "women's worship in the Temple." However, most of the speakers at the conferences are men active in the work of the Temple Institute, such as Israel Ariel and Menachem Makover, the former director of the institute.[42] Although this movement defines itself as apolitical, its rhetoric is clearly drawn from that of the Temple Mount movements and the religious right. The movement works to collect gold, silver, and copper jewelry for the institute's work to recreate the Temple vessels. It also organizes informational evenings for women, and the founder of the movement reports that it has a mailing list of approximately one hundred women.

A key problem facing the movement is that most of the rabbis who permit Jews to visit the Temple Mount state that women are prohibited from doing so, due to problems of purity and menstrual impurity. As will be recalled, it was Shlomo Goren's concern at the possible entry of women into the site that led him to refrain from issuing a categorical ruling permitting visits to the Mount. Israel Ariel has permitted women to enter certain areas of the Temple Mount, but the movement activists are still divided on this question. The women stated to the newspaper *Ha'aretz* that some of them will not visit the Temple Mount until a clear permit is provided on this matter.[43] In any case, the women's movement is barely active for all practical terms.[44]

Conclusion

Although the Temple Institute declares that its objectives lie in the fields of "study, research, writing, publication, development, and teaching,"[45] it is apparent that it does not confine itself to a passive stance on the sidelines. The demand for the construction of the Third Temple forms a basic foundation of its activities, and the institute maneuvers carefully between its internal message and its various external methods, some of which may sometimes present a more restricted vision. Thus, for example, the large oil paintings displayed on the walls of the institute museum depict the ritual activities during the Second Temple period, and do not present a ision of the Third Temple. The large model at the institute is also of the Second Temple, and does not necessarily delineate the form of a future Third Temple. The same is true of the restored Temple vessels, which could be considered to have essential folklore value. Tens of thousands of visitors come to the institute each year and are thus exposed to a softened version of its activities. Indeed, the directors of the institute make precisely this case in their appeals to external agencies and to the secular public.

It would be wrong, however, to interpret this partial approach as representing the dominant thread in the work of the institute. The institute's objectives are very clear, and culminate in the construction of the Third Temple. Starting from the premise that the State of Israel is the "beginning of redemption," the institute then shows its visitors its vision for the end of this process, and substantiates the nature of the desired redemption. Does the fact that the activities of the institute are supported by the official organs of Religious Zionism, thereby providing tacit consent for the extreme positions of its director, suggest that the rabbis see the institute as an avant-garde force leading their entire camp?

The religious establishment has been able to support the institute because its activities take place outside the Temple Mount. Accordingly, leading figures in the Religious Zionist public have been able to visit the institute.[46] Even the Chief Rabbis have been able to attend events under the auspices of the institute; the Chief Rabbinate provides funding for the establishment, on the one hand, while maintaining its traditional position opposing entry into the Temple Mount by Jews, on the other. The delicate balancing game played by the institute takes place along the seam between what is permitted and what is forbidden. Maintaining this balance enables the institute to remain an officially sanctioned part of the establishment. In turn, this enables the religious establishment to continue its paradoxical support for the institute and its reservations regarding its positions.

The institute's activities also reflect the position that it is possible, through purely human tools, to expedite and encourage the building of the Temple. The inspiration behind this position lies in the profound personal crisis experienced by Israel Ariel after the Six-Day War. His demand that the Temple be established here and now may be seen as the product of his effort to cope with the cognitive dissonance caused by the gulf between his upbringing and the sense of elation he experienced on the Jewish return to the Temple Mount and the fact that redemption did not immediately follow. The Temple Institute constitutes a prominent and important component in the overall picture of activities relating to the establishment of the Third Temple. Chapter 3 will examine Yehuda Etzion's Redemption movement, a far more aggressive demand for the Third Temple.

A different outlook on the activities of the Temple Institute can be learned by using the analysis offered by historian Karen Armstrong, which tries to define fundamentalism in the balance between mythos and logos.

Central to her reading of history is the notion that premodern cultures possessed two complementary and indispensable ways of thinking, speaking and knowing: mythos and logos. Mythos was concerned with meaning; it provided people with a context that made sense of their day-to-day lives; it directed their attention to the eternal and the universal. Logos, on the other hand, dealt with practical matters. It forged ahead, elaborating on old insights, mastering the environment, and creating fresh and new things. Armstrong argues that modern Western society has lost the sense of mythos and enshrined logos as its foundation. Mythical narratives and the rituals and meanings attached to them have ceded authority to that which is rational, pragmatic, and scientific— but which does not assuage human pain or sorrow, and cannot answer questions about the ultimate value of human life. However, far from embarking on a wholesale rejection of the modern emphasis in favor of the old balance, the author contends that religious fundamentalists unwittingly turn the mythos of their faith into logos, giving rational meaning to mythology.

This can explain the role of the literal reading of the scriptures that characterized fundamentalist movements. This is the reason why American fundamentalists went to battle against the teaching of Darwinist theory, that contradicts biblical creation stories. From there, we can understand their attempt to scientifically prove that Jesus is indeed the son of a virgin.[47]

Even though Armstrong's theory is relevant mainly for the understanding of the motivations of Christian fundamentalists, we can still find it useful to explain those who are advocating for the immanent construction of the Third Temple. Jewish traditional literature mostly viewed the construction of the Temple as a miraculous event that will take place as part of the End of Days. It may be possible to view the demand to rebuild the Temple by human effort—thereby rejecting the passive awaiting of heavenly occurances—as a cognitive attempt to make the miracle real.

It seems like from all the activities surrounding the construction of the Third Temple, the Temple Institute is the most prominent force working for the implementation of this vision, in the ways of the modernist trend of fundamentalism.

3

The Movement for Redemption and Yehuda Etzion
Theocratic Post-Zionism

In the spring of 1984, the Israeli General Security Service (GSS) uncovered the so-called Jewish Underground, a group that committed a series of revenge attacks on Arabs. The members planted incendiary devices in the cars of the leaders of the National Guidance Committee, a group of local Palestinian leaders, in response to an attack on a group of Jews in Hebron (May 1980). The mayors of Ramallah and Nablus lost their legs in the action, and an IDF bomb disposal expert was injured while attempting to defuse a third device. At the beginning of July 1983, Aharon Gross, a student at Shavei Hevron yeshiva (which has links with Mercaz Harav yeshiva), was murdered. The Jewish Underground responded by attacking the Islamic College in Hebron, a center of anti-Israeli activities. Three Arabs were murdered in the attack and approximately thirty were injured. An attempt by the underground to booby-trap a bus transporting Arab workers in East Jerusalem was foiled after the underground cell was exposed by the GSS.

Three men initiated the establishment of the Jewish Underground: Michael Livny, Yehoshua Ben-Shoshan, and Yehuda Etzion. The latter two also had a further objective that was not realized, and this was the underlying motivation behind the establishment of the underground. At the beginning of Etzion's trial, he confessed that "the action against the mayors took one month of my life. The thoughts, preparations, conceptions, and actions I undertook with regard to the [Temple] Mount occupied years of my life."[1] Indeed, this was the true objective of the underground—to remove the mosques from the Temple Mount and prepare the site for the establishment of the Third Temple.

51

This chapter examines Yehuda Etzion and his activities after his release from prison, particularly the establishment of the Chai Vekayam Movement for Redemption. Etzion is one of the most original thinkers among contemporary Religious Zionists; his positions constitute a right-wing benchmark and draw the Gush Emunim public toward religious extremism and radicalism. I will present his theocratic perspective, which advocates the "cleansing" of the Temple Mount as a first step toward the reconstruction of the Temple, and I will discuss the steps he has taken to advance his position.

Although Etzion is a product of Gush Emunim, his spiritual positions differ from those of Mercaz Harav yeshiva, which is most closely identified with that movement. Etzion chose to base his worldview on the writings of Shabbtai Ben Dov, whose philosophy will be examined later in this chapter. I will also examine Etzion's perspective against the background of these sources, with an emphasis on the symbolic importance Etzion attaches to the issue of the Temple Mount and the actions that stem from this approach.

"[Yehuda Etzion] is a person who constantly feels he has a role to play in the process of redemption, and who asks himself each day: What am I doing to help the process of redemption." Etzion's wife chose these words to describe her husband.[2] The biographical outline of his life—studies at a yeshiva high school in Pardes Hannah, followed by a Hesder yeshiva, and military service in a combat engineering corps—is relatively routine and carries no hint of the unique course he would later take.

After the signing of the Camp David accords in 1979, Etzion decided to sever his connections with Gush Emunim completely because of his conviction that the task of raising the Jewish people toward redemption could not be based solely on the vision of the settlements. Etzion's ideology, which led him first to the Jewish Underground and later to the Movement for Redemption, is driven by a profound sense of crisis. His approach is that in the absence of positive progress, deterioration and retreat inevitably ensue. The redemption of the Jewish people requires proactive steps, and Gush Emunim, as the leading body carrying the message of redemption, lacks the proper tools for creating the desired breakthrough. Etzion argued that Zionism had reached a dead end; existing mechanisms could not overcome the crisis, and new objectives must be set.

In this chapter I will show that Etzion's approach was the product of his internal struggle with a failure of faith. Etzion is not alone in these feelings. Since the peace process between Israel and Egypt (1978), many Religious Zionists have been forced to confront the growing contradiction of their basic assumptions regarding the nature and destiny of the State of Israel. The withdrawal from Sinai, and, later, the Madrid talks and the Oslo Process, which led to an Israeli withdrawal from parts of the West Bank, led to a severe theological crisis. Etzion's reaction to this crisis was to reinforce his messianic faith, and to engage in forceful action with the goal of expediting the realization of this faith. Etzion developed his solution to this dissonance as early as the late 1970s, and his approach became more determined as time passed. Etzion functions as a "prophet" or a "general without soldiers," as one of his associates described him to me in a personal conversation. He is not a charismatic leader attracting the masses after him, but his position embodies a clear message. The psychological dissonance experienced by Religious Zionism over the past two decades, and particularly since the early 1990s, produced a broader and deeper response in the practical and ideological approach taken by Etzion.

The Foundation of Crisis:
The Background to Cognitive Dissonance

As noted, the messianic role attributed to the State of Israel by Religious Zionists, and the actualization of this concept following the 1967 war, later sparked a crisis among many in these circles following the peace treaty with Egypt and the potential shattering of the vision of the Greater Land of Israel. The situation was exacerbated still further following the Oslo Accords and the withdrawals from parts of the West Bank. The crisis was caused by the inability and unwillingness of those involved to see the State of Israel moving in a direction that was inconsonant with, and even diametrically opposed to, the process of redemption as they saw it. They could not tolerate any concept of retreat, whether territorial or spiritual; the withdrawals constituted irrefutable proof that the process of redemption was reversible, and this is the underlying cause of the dissonance they experienced.

Dov Schwartz argues that this crisis led to two main responses within Religious Zionism. The first advocates a further strengthening of educational efforts to show secular Israeli Jews the path to a "Zionism of faith."[3] The second adopts the opposite approach, focusing on reimmersion in the sacred texts relating to the process of redemption, accompanied by a tendency to passivity and isolationism.[4] In my opinion, an intermediate response may also be noted by Etzion, and it may be described as a post-Zionist theocratic response.

The main thrust of Etzion's criticism of the Religious Zionist leaders is that they allowed secular Jews to lead the process of redemption. The idea that secular Israelis, unaware of the tremendous mission they bore, would deliver their secular enterprise into the hands of a messianic theocracy proved mistaken. The divine mission was neglected by precisely those who were destined to be its bearers—Religious Zionism; and in place of progress came regression. The desire for "normality" led the course of redemption to the edge of oblivion.

The processes of secularization undergone by Israeli society, and the willingness to view the territories occupied in the 1967 war as bargaining chips to secure peace agreements and compromise, while totally ignoring their messianic importance—all this, Etzion believed, proved that the tactic adopted by Religious Zionism had been mistaken, since general Zionism did not have the strength to lead the journey toward an era of total redemption.

For Etzion, the "supreme strategy" of Religious Zionism remained the desire to move closer to a theocratic messianic dominion. In tactical terms, however, an urgent revision was required in the definition of how to lead this process. The answer lay in religious radicalism and theocratic activism. Etzion interpreted the "Return to Zion" as a cosmic process progressing toward the redemption of the People of Israel. However, he argued, the way in which Religious Zionism had sought to channel the people toward this goal had actually led to the traumatic consequences of Israel's territorial withdrawals.

Surprisingly, Etzion argued that the responsibility for this failure on the part of Religious Zionism rested with its adoption of the philosophy of Rabbi Avraham Yitzhak Hacohen Kook, as embodied in the approach of Mercaz Harav yeshiva.

As mentioned, Mercaz Harav yeshiva, which seeks to combine religiosity and nationalism, elevates and sanctifies two principal values: The sanctity of the Land of Israel and the sanctity of the State of Israel. According to the approach of Rabbi Zvi Yehuda Hacohen Kook, as transmitted to his students and followers, the Land of Israel constitutes a single, organic entity that belongs to the entire Jewish people—past, present, and future. Thus, land and people are fused in complete unity. Accordingly, no individual has the right to relinquish any part of the land, since it does not belong to any single group. The fusion of people and land reflects the divine will for the redemption of the Jewish people.[5]

Within this structure, the tool for realizing Divine will is manifested in Jewish nationhood. Accordingly, the doctrine of the sanctity of the Land of Israel is mirrored by the sanctity of the State of Israel, since the State of Israel advances a messianic process, albeit unwittingly. Zvi Yehuda Hacohen Kook went further still: "It must be recalled for once and for all: that which is sacred is sacred! . . . The State of Israel and the governmental regime in Israel are sacred. Everything that belongs to the observance of this commandment, all the tanks and other weapons . . . belong to this sanctity."[6]

Etzion's criticism is that the sanctification of the state by the adherents of approach taken by the Mercaz Harav yeshiva can prevent an effective struggle against the state when it is thwarting processes that can lead to redemption. When the State of Israel decides to withdraw from parts of the Land of Israel, the yeshiva is trapped and cannot take firm action against such a policy. The weakness of the Mercaz Harav school is manifested in the clearest terms in its position regarding the Temple Mount. Etzion argues that if the state were to declare its sovereignty over the Mount and remove the Waqf and the mosques, the followers of the yeshiva would laud its actions. Since the government refuses to do so, however, they justify this inaction by resorting to the traditional formula that "the generation is not yet prepared" for such a step.

Accordingly, Etzion argues, a different ideology and solution are required. Etzion finds these among the veterans of the Lechi underground movement. The formative figure in shaping Etzion's worldview is Shabbtai Ben Dov. Ben Dov, an autodidact and a prolific writer, became an ideal and an idol for Etzion. He stated that Ben Dov's vision inspired his plan to blow up the mosques on the Temple Mount. In any case, Etzion's activist stance on the question of the Temple Mount and the Temple obliged him to go beyond the confines of the Orthodox Zionist camp to find a philosophical foundation for his approach. Accordingly, a brief review of Ben Dov and his political philosophy is appropriate.

The Ideology of Shabbtai Ben Dov

Shabbtai Ben Dov was an activist in the Lechi underground movement. In his writings, he elaborated a plan to transform the State of Israel from a parliamentary democracy into a theocracy. Ben Dov was not an influential figure during his life, although he gave lectures and met with groups of young people. Little attention has been given to examining the philosophy of this spiritual mentor and the political and theological principles that emerge from his writings; this section will attempt to fill this void. It is important to note, however, that Ben Dov worked and developed his philosophy within an ideological circle that included other veterans of the Lechi movement who published their ideas in the journal *Sulam*. I have chosen to concentrate mainly on the thought of Ben Dov, rather than the other writers in *Sulam* because of his central role in the revolutionary discourse of the Temple Mount activists.

Shabbtai Ben Dov was born in Vilna in 1924, and grew up in a Jewish home with a strong sense of national identity. His parents employed a tutor when Ben Dov was only six years old to teach him Hebrew and Jewish studies. His father, Dov Dravinsky, was a prosperous man who provided an aristocratic education for his son. His mother, Miriam (née Levinson), a music teacher by profession, ensured that Shabbtai observed the religious commandments. At his father's insistence, he also used to study the writings of Polish and Lithuanian nationalist writers. Approximately one year after his father died, when Shabbtai was eleven years old, Shabbtai emigrated to Palestine.

He was accepted into the third grade of Geulah High School of Commerce in Tel-Aviv; he later described himself as a fairly mediocre student. As a youngster, Ben Dov had already begun a series of political shifts; he first supported the Haredi party Agudat Israel, and later transferred his allegiance to Jabotinsky, before eventually joining those who broke away to form the Lechi group. After the assassination of Yair Stern, the Lechi leader, Ben Dov was arrested due to the actions of informers; he was not yet eighteen. He was first held in detention camps in Mizra, Latrun, and Akko, and later was exiled to Kenya and Sudan, together with two hundred fifty of his comrades from the underground movements.[7] Six years behind bars gave Ben Dov an opportunity to acquire knowledge in the fields of history, psychology, political economics, and the Hebrew language. He returned to Israel in May 1948, ten days after the declaration of independence. Israel Eldad noted that Ben Dov spoke eight languages, could read a further three, and had a basic knowledge of two others.

After the 1948 war, Ben Dov began to study law at the Hebrew University. However, after reading Asher Golak's book *The Foundations of Hebrew Law*, he became aware of what he considered a fundamental flaw: his obvious lack of knowledge of the Hebrew sources. Accordingly, he began to study the Bible, Gemara, and Mishnah, as well as completing his broad-based general education. As the years passed, he saw the light and adopted a religious lifestyle. He worked as a legal adviser in the Ministry of Trade and Industry for his living, and, after the Six-Day War in 1967, was the first person to petition the Supreme Court, demanding that the State of Israel expropriate the control of entry into the Temple Mount from the Waqf and transfer it to persons charged with protecting the Mount as a sacred site to the Jewish religion. In 1979, Ben Dov died; he was just fifty-five.[8]

Ben Dov's first essay was published in 1953 in *Sulam*, and he continued to write extensively regarding his vision of the course by which Jewish redemption should be advanced. He expounded on his approach in two key books, on which my presentation of his philosophy is based.[9]

I begin the examination of his legacy with the central argument presented in his second book *Prophecy and Tradition in Redemption*, which was written in the form of a series of debates challenging the findings of Gershom Scholem, the renowned researcher into the Kabbalah and Jewish mysticism. According to Ben Dov, Scholem saw the mystical perception of the Messiah as depicted in the Lurianic Kabbalah (Rabbi Isaac Luria) as the sole manifestation of the concept of messianism. Accordingly, the crisis following the apostasy of Shabbtai Zvi—as an attempt to realize the vision of redemption in concrete terms—was perceived as the logical and inevitable result of the presumptive desire to realize the messianic ideal per se.[10] The conclusion that emerges from Scholem's works, and which Shabbtai Ben Dov challenged, was that a similar outcome will always be produced whenever an attempt is made to realize the messianic idea. Accordingly, if Judaism will face apostasy during the attempt to realize the vision of redemption, it is better for it to continue its course without such attempts, and without a living, acute, and binding messianic tradition.

Scholem's positions in this respect may have been influenced by his personal worldview, by his fear that Zionist endeavors would become colored by a messianic or apocalyptic hue, and, above all, by his concern of the possible ramifications of such an approach regarding the status of the Temple Mount.[11] Be this as it may, Ben Dov felt obliged to challenge Scholem's assumptions. His position was diametrically opposed to that of Scholem; he passionately believed that it was only the aspiration to redemption that could grant vitality and meaning to Zionist political life in the revived Jewish state.

Ben Dov, who, as noted, was among those who left the Etzel underground movement along with Yair Stern, saw the philosophy of the Lechi movement as the key to realizing the Jewish people's longing for redemption. He sought to develop the political ideology of the dissident group, as reflected, among other sources, in the poems of Uri Zvi Greenberg, and to imbue this ideology with religious content rooted in Jewish tradition. Thus, he sought to synthesize the romantic political messianism characteristic of this group, which drew extensively on traditional messianic myths, though not always in their traditional context,[12] and the naturalistic religious messianism that constitutes a distinct thread within Jewish tradition, particularly in the political Halachic codex included in Maimonides's *The Laws of Kings and Their Wars* in his Halachic work *Mishneh Torah*. In other words, Ben Dov sought to offer a conceptual fusion of political messianism and ideas that view ideal Jewish dominion as the manifestation of the Divine kingdom.

After the establishment of the state, some of the veterans of the Lechi movement expressed their approach in the journal *Sulam*, edited by Israel Eldad (Scheib), who was also a prolific contributor to the journal. Eldad was profoundly influenced by Nietzschean philosophy, which he openly expounded after translating his works into Hebrew.[13] By contrast, Ben Dov adopted his own approach to the merging of Western philosophical influences; he did not quote these directly, but integrated them in his writings.

As was the case with Eldad and his circle, Ben Dov also seems to have seen the Fascist regime in Italy as a model for the desirable system of government in Israel and for the character of the Hebrew kingdom. The governmental system that emerges from his writings is certainly reminiscent of this regime.

Israel Eldad argued that the proper system of government for the State of Israel should be dictatorial and theocratic: "The truth is that Mussolini's dictatorship contained nothing bad for the Jews of Italy or for

Zionism until that last, foolish, and unnecessary step that Mussolini took toward what seemed to be the victorious side."[14] He believed that the Hebrew revolution could not be borne by a democratic regime; accordingly, Israel should become a governmental dictatorship in the spirit of Italian Fascism: "The dictatorship of an authoritarian regime is the solution and alternative to rotten democracy. Free of the egoistical interests of the electors [=elections], they [the leaders] will be able to take the nation forward toward the ideal kingdom of Israel".[15] This circle also rejected universal and humanistic morality, and was particularly critical of those who presented this morality as an authentic Jewish value. For their part, they were convinced that universal morality is inherently alien to Judaism,[16] and that humanism is a distortion of the foundation of Jewish faith resulting from the other distortions of the Jewish Emancipation.[17]

However, Ben Dov differed from Eldad's circle in his effort to find a genuine interface between these two approaches. Whereas for Eldad Jewish tradition was essentially an instrument for the development of national identity and myths, and less a prescription of ritual requirements, Ben Dov was concerned mainly by the intellectual attempt to overcome the barrier of messianic passivity in Jewish tradition. To this end, he drew on theories of totalitarianism that grant a topical dimension to the utopian messianic myth, which is transmuted into the secular, mundane, and political realm. Ben Dov sought to transform redemption into an instrument for human execution, with no place for Divine intervention. In his notebooks, he undertook an exercise designed to return the idea of totality to the religious sphere in the form of theocracy. The replacement of the kingdom of God on earth with the kingdom of humanity on earth; the perception of the ideal of the End of Days as an achievable reality that must be brought about here and now through the actions of believers; the need for revolutionary political action by an informed vanguard to restore history to its proper path; and the construction of a new social, national, or world order—all these characteristic components of political messianism may be found in the religious ideology of Shabbtai Ben Dov.[18]

Immediately after the establishment of the State of Israel, Ben Dov felt that the Zionist movement had lost its drive and was stagnating, leaving a sense of emptiness and a loss of values. Zionism had reached a point where it no longer had any reason to rebel; accordingly, it was in a process of degeneration. The Zionist rebellion was a rebellion against the essence of Jewish life in the Diaspora, and the Hebrew resurgence opposed Jewish culture, which could not meet its national needs. However, whereas the assimilators sought to adopt a different identity, the Zionists maintained their essentially Jewish identity, and were thus left disconnected from any foundation on which they might draw.

Ben Dov argued that modern Jews had not fully internalized European culture, and that this was particularly apparent among those who emigrated to Israel. Accordingly, Zionism was trapped in internal contradictions due to its refusal to accept the Jewish religion as its basis and due to its self-perception as a purely political movement with no over-arching objectives.

In his first book, *Jewish Redemption in Political Crisis*, Ben Dov analyzed the alienation of the various Zionist ideologies. He argued that Socialist Zionism faced an inherent contradiction; by its nature, Socialism was a cosmopolitan movement; however, as the result of anti-Semitism, the Jews had no choice but to wage their class war in the Land of Israel, separate from their fellow revolutionaries in Europe. Accordingly, the Zionist class war contradicted the basic assumptions of Socialism: Jewish Socialism sought first to establish a political entity and then to join the Socialist Utopia, thus distorting the entire essence of Socialism.

The same was true of liberalism and humanism. While English liberalism centered on the English way of life, and was intrinsically bound with English democracy, Zionist liberalism, like Zionist Marxism, could not connect with its thematic values, and was the product of the need to escape and reject Jewish values. Ben Dov argued that the root of the problem lay in the democratic liberal regime, which has no interest in supreme national goals in the spirit of political messianism. Democracy serves as an instrument for realizing the desires of its constituent individuals, through free, organic, and independent competition. Such a regime can carry no purpose other than the bourgeois purpose of increasing capital, and this situation is created by means of the division of government and ensuing competition. These values, he posited, are contradictory to the purpose of the Jewish people, which is complete redemption. Existence without an overarching goal, without the demand to realize redemption here and now, renders the reality of the Jewish people under the democratic regime pointless and meaningless and, accordingly, both foolish and dangerous. Democracy is "foolish—since it complicates our morality with . . . values whose entire import is historically alien, and destructive since it deprives our culture of its internal Hebrew historical development and transplants it into an alien tradition."[19]

The supreme goal nurtured by Zionism was a restricted political goal: the establishment of a state for the Jews in the Land of Israel. Once this goal was realized, and the movement lacked any new and ultimate goals, a psychological crisis developed, leading to a new goal: to be "a normal people."

However, the value of normality is contradictory to the nature of the Jewish people as the "Chosen People." The concept of the chosen character of the Jewish people was denuded of any practical content in the everyday reality of Zionism, and was left as no more than a debilitated reference in the synagogue. In its current state, the Jewish people are so convinced that they are no longer the Chosen People that they feels no need to tell themselves any more that they are such a people and, as a result, are drawing further away from the religious tradition. Since the people have such a strong desire to free themselves of the recognition that it is different from the Gentiles, yet still wish to maintain their national existence, the simplest course open is for them to attempt to mimic the Gentiles in political terms. Accordingly, the aspiration of messianism was replaced by the aspiration of normality, and, as a result, once Zionism realizes its goals it will be no different from any other nation, without any unique status or purpose.[20]

The solution lies in an ongoing effort to act in accordance with the original destiny of the people: their messianic destiny. However, such a driving force cannot come from the rational world of Zionism. The necessary ideological resurgence must focus on the desire for Jewish redemption; this will complement Zionism and "take over the reigns." The Torah must take its rightful place in practical life, and it must do so immediately:[21]

> The overall condition for drawing out of the crisis is that an ideal-istic resurgence emerge among us that will no longer be reflected merely in the experience of Hebrew nationhood, associated with a number of partial problems and subject to a structure of random and contradictory values, as was the case with Zionism, but rather which shall appear as a complete psychological entirety in a Hebrew awareness that embraces and clarifies through faith the entire extent of national content, rejecting all that is alien and irksome, and drawing its aspirations autonomously from its own sources; a resurgence that is rooted and based in the Torah, and which draws from the Torah the full sacred strength of the aspiration for Israeli redemption, in order once again to reestablish the Holy Dominion of Israel; and, in a nutshell, and in the full sense of the phrase—messianic resurgence.[22]

What exactly does Ben Dov mean by "messianic resurgence"? In Jewish tradition, messianic expectation did not demand any active step to realize redemption, with the exception of the requirement to pray and to maintain ritual purity to enable the arrival of the redeemer. The Zionist consciousness sought to break this cognitive mold, advocating concrete political action while rejecting and negating the passive tradition.[23] Shabbtai Ben Dov argued that activism and traditionalism could be combined, and that the realization of redemption could come through mundane actions in the present world. To this end, the concept of redemption, which is a principle of mundane realization, must be distinguished from the concept of the End of Days, which includes the redemption of the world and the resurrection of the dead, and relates the miraculous aspects of redemption and, accordingly, to its passive sides.

The plan developed by Ben Dov demanded practical responsibility and actions. He believed that there was no need to change the Jewish religion and no need to negate Torah. The central idea in his platform was that the world is defective and needs the tradition of Torah to be repaired. The Halacha is the objective yardstick by which the vision of redemption is to be gauged, with no need for antinomian innovations. He argued that everything could be found in the Torah—the kingdom of Israel could be ordered and managed in accordance with the laws presented in the Torah.[24] This is the fundamentalist element in his thought, connected with his rejection of modern liberalism; he seeks to provide an overall goal for the Zionist enterprise in the form of the reinstatement of the monarchy, drawn from naturalist messianic tradition and integrating aspects of political messianic thought.

The proposed state is supposed to operate in accordance with several basic principles derived from the Torah, as interpreted by Ben Dov:[25]

1. *Hebrew morality of war*—"a morality free of any European-Christian ambivalence"; a morality that is not based solely on defensive values. Ben Dov was influenced here by the approach that sanctifies militarism, as a force for building and galvanizing the nation, and that despises humanistic and pacifistic tendencies.

2. *The Jews are the Chosen People*—for Ben Dov, the concept embodied in the scriptures that the Jews are the Chosen People negates the possibility that they might employ Gentile systems of government. This approach is analogous to certain circles within political messianism, and particularly Mussolini's theory of Fascism, which emphasized the unique identity of the nation as a supreme value, as the antithesis of the universalistic concepts of democracy and Socialism, and as a rebellion against the panhuman tradition of humanism.[26] The same approach leads to the next principle.

3. *The vision and model of the Torah*—secular thought cannot provide the mental strength needed for the national revival of the messianic standard. To this end, the model must be found in the Torah and Halacha. Accordingly, the future society will take the Halachic lifestyle as its ideal.

4. *The kingdom of God*—that is, theocracy; an approach that sees the Jewish kingdom as a form of government that seeks to execute God's will. This will is manifested indirectly through emissaries—the sages of the Sanhedrin. The Divine Presence

rules over the Sanhedrin, the bearers of the Torah and the bearers of the nation's vision. Ben Dov argues that the denial by the State of Israel of the principle of the kingdom of God does not bind the people; accordingly, it is permissible to revolt against a government that is not the government of Torah.

5. *The Jubilee system*—the desired economic regime is a military regime based on a national economy. This regime will enable the implementation of the vision of the Jubilee as a mechanism for the redistribution of land. This economic regime neutralizes individual capitalism, while avoiding the opposite extreme of collectivism. In my opinion, echoes of this approach may also be found in the economic policy of Italian Fascism, which nationalized the economy while permitting free competition.[27]

6. *The Arab problem*—according to Ben Dov, the non-Jewish residents of the Land of Israel must choose between the three options presented by Yehoshua Bin Nun during the biblical conquest of the land: Those who wish to leave may do so; those who accept the Jewish faith—not by way of surrender, but ab initio, wholeheartedly, and genuinely—may remain; and those who wage war "shall have no pardon even in surrender."[28]

7. *The exile in Diaspora*—According to Ben Dov, the Jewish Diaspora is merely an annex of the Land of Israel; it has no importance except in terms of its affinity to the land. The endeavor of national revival is the responsibility of the entire Jewish people, including both those who live in the Land of Israel and those in the Diaspora.

Ben Dov believed that while Zionism had developed in the context of European political thought, it was indirectly activated by the Hebrew longing for redemption. It was this longing that had guided the movement to the Land of Israel, rather than Uganda, for example; and it would provide the impetus for its own completion through the course of religious redemption. His conclusion was that it was essential to act within this imperative, and not within the cultural hybrid of Zionism. The transition from the existing consciousness to the Hebrew consciousness of sanctity must be free of any reliance on alien cultures; to this end, all the members of the new Jewish community in the Land of Israel must be educated in the spirit and values of the Torah.[29]

The clearest weakness in Ben Dov's theory as present hitherto would seem to be the fact that the ideal Jewish kingdom is the kingdom of God. Indeed, this is the essence of theocracy: the dominion of God is implemented by mundane forces. It is not a human dominion, and the function it grants to the human is that of a servant of God's will.

The question that inevitably arises, however, is, Who knows what is God's will? Accordingly, a truly theocratic regime requires the resumption of prophecy. Only a prophet can communicate directly with God and convey the sublime messages to mere mortals. However, Judaism teaches that prophecy has vanished from the earth and there are no more prophets. How, then, can a theocracy be maintained in the absence of prophets?[30]

Ben Dov was aware of this dilemma. His solution was that the institution of prophecy could also be reinstated through mundane tools. He argued that prophecy had vanished from the world due to Jewish passivity, which had adapted to the realities of exile and was unable to renew itself according to the "messianic standard" that could lead to Jewish redemption. He argued that the reinstatement of prophecy required a messianic vision for the Jewish people in the spirit of the mundane program of redemption. It would then be possible to witness new prophecy, and the conditions for the redemption of the people would be complete.

Ben Dov draws on the definition offered by Max Weber regarding the distinction between bureaucratic and charismatic behavior, arguing that since the destruction of the Second Temple, the Jewish people acted, in religious terms, according to the bureaucratic model, lacking charismatic leadership with the vision to bring the people back to their homeland. Charismatic figures certainly emerged among the people, but either they lacked a message capable of leading to change, or they transpired to carry a false message and were rejected by the people. "In the final analysis, therefore, the people remained stuck in a double paralysis, lacking any prophetic message of progress that could remove them from their miserable state, and lacking a prophet who might bear the true message of such a transformation."[31]

The bearing of the vision of Jewish redemption in accordance with the messianic standard, and the shaping and consolidation of this standard within Jewish tradition, entails the model for the reinstatement of prophecy. The figure of the prophet that emerges from Ben Dov's writings is that of an ideologue acting to find religious solutions to develop the dominion of religion. Shabbtai Ben Dov fiercely rejects the assumption that the prophet is a passive and metaphysical intermediary who is granted a Divine mission, and who proclaims this message like the Oracle of Delphi. He argues that the Jewish prophet must experience the message of prophecy from the grassroots, seeing that which requires repair; through this process, the message will descend from "above," and the will of God will be revealed to him.[32] The truthfulness of the prophet is gauged by the extent to which his prophecy materializes. Accordingly, prophecy will be renewed before the construction of the Temple, and not after. The new prophecy will emerge as a derivative of the mundane realization of the goals of redemption—the reinstatement of the ritual on the Temple Mount in the a theocratic political framework.

Ben Dov argued that the founders and thinkers of the Zionist movement constitute a manifestation of the renewal of the spirit of prophecy among the Jewish people. However, this is a lower form of prophecy, since it is not rooted in the Jewish tradition. A higher type of prophecy may be found in the principles that led Yair Stern to leave the Etzel movement, as well as in the poetry of Uri Zvi Greenberg. Both these figures reflected a higher level of prophecy, since their vision of the dominion of Israel may be found in their poetry. Nevertheless, their prophecy was also tainted by the "diseases" of excessive humanism and by the direct influence of secular European political theories.

A further condition for securing the prophetic spirit lies in a total disconnection from the Orthodox establishment to overcome its "bureaucratic" influences and to develop the foundation for completely new institutions. Only through the rebellion against the religious establishment, or at least by circumventing its authority, can a message be offered for the future and can the process of redemption be advanced. There can be no message of redemption without such a disconnection; there can be no message while the tradition of the Diaspora continues to be institutionalized as in the past.[33]

The process of reversing the current course, which has reached an impasse, and of moving toward the desired redemption demands revolutionary tactics of an essentially political nature. The goal of these tactics is to change the patterns of government and to introduce a regime whose leadership possesses a messianic consciousness.[34]

Accordingly, the pattern of the struggle should remain within the confines of democracy:

> Who holds authority? The current regime holds authoritative validity. But our authority rests on the validity of the destiny of the mission imposed on us in accordance with the spirit of God, which seizes us in sanctity. . . . We are commanded and entitled to remove the current establishment, to replace and change it, and to bring in another in its place; in any case, however, we are not permitted to rebel against it through hostility. . . . It must be noted that the regime in Israel is improper and distorted . . . since the alien principle of democracy is itself one of the main foundations against which our revolution is to be directed. *Accordingly, we can accept democracy only as a potential factor to be exploited* . . . and in the context that it is not the laws of the state themselves that shall determine what is permitted and prohibited for us in our revolutionary subversion against it, but rather the Torah of Israel and the sense of national responsibility we bear shall determine to what

extent we shall recognize or reconcile ourselves to the laws of the
state in our practical struggle. . . . We consider our authority
superior to that of the existing regime, even to the point of negating the validity of the latter in accordance with our approach, and
it is as we already constituted a type of "shadow government"
behind and above the existing regime. (emphasis added)[35]

To implement this revolution, several steps are required: The reinstatement
of the Sanhedrin, functioning as the antithesis of the Israeli legal system;
the establishment of a yeshiva open to prophetic inspiration; and the renewal of the Levite tribe, whose function is to guide the people in consolidating the dominion and to serve as the flagship of the rejuvenated state.

As is evident from Ben Dov's comments, his attachment to democracy
is purely for tactical reasons. In 1979, he proposed that the revolutionary action could begin with a struggle against "governmental treachery," since the
state was failing to settle all the territories occupied in the Six-Day War. The
movement of redemption would seek to "disrupt this treachery" by settling
the land against the wishes of the existing regime. If the regime acted against
them, it would "no longer be a regime bearing historical Israeli sovereignty,
and even the use of force cannot be considered a prohibited rebellion; on
the contrary: This is a choice commandment, and provided that the tactical effectiveness of the contest shall indeed be reasonable."[36]

The ideal group for leading the revolution is none other than Religious
Judaism. This sector can light the spark of the messianic movement—if only
it so wishes. Herein, however, lies the problem: it does not wish to.[37] Ben
Dov argues that traditional Judaism has freed itself of the messianic dilemma
posed by the Zionist enterprise, which has realized significant portions of
what was supposed to constitute the vision of religious redemption, by separating itself from Zionism and by declining to take part in the historical
course of the nation. Accordingly, this section of the people saw itself as the
bearer of Torah, rather than the bearer of the nation, and is now no more
than another party within Judaism. This explains the adoption of the label
"Religious Judaism," by way of apposition to "Secular Judaism"—the former
is engaged in affairs of faith, and the latter in the affairs of society.[38]

Through this process, Religious Judaism came to focus solely on ritual: "exercises of order and the parade of the Lord's army. Disconnected
from bearing the Covenant and from the core commandments of the
Torah, and disconnected from any genuine sacred experience."[39] Thus
from a way of life, religion became a routine and a degenerative conceptual rut. This weakness convinced the public that religion could make no
meaningful contribution to contemporary life.

Despite this criticism, Ben Dov felt that religious circles could provide the springboard for the solution. Their advantage is that the religious

population maintains the spark of the Torah, and therefore has the necessary foundation for the revolution. The problem of the religious public lies in a mediocrity that prevents it from overcoming the routine of the Diaspora and halting the process of degeneration. Only by actualizing the values of redemption may it be possible to lead to the growth of a powerful movement toward the concept of revolution within this sector. Activism is the only way to secure revolutionary change.[40] Accordingly, Ben Dov believed that this psychological process within Religious Judaism could be led only by the veterans of the Lechi movement—the followers of Yair and Uri Zvi Greenberg.

The ideology of Lechi was also rooted in "alien" European culture. The movement blended foreign ideas alongside Jewish ones, creating "a schizophrenia and Machiavellianism just as in any other Zionist doctrine." After the establishment of the state, however, Israel Eldad attempted, through the journal *Sulam*, to encourage deeper study of Jewish tradition and to reject alien values drawn from secular approaches. Accordingly, this grouping would be able to lead the way to the regime of mundane redemption.[41]

Ben Dov's dream of realizing Jewish dominion through political means positions him as the "missing link" in an ideological structure linking secular millennialism, in the form of the political messianism that became the "state religion" of the totalitarian regimes, and theocratic and fundamentalist ideals.[42]

The Ideology of Yehuda Etzion

Yehuda Etzion argues that the Torah constitutes the proper standard for the life of the Jewish nation. The Utopia is represented by Jewish dominion. This should be guided by the Great Court, sitting in the Hewn-Stone Hall in the Temple, where the religious rituals of the sacrifices are carried out. The Jewish people should seize, farm, and guard the Promised Land from the River Jordan to the Mediterranean Sea. This is the balance of perfection, and from this basis the culture of the Jewish people springs.

Etzion argues that the Torah does not permit a state of exile. The perfect state comes when the people live in their own land and worship their God. Accordingly, there is no commandment to reconquer the land, since no permit was ever granted to leave it. Neither is there a commandment "to remove the impurity and cleanse the Temple Mount" and to build the Third Temple—since the Temple was supposed to be eternal.

The destruction of the Temple and exile were the result of sin and the outcome of the reprehensible behavior of the Jewish people. The Torah teaches that the people must repent their sins and return to the fold; this entails returning to the Holy Land and reinstating their sovereign life as in ancient times. The Torah commands Jews to choose life: "For I have set before you life and death . . . choose life" (Deut. 30:19). Exile carries the essence of death and the absence of national life; its contrast lies in the return to the Land of Israel and the maintenance of life therein. The Torah demands life as a nation in the Land of Israel; accordingly, life outside the Holy Land is tantamount to the rejection of the entire foundation of the Torah and analogous to idolatry.[43]

The existence of the people has a purpose and the nation has a destiny: to establish a kingdom of priests and a holy nation. This is the principle that should dictate national laws and behavior. "We exist in the world in order to realize our destiny." Such a life cannot be merely biological; its meaning rests in the renewal of the Covenant with God. Accordingly, national existence must be independent and free of any involvement or collaboration with alien values of the nations, which "oppose the standard of life our Torah demands and impede our efforts for its realization."[44]

However, the ability to act toward this destiny was blunted during the course of exile, and framed in the terms of a miracle: "The Holy One, blessed be He, will send us Messiah on a white donkey, will lead us to the Land of Israel, and will bring down the Temple from the heavens."[45] Thus, Etzion explains, a life of destiny was replaced by a life of survival. Redemption became an abstract concept, beyond reality, and connected with the expectation of miracles.

Although it is a movement of national resurgence, Zionism operates outside the bounds of this destiny. Rather than being drawn to the destiny of establishing sovereign life in the Land of Israel, it was pushed into this position by anti-Semitism and global developments. As a result, it developed its ideology on the basis of the idea of finding a solution to the Jewish question and of locating a refuge for the Jews. In other words, Etzion argues, Zionism sought to find a life of survival and aspired to become "a normal nation." The Zionist leaders turned their backs on Jewish study and tradition, which was perceived as an impediment and an obstacle along their course.[46]

The pointlessness of Zionism weakened the people's resolve to strive toward its destiny and its ultimate objective. Accordingly, that section of the public that has a consciousness of destiny must strive to replace Zionism. The Movement of Redemption that Etzion began to envisage was intended to alter the course of Zionism:

> To take the initiative, to accept responsibility and authority to act for the redemption of Israel, is the basic logic behind our Torah, and accordingly it is God's will of us.[47]
>
> It is our obligation to observe that the cart of Zionism, which has for a long time now—from the outset, in fact!—has been moving along a no-through road, has now indeed reached an

impasse. . . . Just as we have grown up and abandoned the child-
ish naivety of awaiting a miracle, so we have matured beyond the
approach that seeks to cast our redemption in the secular mold
of mundane existence.[48]

In light of Etzion's anticipation of the end of Zionism and its replacement with a theocracy, I term his positions "theocratic post-Zionism." The
perceived obligation is to impose the Torah as the ruler of the nation's
life, and this kingdom will constitute the end of exile. The heart of the
kingdom is the Temple Mount.

PURIFYING THE TEMPLE MOUNT AND REBUILDING THE TEMPLE

On learning of the price the Israeli government was willing to pay in return for the peace treaty with Egypt, a number of members of the Movement to Stop Withdrawal from Sinai and of Gush Emunim began to
develop the idea that blowing up the mosques on the Temple Mount
could thwart the treaty.[49]

In his analysis, Gideon Aran determines that a clear sociological con-
necting thread may be seen between the withdrawal from Sinai and the
plan to blow up the mosques. The eviction of Yamit was the point at which
the barriers preventing this move fell. The traumatic experience of the
withdrawal from Sinai, despite the struggle waged to prevent this development, led a number of key activists in Gush Emunim to advocate this
idea more forcibly than before. According to Aran, this may be considered a manifestation of frustration and despair, as well as one of destiny,
fulfillment, and hope.[50]

Yehuda Etzion acted on the basis of the same logic. The post-Zionist reaction he developed was rooted in the sense that the approach of the general Zionist movement had failed; this was compounded by disappointment
with Religious Zionism, which had granted its approval for the weak will
that led to the withdrawal. Etzion identified the cause of this weakness, and
conceived a dramatic move that would put the proper process back on
course, accelerating the process of redemption. He argued that the Temple Mount held the mystical key for ending the period of meek Zionism.
The removal of the mosques would put redemption back on course.

The booklet *The Temple Mount*, published during the course of his trial
(1985), is written in the form of a statement of defense. Etzion argues that
his plan to blow up the mosques on the Temple Mount was developed
against the background of the refusal of the State of Israel to perform its
duty in terms of the deterministic destiny of redemption. Etzion began his
argument by proposing that the property of David on the Temple Mount
is the eternal property of the Jewish people; this ownership has never

expired and will never do so. The State of Israel is required to realize this ownership by virtue of the eternal Covenant between Israel and God. This obligation must be met "here and now," and no one may rest until it is fulfilled. The longing for the rebuilding of the Temple embodied in the Jewish prayers demands concrete action, and the public is obliged to realize this. "Accordingly, we reject here the evasive approach that leaves the responsibility of the burden of redemption to the Lord in an abstract and vague manner; and we demand here, first and foremost of ourselves, but no less of the state of which we are the children—that the overall responsibility for Jewish redemption be accepted."[51] The object of the prayers lies in Jerusalem, and during his prayers the worshipper turns toward the Temple Mount and the Temple. Generations of worshippers never abandoned the idea of the full return to Zion, and longed for tangible and actual redemption. This is the purpose of Jewish destiny.

In the present, however, the Temple is not being built. Etzion does not argue that this work should begin rashly; rather, the Mount must be "redeemed." This may be done immediately, and strangers must be prevented from entering the site. Just as Halachic authorization was received for IDF soldiers to enter the Temple Mount area for the purpose of its conquest, so they must return to the site to concretize this conquest by removing the alien presence. "Cleansing" the Temple Mount of the mosques will create the necessary support and understanding for full redemption. The cleansed mount will be the catalyst for the people's ascent up the scales of sanctity.[52]

It should be noted that Etzion came under severe criticism from Religious Zionist circles. Yoel Bin-Nun, Etzion's teacher at Alon Shevut yeshiva, stated that if the nation's leaders asked his opinion on the matter, he would recommend that they refrain from damaging the mosques on the Temple Mount. He accused Etzion of Sabbateanism (which he viewed as a synonym for false messianism) due to the plan to blow up the mosques on the Temple Mount, and explained that the cleansing of the Mount must occur as a supernatural and miraculous event ("the nonhuman destruction,") such as by earthquake, for example. Etzion replied that Ben-Nun's position was actually reminiscent of that of Shabbtai Zvi, who anticipated assistance from the legendary army of "Gad and Reuben"—two of the Ten Tribes who settled to the east of the River Jordan: "What is the difference between Shabbtai Zvi waiting for . . . the army of Gad and Reuben to spring from beyond the Sambatyon to take us and conquer the land, and Yoel Bin-Nun waiting for 'the nonhuman destruction' to redeem the Mount?"[53]

THE CHAI VEKAYAM MOVEMENT

After his release from prison in 1989, Etzion initiated the establishment of the Movement for Redemption, reflecting the ideas he had advocated since the uncovering of the Jewish Underground. The difference in Etzion's position after the Jewish Underground affair was that he became convinced that violent action on the Temple Mount, or anywhere else, was inappropriate until public support had been ensured. He refused to express remorse for his plans in the underground, but admitted that his plan to blow up the Muslim shrine was ill advised. Etzion admitted that until such time as a new, firm movement would arise and challenge the legitimacy of the current regime in the State of Israel, offering a complete spiritual and religious alternative, no individual or small group was permitted to act on their own accord on such a fateful matter.[54]

This approach was also reflected with regard to the 1995 assassination of Prime Minister Yitzhak Rabin by Yigal Amir. Etzion rejected the assassin's approach, arguing that "no good will therefore come of the physical elimination of the leaders of the regime of disorder, as long as the culture of disarray is intact . . . [s]uch a step—as we can see—causes a grave reaction and broad cohesion around the existing regime." Etzion saw Yigal Amir as a confused child of the transitional season between "the democratic, alien, and imported culture of Israel" and "the culture of the Third Temple that is knocking at the door." However, the difference between Etzion and Amir was only a matter of methodology:

> In a flash of impatience, Yigal Amir chose to injure the existing regime by shooting its leader, rather than shooting with us the foundation stones and basis of the future regime, and laying with us the rocks of the foundation, layers as we come to build the Hewn-Stone Hall.[55]

His search for supporters for his approach brought Etzion to Bat Ayin, a settlement in the Judean Hills where he found an attentive audience and emotional support. Most of the settlers in Bat Ayin are newly observant Jews who hold spiritual and mystic worldviews. This is a growing trend among the second generation of Gush Emunim settlers, and is an antithesis to the bourgeois lifestyle that has developed in the well-established settlements. The residents of Bat Ayin form a radical ideological hard core. The settlement was the base of a Jewish terror group that placed a container of explosives outside an Arab girls' school in Jerusalem in 2002.[56]

The Chai Vekayam (Alive and Well) movement was also established in Bat Ayin by Motti Karpel and Chaim Nativ in 1993. Etzion joined the original core group and established the course of the movement.[57] In the movement's "Identity Card," a three-page document printed for distribution at a press conference, several principles were presented relating to the delegitimization of the laws of the State of Israel. The document requires no interpretation:

1. We ask every citizen this question: Do you realize that your money—taxes and levies to the authorities—is now being poured into the establishment of a PLO state in the heart of your land? Has the time not come for civil disobedience and refusal to give your money to a regime that has betrayed the objectives of the nation? You must choose between your allegiance to a mistaken regime and your loyalty to your people and your G-d, the Eternal of Israel.

2. We ask every civil servant this question: Will you collaborate—"in the course of your function"—with the government that collaborates with the PLO? Will you work with it to establish the enemy state? Will you, for reasons of livelihood, share the awful responsibility for the sin of the leadership? You must choose between your allegiance to a mistaken regime and your loyalty to your people and your G-d, the Eternal of Israel.

3. We ask every soldier this question: Will you obey the instructions and orders of a regime that is using you to establish a Palestinian state in the heart of the Land of Israel? Will you load your brothers and countrymen onto trucks? Do you realize that these commands are grossly unlawful in accordance with the laws of the State of Israel, and are "marked by a black flag?" You must choose between your allegiance to a mistaken regime and your loyalty to your people and your G-d, the Eternal of Israel.

4. Neither 120 Members of Knesset nor a referendum nor elections can change the declaration of the people. The Eternal of Israel shall not lie, for He is not a human. The land was bequeathed to the people for all its generations; we hold it in deposit—and no single generation . . . is empowered to abandon and destroy the nation's enterprise through the strength of its God.[58]

As Ehud Sprinzak shows in his analysis, the messages of this movement embody a clear statement that the laws of the state, and particularly those relating to the settler community in Judea and Samaria, are no longer binding, and that anyone who can do so is required to cease to observe them. Etzion raised the possibility of civil disobedience and a refusal to pay taxes. He also praised those rabbis who urged soldiers to refuse to obey orders to evict settlements.[59] Motti Karpel, Etzion's partner in the movement, refused to perform reserve duty and went to prison rather than obey army orders.[60]

The best-publicized and most prominent actions by the Chai Vekayam movement have been its efforts to enter the Temple Mount for the purpose of praying on the site. The supporters of the movement have attempted dozens of times to enter the Temple Mount site draped in prayer shawls. Some of the attempts have been accompanied by press crews. These visits have not been coordinated with any official body, such as the police, since the followers of the movement consider that they are "free from the yoke of the law in matters concerning our entry into the Temple Mount in order to pray."[61] Members of the movement have been arrested during these events and criminal files have been opened. In some cases, they have been held in detention and not released on the completion of the interrogation. One of the aims of these actions is to provoke a widespread public outcry regarding the question of Jewish prayer on the Temple Mount.

With hindsight, it is evident that this activism has led to a tightening of the police supervision of those entering the Temple Mount site. Those most affected by this change are the members of the Movement for the Establishment of the Temple (whose activities are described in depth in Chapter 5), whose visits previously took place discretely, and who now face harsher conditions in their efforts to enter the site. In terms of public impact, however, the photographs of Etzion and his supporters being removed from the Temple Mount by force underscore for the Jewish public (and particularly the Religious Zionist public) the prevailing reality on the site, which is effectively managed as a broad Muslim autonomy, and which Jews are prohibited to enter for public prayer. The heightened awareness of this situation has led many to demonstrate against the denial of the right to pray at the most sacred site to Judaism, while Muslims act as the owners of the site. This has drawn additional figures into the circle of those supporting the movement, such as Moshe Feiglin, leader of the Zo Artzenu (This Is Our Land) movement, which organized massive demonstrations against Israeli government policy and the Oslo Process; and Hillel Weiss, a professor of Hebrew literature at Bar Ilan University and a prominent ideologue in contemporary Religious Zionist circles. Both these figures have publicly announced their support for activities opposing the prohibition against Jews praying on the Temple Mount.

Etzion has also been involved in several other provocative actions: Holding a model example of the Passover sacrifice; establishing the Census of Priests and Levites; and running ceremonies for the sanctification of the new month. The objective of these activities was to challenge the authority of the Orthodox rabbinical establishment.

During a period of five years, Etzion held annual model examples of the Passover sacrifice. The ceremonies took place on the day before Passover in the Abu Tor neighborhood of Jerusalem, opposite the Temple Mount. The events included speeches followed by the slaughtering of young male goats, in an effort to recreate the sacrifices in the Temple. After the goats were slaughtered, they were roasted by the participants in the event. The model Passover sacrifice is a symbolic event reflecting the yearning for the reinstatement of the sacrifices; however, it includes a strong subversive message against the Halachic authorities in Israel, who do not carry out such ceremonies due to a rabbinical prohibition.

The idea of holding the Passover sacrifice in the Temple Mount area was raised immediately after Etzion's release from prison, during a meeting at the Jewish Idea yeshiva, which is associated with the Kach movement. On the initiative of Noam Livnat, a proposal was raised to smuggle the sections of the altar into the Temple Mount in modular form, and to hold the sacrificial ceremony without warning. The members of the Movement for the Establishment of the Temple—Yosef Elboim, Yoel Lerner, and others—also participated in the meeting. The idea was eventually rejected as impractical.[63] Two years later, the Movement for the Establishment of the Temple again attempted to arrange such an event—this time not in a clandestine manner, but with all the necessary authorizations. The movement petitioned the High Court of Justice asking that it be enabled to hold the event, but the petition was rejected.[64] Permission was granted only to hold the ceremony outside the Temple Mount; accordingly, Etzion chose to hold model ceremonies at a site overlooking the Mount.

At the festival of Sukkot in 1998 and 2000, Etzion held the "Temple Conference." These colorful gatherings took place in the auditorium at the International Conference Center in Jerusalem and were well attended. The conferences received wide coverage in the media, exposing the public to the activities of the Temple Institute and its recreations of Temple vessels. Speeches were made by rabbinical authorities supporting the demand for Jews to be permitted to pray on the Temple Mount. At the second conference, in 2000, the Census of Priests and Levites was announced. In the spirit of the approach delineated by Shabbtai Ben Dov, the Levites are supposed to play a key role in educating the people toward the objectives of redemption. Yehuda Etzion and Baruch Ben Yosef, a member of the Movement for the Establishment of the Temple, sought to establish a center that would register all the priests and Levites in Israel. Following the example of King David, who divided the Levite tribe into twenty-four units, they also sought to establish twenty-four guards of office on a geographical basis. "This will enable the development of a system of 'reserve duty,' whereby each priest and Levite who volunteers will serve for one week every six months."[65] The idea never came to fruition, due in part to the lack of cooperation among the public, and also to a lack of funds.[66]

A further ceremony initiated by Etzion is the Sanctification of the New Month, held to honor the beginning of each new Hebrew month. I have attended this ceremony on several occasions, and I can report that the number of participants is small; on some occasions, not even an Orthodox quorum of ten men is present. The ceremony was held at the foot of the Hulda Gates, to the south of the Temple Mount at the end of each month, and sought to replicate the ancient custom of sanctifying the month—determining the beginning of the new month by a religious court—as was the practice in ancient times. Due to the absence of a high court, the rabbis ruled that this commandment would be resumed after redemption. According to Maimonides, when the age of redemption comes, the Sanhedrin will set the Hebrew calendar, after witnesses come to report the sighting of the new moon. According to Etzion, this ceremony symbolizes the revitalization of the people, since, from now on, the new month will be set by a court, and not by the astronomical readings, which was the method of determining the months employed during exile and up to the present day. The blessing for the moon is recited during the period between the third (or seventh) day following the new moon and the middle of the month—the day after which the moon begins to wane. However, the sanctification of the month is not the same as the blessing for the moon. The sanctification of the month requires a court ruling, while the blessing for the moon has the same status as any other Jewish blessing.

The ceremony I attended began with a declaration of the "impregnation" of the moon, in the presence of a court (three men). Etzion then read a text he had prepared in advance. The participants raised their glasses and made the traditional *Shechechiyanu* blessing for new occasions, ate sweet items, and danced. Etzion believes that this event has a messianic dimension of subversion. Just as the moon is renewed each month, so the nation is renewed and revived.[67]

Etzion's activities in the framework of the Chai Vekayam movement indeed include a strong element of religious subversion. It is important to emphasize that religious millennialism is by its very nature a revolutionary phenomenon that seeks to challenge the existing religious and political order. Millennialism seeks to replace the mundane order, which is perceived as fundamentally rotten and corrupt, with a new governmental strength drawing on Divine authority. The proposed millennial social structure carries a subversive message against the very foundations of existing religion; accordingly, millennial activism can sometimes be channeled toward religious revolution.[68]

On the basis of his revolutionary approach, Etzion developed his overt criticism of the mainstream theological perspectives of Religious Zionism, sharply attacking those who embraced these perspectives and, in particular, the two Rabbis Kook. Etzion's bold opposition to the leading rabbis of the generation is not typical in Orthodox Jewish circles, particularly since he is not a rabbinical authority and has never been ordained. Indeed, he shows little sign of seeking support among Religious Zionist rabbis. On the contrary, he criticizes the rabbinical authority of the national yeshivot. His theocratic approaches undermine the status of the rabbis, with the objective of replacing them with a different, genuine religious leadership. Thus, for example, the attempts to enter the Temple Mount to pray on the site took place without the authorization or support of the rabbis. The census of priests and Levites was intended, in part, to create a new pool of potential religious leaders based on biological origin rather than on training and Halachic proficiency. Contrary to the current practice for determining the Hebrew months, Etzion appoints a court to declare the new moon, thus challenging the fossilized state of the Halacha. The Passover sacrifice symbolizes the longing for the reinstatement of the Temple ritual as a manifestation of Jewish redemption, and the preference for this ceremony over the synagogue services—despite the fact that the event is prohibited in Halachic terms.

In the same revolutionary spirit, Etzion has also proposed changes to the format of the prayers: "When we have a proper spiritual leadership, far-reaching changes will be required to the prayer book. . . . For example, when Jerusalem is already being rebuilt, we shall no longer recite 'And build Jerusalem, Your city, speedily in our days.'" On the basis of this assumption, Etzion proposes that even before such leadership is present, the format of the prayers for the three pilgrim festivals should be changed, deleting the line that states: "Because we are distant from our land, we cannot again ascend and see . . . and perform our obligation in Your Chosen House."[69]

In presenting this perspective, Etzion is continuing the approach developed by Shabbtai Ben Dov, which argues that only by withdrawing from the religious establishment will it be possible to bring the message of redemption. As discussed, Ben Dov longed for charismatic spiritual leadership that would develop the message of redemption, circumventing the authority of the degenerated and unwieldy rabbinical bureaucracy. Accordingly, Etzion has continued this approach, rebelling not only against Zionist thought, but also against the behavior of Orthodox Judaism.

THE ATTITUDE OF THE RELIGIOUS ZIONIST ESTABLISHMENT TO YEHUDA ETZION

The question of Etzion's status within the Religious Zionist camp is of particular interest. Despite his activities in the Jewish Underground, which led to fierce public criticism of the settlement enterprise;[70] and despite his fierce criticism of the spiritual leadership and his challenges to religious authority—he has not found disfavor; as a matter of fact, the contrary is the case.

Etzion regular receives generous space to present his views in *Nekudah*, the journal of the settlers. After his release from jail, he was employed by circles within the Council of Judea, Samaria, and Gaza, working to promote the immigration to Israel of the Ethiopian Jews. This activity was also intended to advance the activist messianic goal of ingathering the Jewish exiles. Etzion is on close terms with the leaders of the council and works together with them in various public activities.

Despite his unusual views and his fierce criticism, Etzion has not been obliged to leave Ofra, the "flagship" of the settlement movement. By contrast, his neighbor in the same community, Yoel Bin-Nun, was forced to leave after criticizing the spiritual leaders of Religious Zionism. Bin-Nun's criticism was in a different context and from the opposite direction: After the assassination of Prime Minister Rabin, which had a profound effect on Bin-Nun, he sharply criticized the atmosphere within the religious public prior to the assassination, which he claimed created legitimacy for the act. He threatened to present to the police the names of rabbis who approved the assassination. Following this threat, which he never realized, Ben-Nun was subjected to fierce criticism, to the point that he preferred to move to Gush Etzion, where he found the atmosphere more congenial.[71]

The comparison with the experience of Yoel Bin-Nun may reflect the unique public status of Yehuda Etzion, who is considered to be an exemplary figure and a "prophet." Etzion is a "zealot,"[72] someone who is faithful to the absolute truth and does not surrender to pragmatism and compromise. For many, therefore, he represents a pure ideal—something others may aspire to even if they do not dare to put it into practice. He has acquired this status through his rigorous quest for perfection. He is perceived as someone who is totally honest and faithful to his ideas, even at a heavy personal price. Moreover, Etzion's criticisms are not designed to weaken the Religious Zionist camp, but to lead its course. As a leader, Etzion establishes a right-wing benchmark and urges the remainder of the camp to follow suit.

Etzion's nonconformism and the weakness of the system in confronting him may also be an example of the "messianic dilemma" facing mainstream contemporary Religious Zionism, which cannot unequivocally oppose religious zealotry. Although the zealots may be unrepresentative of the "bourgeois" character of Religious Zionism and the settlement movement it has spawned, zealotry is still perceived as the prototype for the "authentic" Religious Zionist. This ideal represents the pinnacle of aspirations and arouses admiration through its determination. The zealot seeks to implement immediately the most fundamental positions of Religious Zionism regarding the dialectical destiny of the Zionist movement—something the pragmatic majority finds difficult.[73]

Given this situation, it is hardly surprising that such approaches can set down roots and secure a growing measure of support.

Conclusion

In this chapter, I have sought to illustrate how the theological crisis created by the threat to the vision of the Greater Land of Israel led to a counterreaction of reinforcement and radicalization in religious terms, and how this, in turn, led to violence and nonconformism, culminating in the plan to blow up the mosques on the Temple Mount.

The "crisis of Zionism," reflected in the clearest terms in Israel's willingness to relinquish territories in return for peace with its neighbors, demands acceptance of the fact that the State of Israel has no intention of becoming a theocracy or a messianic entity, and seeks to act in accordance with the accepted patterns of behavior in Western society and the international community. Accordingly, a crisis of consciousness may emerge due to the discrepancy between the fundamental essentials of faith and the reality that confronts believers in the field. Etzion identified the potential crisis as early as the late 1970s, and the solution he found was to adopt a radical and activist form of messianism. The personal crisis experienced by Etzion was felt with full force by many others in Religious Zionism following the implementation of the Oslo Accords in the mid-1990s. Etzion's response and the answers he had developed met with a much more positive response during this period. As Ehud Sprinzak shows in his analysis, the force of this ideology may be enhanced significantly following the eviction of settlements as part of peace treaties (or as a unilateral measure). "The importance of the Chai Vekayam movement rests, in my opinion, not in the number of its supporters, but in the leadership qualities of its few followers; in the systemic challenge it presents to the tendencies of pragmatism and acceptance among the majority of the members of Gush Emunim; and in the difficult questions it raises for those who have still not lost their faith in the legitimacy of the State of Israel and the IDF."[74] These dilemmas where manifested in the most blunt way during Israel Disengagement plan, and will be discussed in the concluding chapter.

In chapter 4 I will examine sections of Israeli society that are involved with the demand for the Temple, although they do not form part of Religious Zionism.

4

Gershon Salomon and the Temple Mount Faithful

Apocalyptic Messianism

The Temple Mount Faithful movement is the oldest and best known of the groups devoted to the Temple Mount and the Temple vision. Gershon Salomon is the founder and the unchallenged leader of this group and has an international reputation due to his indubitable rhetorical capabilities that have kept his actions on the public agenda over a period of almost three decades. In many cases, the media tend to group all the Temple movements together under the name "Temple Mount Faithful," and find it difficult to distinguish between the wide range of movements in this field—a phenomenon that reflects the status the Temple Mount Faithful has attained in Israel and internationally. Salomon openly advocates the "judaization of the Temple Mount," and organizes several ritual events each year demanding that the Muslim presence be removed from the Mount, and that it be transformed into the spiritual and political center of the State of Israel. Of all the Temple activists, the Muslim Waqf seems most alarmed by this determined man and his followers in the Temple Mount Faithful. The symbolic and demonstrative activities they undertake each year, including their declared intention to lay the cornerstone for the Temple, raise the level of anxiety among the Arab public, which is called on in turn to protect the Temple Mount against Jewish efforts to seize control of the Muslim holy site.

These demonstrations are used to cause provocations and riots bordering on hysteria among the Muslim public. In this way, Gershon Salomon and the Waqf play into each other's hands. An example of the bloodshed caused by these mutual provocations was seen in October 1990, when mass riots erupted on the Temple Mount in response to the intention of the

Temple Mount Faithful to lay the cornerstone for the Temple. The Israel Police stormed the Mount and seventeen Muslim demonstrators were killed.[1] Indeed, well-publicized visits by leading Israeli figures intended to emphasize Israeli sovereignty over the Temple Mount on several occasions have led to Muslim riots. This was the case in 1986, when the Knesset Internal Affairs Committee visited the site and was rescued with great difficulty after they came under attack from a large crowd of Muslims. Similarly, the Al-Aqsa Intifada erupted after Ariel Sharon visited the Temple Mount in September 2000, leading to tension and an atmosphere of hysteria that indirectly led events to spiral out of control.[2]

The Temple Mount Faithful was the first significant group to demand the removal of the mosques from the Mount and its transformation into a Jewish center, and the movement drew together most of the activists in this field. Its supporters came both from the maximalist circles of the Movement for the Greater Land of Israel, including veterans of the Lechi and Etzel underground movements in the pre-independence period, and from adherents of the messianic religious right. Over time, however, the movement lost some of its prestige, and a number of key activists left and founded other frameworks that gradually grew in strength, such as the Movement for the Establishment of the Temple, which was created from the religious faction in the Temple Mount Faithful. Today, only a handful of activists remain in the Temple Mount Faithful, attending the regular demonstrations held several times a year. This movement, which is not specifically Orthodox in character, seems to have lost its appeal and been reduced to a marginal status among the Temple Mount groups. Alongside this process, however, a significant breakthrough came in the increasing rapprochement between these circles and a new, supportive periphery: the evangelical Christian right wing. From the mid-1990s, these circles became a key target for the movement's activities. Accordingly, the Temple Mount Faithful, which had been the leading Jewish activist group on the Temple Mount issue during the 1970s and 1980s, suffered from declining influence among the Jewish public in the 1990s, but at the same time found a new circle of supporters and a new arena for action of considerable importance. These changing conditions also led to a dramatic change in rhetorical terms.

The Temple Mount Faithful movement differs in its character, activities, and attitudes from the other groups reviewed in this book. It began as a nationalistic right wing, and subsequently—and gradually—acquired characteristics of a new religious movement that includes apocalyptic worldviews. Accordingly, it is interesting to compare this movement to the others active in the same arena. In many senses, the Temple Mount Faithful, under Salomon's leadership, differ radically from the other activists in the Temple Mount and Temple groups—in religious terms, in terms of the patterns of leadership, and in terms of their attitude toward Zionism.

This chapter presents the history and political platform of the Temple Mount Faithful, focusing on a comparison between the movement and the other groups active on the issue of the Temple Mount.

The Temple Mount as the National and Spiritual Center for the State of Israel

Gershon Salomon comes from a well-known family of rabbis that settled in Jerusalem in 1811 out of messianic motives. He is also descended from Yoel Moshe Salomon, one of the founders of Petach Tikva and one of the earliest Zionist pioneers in Palestine. The personal history of Gershon Salomon includes an element that may also be found among other Temple activists: a combination of the horrors of war and the vision of the rebuilding of the Temple. In 1958, as the commander of an infantry unit, he was involved in combat action on the Golan Heights. During the course of the fighting, Salomon was accidentally run over by an IDF tank, sustaining severe injuries to his legs. After spending a year in the hospital, he managed to recuperate, and after a long struggle with the military authorities, he returned to his previous unit and served as an operations officer. He never completely recovered from the injury and suffers from a severe limp to this day. Despite his injury, Salomon marches in demonstrations alongside the other members of his movement, although this is visibly a strain for him. As a soldier, he also participated in the battle for Jerusalem in the Six-Day War.

The connection between Salomon's disability and his activities in the Temple Mount Faithful is explicit and direct. Salomon claims to have experienced Divine revelation on the day he was injured. When the Syrian soldiers came to kill the IDF soldiers lying in the field, they suddenly fled in fear after thousands of angels circled above him, protecting his injured body. Since then, he reports that he has become an agent of God, bearing the message of the reconstruction of the Temple. Salomon states that since this event he has regularly experienced Divine revelation, and his ongoing efforts for the Temple Mount are the product of this direct connection.[3]

Salomon established the Temple Mount Faithful movement at the end of the 1960s. The movement is essentially one of protest, and the activities are arranged according to the Hebrew calendar. In the periods leading up to the Jewish festivals—and particularly festivals that have a connection with the ancient rituals on the Temple Mount, such as the three pilgrim festivals, Hanukkah, and Tisha B'Av—a demonstration takes place in the form of a pilgrimage, including elements from the rituals performed on the Temple Mount as related in Jewish tradition. At the festival of Sukkot (Tabernacles), for example, the procession passes through the Shiloach tunnel to create a symbolic water-related element, which recalls the ritual pouring of water and the joy of the water libation ceremony. At Hanukkah the marchers carry torches, and at Shavuot (Pentecost) the first harvest offerings are brought to the Mount. Similar demonstrations also take place on Zionist occasions such as the Memorial Day for Fallen IDF Soldiers and Jerusalem Day.

Having participated in several of these demonstrations, I can report that they have a uniform character. The event effectively begins a few days before the march, when Salomon asks the Israel Police for permission to hold a prayer service on the Temple Mount on the given date. After receiving a negative response, as is invariably the case, Salomon petitions the High Court of Justice. The judicial ruling that has become established is that the court permits the Temple Mount Faithful to enter the site, but not to pray there. Entry is conditioned on the professional opinion and discretion of the Israel Police, and in practice the police invariably determine that such entry is not to be permitted due to the security situation.[4] This situation has its origins in the status quo arrangement introduced by Moshe Dayan following the occupation of the holy sites, which stated that the Temple Mount would continue to serve as a Muslim place of prayer, while the Western Wall would be a Jewish place of prayer. In 1968, the court decided not to intervene in the question of Jewish prayer on the Temple Mount, ruling that this was a political question rather than a judicial one. The court permitted the Israel Police to establish procedures for entry into the Temple Mount on the basis of security considerations.[5]

Accordingly, the demonstrative procession of the Temple Mount Faithful stops at the entrance to the Temple Mount, on the embankment leading up to the Mograbi Gate. The following is a description of one such procession that takes place every year at Hanukkah. The Temple Mount Faithful gather in Jerusalem and travel together to the tombs of the Maccabis near Modi'in. This location was chosen because of the connection between the festival and the movement's demand to end the Muslim administration on the Temple Mount. Salomon delivers a speech by the side of the Maccabi tombs reviewing the history of the Hasmonean family, which rebelled against the Greeks and purified the Temple Mount from idol worship—a process he compares to modern-day reality, urging the prime minister of Israel to learn the lesson of Hanukkah and remove Islam from Mount Moriah. A symbolic torch race then takes place to Jerusalem—a number of individuals begin to run in the direction of Jerusalem, carrying torches, and after covering a certain distance, they board buses and continue their journey to the capital. After arriving at Jaffa Gate, at the entrance to the Old City, the group carries signs, flags, and a symbolic model made from cardboard, which is intended to denigrate the emblems of Palestinian nationhood, such as a coffin for Yasser Arafat or a Palestine Liberation Organization (PLO) flag. The group marches toward the plaza inside Jaffa Gate to enable the press photographers to record the procession. Here Salomon stops and makes a speech (in Hebrew followed by English) demanding the removal of the Muslims from the Temple Mount. He also addresses current affairs in Israel, emphasizing his hawkish views on various issues relating to Israel and the Arab world. He then proceeds to take the cardboard model and tear it to shreds, sometimes also burning it, as the media cameras flash away. Salomon then holds an impromptu press conference, answering questions from reporters. The group then continues toward the entrance of the Temple Mount, where it is stopped at the Mograbi Gate by dozens, if not hundreds, of police officers. There is a glaring discrepancy between the number of demonstrators, which is sometimes as few as twenty individuals, and the number of police personnel securing the demonstration, which is sometimes as high as three hundred. Salomon again makes a speech, quoting extensively from the Bible. The pilgrimage ends at the gates of the Temple Mount with a sense of pain and disappointment. Salomon urges the government to open the Mount and bemoans what he considers its weak and defeatist behavior. The event ends with Hatikva, the Israeli national anthem, and with words of thanks to the Israel Police for protecting the demonstration.

The application for police permission, followed by the petition to the High Court of Justice, as well as the words of thanks to the police and the singing of Hatikva all reflect the first point of difference between Salomon and the other Temple Mount groups. Salomon is essentially a Zionist. He views the Mount as a national symbol that should be the home of the national institutions; the military ceremonies that currently take place in the plaza by the Western Wall should properly be held on the Mount itself. It is Salomon's Zionist perspective that leads him to request a permit for the demonstrations, and to contact the official bodies of the Israeli state (the police and the courts). He is extremely careful to ensure that the members of the movement observe the legal instructions and refrain from confronting the police. The same approach leads him to thank the police for their protection. In a personal interview I had with Yoel Lerner, a member of the executive board of the Temple Mount Faithful, he stated that Salomon revoked his membership of the movement after he was convicted of planning to blow up the mosques on the Temple Mount and was sentenced to three years in jail. Lerner attributed this response to what he referred to as Salomon's "obsessive" desire to avoid the movement acquiring any semblance of a violent or dangerous gathering.[6] This point illustrates the difference between the Temple Mount Faithful and Yehuda Etzion's movement Chai Vekayam. The supporters of Chai Vekayam broke into the Temple Mount area without authorization and without asking permission to pray on the site; accordingly, they were arrested by the police and prosecuted for their actions. Salomon, unlike Etzion, does not lead illegal action; he refrains from entering the Temple Mount without permission and repeatedly files requests with the authorities. Although he has received a negative response for almost thirty years, this has not led him to despair or anger, and he has steadfastly maintained his position. Indeed, his movement publicly condemned the plan by the Jewish Underground, led by Yehuda Etzion, to blow up the mosques on the Temple Mount. "The Temple Mount Faithful Youth announced that while it supports any action to end the disgrace on the Temple Mount, it believes that independent actions of this type can at present only damage the struggle, since there can be no greater disgrace than for the Israeli government to rebuild with its own hands the mosques on the Temple Mount."[7]

The other Temple Mount organizations often depict the police as the enemy, and vent their anger on the police officers who prevent them from praying in the holy site. Salomon distinguishes between the police, as a law enforcement agency, and the government, against whom he wages a legitimate public campaign. The singing of the Israeli national anthem, Hatikva, also illustrates his total identification with the State of Israel and the Zionist enterprise. Unlike other Temple activists, such as Yehuda Etzion and Israel Ariel, who do not consider themselves Zionists, Salomon's struggle reflects a maximalist Zionist position that perceives the Temple Mount as its zenith. Salomon believes that the institutions of Israeli authority should be located on the Temple Mount as a symbol of the height of the Jewish people's return to their land. This explains why the movement also organizes ritualized demonstrations on dates relating to the revival of Jewish statehood, such as Jerusalem Day, Holocaust Memorial Day, and the Memorial Day for Fallen IDF Soldiers. Salomon does not claim, as Yehuda Etzion does, to offer a post-Zionist perspective that views the demand to enter the Temple Mount as a reflection of the termination of the function of Zionism and the transition to the messianic age that will replace it.

Although Salomon ensures that his movement does not engage in any illegal or violent activities, its central message—the removal of the mosques from the Temple Mount—may be perceived as conveying an aggressive message for Islam and, thus, may cause serious conflicts on the Mount between Muslim worshippers and the Israeli law enforcement agencies. In 1987, for example, thousands of Muslim worshippers protested against the entry into the site of the Temple Mount Faithful, throwing stones at the Western Wall plaza. This incident ended after intervention by the mayor of Jerusalem at the time, Teddy Kollek. In October 1990, however, during the height of the first Intifada, mediation efforts were to no avail, and a demonstration by the Temple Mount Faithful led to a bloodbath. The incident occurred during the festival of Sukkot, when the Waqf exploited the announcement by the movement of its intention to lay the cornerstone for the Temple (an announcement lacking any real substance) to incite passions, calling on the Muslim masses to come in person and defend the holy sites of Islam. The clarifications by the police that Salomon would not be permitted to enter the Temple Mount, and that there was no intention of laying a cornerstone for the Temple, were of no use. Thousands of Muslims gathered at the site, and were incited by slogans called by the muezzin in the Al-Aqsa Mosque. A mistake by a Border Guard policeman, who accidentally dropped a gas grenade close to the plaza by the Dome of the Rock, led to a mass riot. Protracted clashes erupted between the police and the crowd, and the Muslims managed to take control of the police station on the Mount, forcing the police forces to retreat from the site. The police action to retake the Mount resulted in seventeen fatalities and several hundred wounded on the Palestinian side, and thirty-four injuries among the Border Guard police and Jewish worshippers at the Western Wall. This incident is considered the most serious on the Temple Mount since the site was conquered by Israel in 1967.[8]

As I have noted, the Temple Mount Faithful was once the central grouping of Temple activists. During its early years, the movement was joined by right-wing maximalists, both religious and secular, and managed to include the divergent perspectives within a single framework. As time passed, however, it became impossible to maintain this combination, and the religious circles left the movement. The crisis was initiated by Yosef Elboim, a Jerusalemite and a member of the Belz Hassidic sect. In a personal interview, Elboim explained to me that the purpose of the split was to increase the number of people involved in the Temple Mount issue. He claimed that after a number of activists from the settlement of Kiryat Arba, near Hebron, refused to remain in the Temple Mount Faithful because of Salomon's "secular" approach, he realized that there was no alternative but to establish a new, Orthodox group.[9] While for Salomon the Temple Mount was a Zionist and national symbol, for Elboim the site first and foremost held a religious and ritual importance. Therefore, Elboim and his friends felt that the Temple Mount Faithful could not meet their needs, since Salomon attached less significance to the religious function embodied by the Temple.

Yosef Lerner and Israel Ariel joined Elboim, and, in 1987, the Movement for the Establishment of the Temple was founded (see chapter 5). These breakaway groups did not consider themselves bound by the approach taken by the Temple Mount Faithful, and anticipated that the divisions would increase the number of people involved in the field by creating alternative frameworks for different target populations. A further reason for the division, as noted by Elboim and Lerner (and by other activists I spoke with during my research), relates to Salomon's forceful personality and his centralized approach to leadership; I will discuss this aspect later in the chapter.

A further point of disagreement between the Temple Mount Faithful and the Movement for the Establishment of the Temple related to the question of the ideal of rebuilding the Temple. During its early stages, the Temple Mount Faithful did not include the construction of the Temple as a practical objective; its messages focused on the national aspects of sovereignty over the Mount. For example, the movement's "Declaration of Allegiance" included the following:

> I declare allegiance to the Temple Mount, the sacred national and religious center of the Jewish People and the Land of Israel, and I undertake to act with all my strength for the return to the Jewish People of this national symbol of the resurrection of the Jewish People in its Land.
>
> I shall bear allegiance to Jerusalem, the eternal capital of Israel.
>
> I shall be proud to serve as a soldier in the IDF in all the liberated sections of the Land of Israel, and to carry the message of the Temple Mount wherever I may go.[10]

This declaration does not state that the movement seeks the rebuilding of the Temple; neither does the name of the movement embody this objective. The constitution of the movement states that its goal is "to bring about the realization of the belief and the historical aspiration of the Jewish People . . . that the Temple Mount is the national, religious, and spiritual center of the Jewish People and the Land of Israel."[11] Another declaration by the movement demanded the "removal of the disgrace" and the opening of the Temple Mount to the Jewish people "to transform it into the national, religious, and spiritual center of the Jewish People and to remove our alien enemies from it."[12] Once again, these publications do not mention the rebuilding of the Temple. Accordingly, the breakaway faction decided to emphasize its distinct identity in the name its chose—the Movement for the Establishment of the Temple— and by positioning this objective as its central operational goal.

It should be stressed that the Temple Mount Faithful did not ignore the question of the rebuilding of the Temple; however, the issue was presented in a muted manner. In the first issue of the movement's newsletter, for example, Salomon wrote an article protesting the neglect of the Temple Mount by the State of Israel and its "abandonment" as a site of Muslim worship. His comments include the objective of rebuilding the Temple, albeit by way of allusion:

> The two thousand year dream of returning to the Chosen House is fading, ironically after the State of Israel has been established.

How can we live our lives now as if nothing has happened, and
the Temple Mount is now left abandoned by the people that
once gave its life for this place? And how indeed can there even
be Jewish life in the Land of Israel without the Temple Mount
and its holinesses?[13]

At this point, the aspiration of rebuilding the Temple appears to have
been perceived as a distant goal that should follow more immediate—and,
for Salomon, more important—objectives such as the removal of Islam
from the Temple Mount and the transformation of the site into the center
of Jewish nationhood. In my opinion, the absence of a serious effort to confront the issue of the rebuilding of the Temple also reflects the absence of
a consolidated messianic and religious vision, with the result that the movement focused on a nationalist ideology. Salomon realized that the definition of the goal of building the Temple was a complex one that could not
be addressed on the level of simplistic declarations, and required a clear
programmatic direction that he did not have at the time—or, at least, which
he could not present in public. Moreover, the movement newsletter published an article arguing that while Jews are now permitted to enter the
Temple Mount and demonstrate their presence in the site, it is not appropriate to rebuild the Temple. According to the author, Yoram Gidron, the
public does not have the right to decide to rebuild the Temple. This vision
should not be abandoned, however, but should remain on the level of an
ideal to maintain the unity of the people.[14] The approach presented in this
article, which depicts the rebuilding of the Temple as no more than a spiritual ideal, seeks to avoid division and conflict with Orthodoxy and, in my
opinion, faithfully reflects Salomon's own views on the matter, which explains the publication of the article. A response to this article published in
the following issue of the movement's newsletter did not challenge the perspective it presented on the building of the Temple.[15]

Salomon's perception of the Temple Mount as a national, rather than
religious, center is reminiscent of the position that developed in the Lechi
movement, a small underground organization that was active under the
British Mandate (1942–1948). In the "Principles of Rebirth," the presentation of the principles of Lechi, the last section (section 18) advocates
"the building of the Third Temple as a symbol of the age of complete redemption." According to Zeev Ivinsky, it should not be assumed that Yair
Stern, the leader of Lechi, took a traditionalist position on this issue.
Rather, he perceived the Third Temple as a manifestation of admiration
for Hebrew religion and culture, as part of the future Kingdom of Israel:
"This principled position was grounded not on a messianic tendency, but
on the need to form a connection, through a secular interpretation, to
the dreams and prayers of the generations, through the construction of

the Temple as a symbol."[16] Although Salomon informed me that he was not influenced in ideological terms by the approach of Lechi, I believe that a similarity may be noted between the two in terms of their nationalist, rather than religious, approach to the Temple Mount issue.

In this context, it is worth noting a disagreement regarding the characterization of the Temple Mount Faithful in religious terms. Salomon adheres to an alternative and distinct brand of religiosity. Some have referred to him as secular, erroneously in my opinion, since his pattern is not religious in the Orthodox sense of the term. Salomon does not consider himself bound to the 613 commandments of the Jewish religious law and his rhetorical style does not draw on the Halacha. The political declaration of the movement states that it is committed to observing every detail of God's laws as written in the Bible. The word "Bible" appears in bold, thus underscoring the movement's ambivalent approach to the Jewish commandments. Salomon frequently quotes from the vision of redemption as embodied in the writings of the biblical prophets, which he regards as an obligation for urgent action, but this cannot be taken as implying that he is committed to the Halacha. Neither, though, should his approach be considered secular. His rhetorical style is replete with biblical quotes, and he views the Bible as an ideal for national conduct, and as a mechanism for prophesying the future through to the End of Days. His approach constitutes what might be considered a "new religion"— the "Zionist religion"—rooted in Salomon's familiarity with the Bible and his direct experience of God, he feels able to judge the political behavior of the state and ascertain whether it is moving in what he considers to be the right direction.

The division in the Temple Mount Faithful in 1987 led to a gradual reduction in the influence enjoyed by the movement. Over the years, confrontations took place between the Temple Mount Faithful and the Movement for the Establishment of the Temple. During Hanukkah 1992, for example, the Movement for the Establishment of the Temple planned a mass visit to the Temple Mount. At exactly the same time, Salomon scheduled his demonstration by the gates to the site, and the Mount was therefore closed to Jewish visitors. The supporters of the Movement for the Establishment of the Temple, who had coordinated their visit to the Mount with the police, were forced to retrace their steps. This incident provoked the wrath of the movement activists, and particularly of Baruch Ben Yosef, who lost control of himself and was arrested by the police for rioting. The members of the Movement for the Establishment of the Temple criticized Salomon, whose demonstration had prevented them from entering the Temple Mount. In particular, he was criticized for failing to come to the support of Ben Yosef.[17] By 2000, Salomon found himself left outside the main circle of Temple activists. The other groupings—the

Movement for the Establishment of the Temple, the Temple Institute, the Jewish Leadership faction, Chai Vekayam, the El Har Hamor association, and the Women for the Temple—formed an umbrella organization called the "Temple Admirers" that did not include the Temple Mount Faithful.

A House of Prayer for All Nations

The new body did not halt the development of the Temple Mount Faithful. During this period, Salomon began to become acquainted with the Christian fundamentalist sector, first through the mediation of the former Lechi activist Stanley Goldfoot,[18] and later through contacts he developed himself.

The strategic ties between the Temple Mount Faithful and Christian circles represented the beginning of a new period in the life of the movement, and required adjustments to its ideology and rhetoric. These contacts led Salomon to refine his messianic stance to meet the needs of his new audiences. Modern technologies such as the Internet and satellite television provided simple tools for disseminating the movement's ideas. The central importance of this target population in the work of the Temple Mount Faithful is reflected in the fact that the movement's Web site appears entirely in English—Salomon did not even bother to prepare a Hebrew-language site for the Israeli public.[19]

One of the main ideological developments in this new era for the Temple Mount Faithful has been an increased emphasis on the rebuilding of the Temple as a central objective of the movement. The rebuilding of the Temple, the movement argues, will be possible as the result of apocalyptic end-time events, and due to the fact that the future Temple will be a house of prayer for all the nations. It may be assumed that this change reflects the belief of the Christian fundamentalists that the rebuilding of the Temple is an essential component of the millenarian end-time scenario.[20]

As noted earlier, the publications of the Temple Mount Faithful during the 1980s did not present a detailed vision, and the written efforts of the movement, and of Salomon as its leader, centered on the question of the status of the Temple Mount. However, the movement's Web site, established around the turn of the century, includes extensive details on Salomon's messianic beliefs. In 1999, Salomon published the first English-language version of the movement newsletter (*Voice of the Temple Mount*). These newsletters may be viewed on the Web site, and since this point all the movement's publications have appeared exclusively in English.

The messianic stance raises a further aspect of comparison between Salomon and the other Temple Mount activists. Most of the activists in the field hold naturalistic messianic perspectives that view redemption as a gradual process stemming from human actions. In this approach, they base themselves mainly on the perspectives of Maimonides regarding the Messianic era. By contrast, Salomon's approach, as reflected on his Web site and at the gatherings I have attended in recent years, reflects an apocalyptic messianic perspective. Salomon envisages dramatic events in the relatively immediate future that will announce the End of Days. He argues that redemption will come after the war of Gog and Magog, an event epitomizing the war between absolute good and evil. This process will end with the ultimate salvation of humanity, and with the crowning of God as king on the Holy Mountain in Jerusalem. Redemption, therefore, is both immediate and achievable. Accordingly, the current period, leading up to the war of Gog and Magog, is a time replete with cosmic actions manifested in the realities of contemporary Israeli politics.

Apocalyptic messianic approaches tend to distinguish between the community of those who follow the messianic message, which will be worthy of redemption, and all those demonic and dark forces that seek to prevent its realization.[21] In Gershon Salomon's version of this cosmic drama, the role of demon is reserved for Yasser Arafat and the Palestinian national movement, who represent the apocalyptic enemy that must be annihilated for the Divine plan to be realized in full.

> In G-d's end-time plans there is no place for the cruel enemies of G-d. The terrorist Arafat, and his "Palestinian Authority" will not succeed with their war. We do not fear them nor their violence. The great event of the redemption of Israel cannot be stopped. Who can stop the G-d of Israel?[22]

Salomon is convinced that the vision of the Prophet Ezekiel regarding the war of Gog and Magog is about to come true at any moment. He views this war as the peak of traumatic experiences the State of Israel is undergoing. The way to survive this war, which may be unconventional in nature, is to trust in God.

Salomon argues that there are four stages to be undergone leading to the ultimate redemption of the entire world. The first is the foundation of the modern Israeli state and its miraculous victories over the hostile Arab armies; the second is the return of all the Jews to their promised land; the third is the liberation of the Temple Mount and the construction of the Temple; and the fourth is the return of the King of Israel, the Davidic Messiah. The miraculous return of the Jews to their land was predicted by the prophets, and Jewish redemption will be completed by the redemption of the world.[23]

As the movement has developed its ties with the Christian public, Salomon also appears to have reinforced his centralist approach to leadership. As I have noted, Salomon claims to enjoy direct contact with God. The encounter with the Christian public has given Salomon greater latitude to express such messages, which are somewhat unacceptable in Israeli circles. Thus, for example, he told his Christian audience of an encounter with the angels of God immediately after the conquest of the Temple Mount. Salomon reports that while he was on the Temple Mount on the day on which it was occupied, a mysterious figure came up to the group. The figure showed them the site of the altar and explained the function of each place in the holy site. The movement's newsletter continues:

> All the group were sure that this mysterious "person" was an angel sent by G-d to tell Israel that He was expecting her to immediately rebuild the Temple, to renew the days of Israel as it was in the biblical times, and to open the door for the coming of Mashiach ben David. Gershon will never forget this event.[24]

The connection between the Temple Mount Faithful and Christian circles raises a further point for comparison regarding the role of the Gentiles in Jewish redemption. In the other Temple Mount movements, the universalistic dimension of the Temple is a marginal feature of rhetoric and practice, and the image of the Temple focuses mainly on the particularistic function of the redemption of the Jewish people. Salomon, by contrast, presents an approach that emphasizes the promise of redemption for all the peoples of the world, among whom he has found his allies in recent years.

Of all the Temple Mount activists, Gershon Salomon and the Temple Mount Faithful would seem to provide the most fertile basis for Jewish-Christian cooperation. The reason for this is that this movement is not Orthodox in character, and is guided exclusively by its leader.

Examples of the open approach of the movement toward non-Jews can be found on the movement's Web site. Salomon argues that the nations of the world can join in the process of redemption—a process from which they will also benefit. To that end, Salomon invites "all those whose Scriptures contain hope and faith in one God" to participate in the activities of the Temple Mount Faithful:

> God has given this great vision to our generation and we cannot run away from our responsibility to Him. The redemption of the people and Land of Israel and the rebuilding of the Temple in this generation will open ways for the fulfillment of this vision all over the world. However, it must first be accomplished here in Israel. According to the Word of G-d the Temple must be rebuilt on Mt. Moriah in the midst of Jerusalem. Mashiach ben David will not come to Washington, D.C, not to London, Paris or Rome,

not to Cairo or Damascus, but to the place which G-d chose, Jerusalem. So my call to all the nations is to stop putting pressure on Israel to sign anti-godly so-called "peace" agreements which give the land, Jerusalem and the Temple Mount to the most cruel enemies of the G-d and people of Israel. Do not join the enemies who want to destroy Israel. When you join with the enemies of Israel to destroy her you bring yourselves under the judgment of G-d which he promised to execute on the enemies of Israel.[25]

Salomon invites his readers to make a moral, spiritual, and financial contribution to the work of his movement. He exploits the sense of messianic urgency in requesting this support. "We have now reached a critical stage in our campaign," he states. "We are soon to see the fulfillment of our vision, but this final stage needs additional efforts. All donations will be very much appreciated by G-d and your messengers—the Temple Mount Faithful members." Salomon also urges people to volunteer, and offers guide services for groups visiting Israel, as well as lectures for Christian congregations in the United States.[26] This connection was manifested in concrete terms in 1991 when Salomon was invited to appear on the television show of the popular preacher Pat Robertson.[27]

Conclusion

The Temple Mount Faithful was the first group to initiate Jewish activities on the Temple Mount, and its actions were sufficiently provocative to raise its demands repeatedly on the national and international agenda, heightening discussion of the status of the site among the Israeli public. Though weak in number, the movement's activities are enhanced due to the enormous sensitivity of the Israeli-Arab conflict, as evidenced by the violent events of October 1990. Teddy Kollek, the former mayor of Jerusalem, demanded that the police refrain from enabling the Temple Mount Faithful to demonstrate near to the site, due to the enormous tension created by such demonstrations.[28]

As I have explained in this chapter, the Temple Mount Faithful has been marginalized among the Temple Mount groupings, despite the public interest it has aroused. The clearest evidence of this came when all the Temple Mount movements decided to join forces, but without including Salomon and his movement, who have continued to pursue their own independent agenda.

A comparison of the profile of the Temple Mount Faithful by comparison to the other movements reveals profound and substantial differences. First, the religious foundation is different. Most of the Temple activists define themselves as Orthodox religious Jews whose actions are delineated by religious law (as they interpret it). By contrast, the Temple Mount Faithful has developed its own religious ritual framework that draws only on such elements of the tradition as it finds convenient. A further point of difference relates to messianic perceptions. While the Temple Mount Faithful has, over the years, developed an apocalyptic messianic ideology, the other Temple movements promote a naturalistic messianic ideology. This aspect also explains the difference in terms of the character of the future Temple: whereas the Temple Mount Faithful anticipate a universal Temple, with a place of honor for all the nations of the world, the remaining movements focus on the particularistic aspects of the Temple regarding the Jews alone, with virtually no consideration of the role of the Gentiles in redemption. In my estimation, this difference reflects the appeal of the Temple Mount Faithful to fundamentalist Christian circles, resulting in a strong emphasis on the universalistic aspects of redemption. In terms of the demographic composition of the groups, the Temple Mount Faithful activists are relatively older than those of the other groups; not all of them wear skullcaps, and they are accompanied by Christians (men and women together) at their demonstrations. The activists in the other groups are generally younger and do not include non-Jews in their activities. A difference may also be observed in terms of the founding texts—the Temple Mount Faithful focuses on the Bible, and particularly on the prophets. This may also reflect the non-Jewish audience of the movement, which is familiar with the Old Testament but less so with the Jewish exegeses of the Bible, and which does not recognize the authority of Halacha. The other Temple movements base their religious arguments mainly on the Midrashic literature.

Gershon Salomon has shifted his long-standing campaign to remove the mosques from the Temple Mount onto apocalyptic and dualistic lines, depicting the Palestinian presence on the Temple Mount as an enemy that must be annihilated in order for redemption to come to the world. The other movements devote less attention in their actions to the struggle against the Palestinians, and their message has a more internal character, directed at the Orthodox section of Israeli society, with the goal of changing attitudes toward the Temple Mount and the construction of the Temple. This aspect relates to the last point of comparison—the attitude to Zionism. The other Temple movements believe that Zionism has reached a dead end and cannot accommodate the breakthrough to the Temple Mount and the Temple; accordingly, they have developed a theocratic and post-Zionist approach. Salomon's perspective is different; he considers himself part of the Zionist collective, and believes that his actions constitute the pinnacle of Zionist endeavors and a national symbol. Salomon was even a member of the Herut movement, and considered running for the Knesset in 1992 in an independent list. He rejects the idea that there is any inherent conflict between a Jewish-Zionist state and the Temple Mount, as is posited by the other Temple movements, since he considers the Temple Mount the symbol of sovereign realization.

During its early years, the Temple Mount Faithful emphasized the function of the Temple Mount as a ceremonial and symbolic site, whereas more recently it has stressed the need to build the Third Temple. This change in rhetoric came alongside the shift in the target audience addressed by the movement. Fundamentalist Christians could not have developed such a strong interest in the movement had it not explicitly demanded the construction of the Temple. The driving theology of the Christian movements is based on the need to build the Temple on the Mount in preparation for the coming of Jesus; no other scenario could bring them to support such a movement. This, I believe, explains the adjustment in the message of the movement to respond to this audience. The rhetoric of the movement also changed, and its content and style became more similar to those of the evangelical Christian leaders. Despite these changes, the movement's message is still somewhat blurred. It is unclear what kind of Temple Salomon envisages in his speeches: a religious one including the reinstatement of the sacrifices; a secular Temple as a national symbol; or perhaps a Temple for all the nations?

The Temple Mount Faithful now finds itself on the margins of those groups that seek to promote a Jewish presence on the Temple Mount. Its leading role has been taken by younger and more dynamic forces from the fringe movements of Religious Zionism. This does not mean, however, that the movement has lost its vitality or its potential for influence. The movement's public relations stunts, such as laying the cornerstone for the Temple or preparing an architectural plan for its construction, combined with its regular demonstrations, can still arouse Muslim passions and stir internecine tension. This enables the movement to retain a prominent profile and, in turn, to maintain the support of fundamentalist Christians who see it as a vessel for realizing their own messianic vision. This connection is vital to ensure the economic strength needed to finance the regular and expensive actions of the movement; to rent and maintain spacious offices; to file petitions to the High Court of Justice every few months; to publicize the movement's activities through billboards and direct mailing; to prepare vessels for use in the Temple similar to those displayed by the Temple Institute; to create a model of the Third Temple; and so on.

It is my assessment, however, that the Temple Mount Faithful has passed its peak and is in a process of decline. Its demonstrations draw no more than a few dozen participants, most of whom are relatively elderly, and some of whom are not Israelis. By comparison, thousands of enthusiastic young Jewish Israelis participate in the monthly marches around the gates of the Temple Mount. Given the lack of leadership structure in the movement, and its total dependence on Gershon Salomon, it is doubtful whether it will be able to survive in the future if Salomon is unable to continue to remain in his leadership position.

In the next chapter I discuss the Movement for the Establishment of the Temple, which broke away from the Temple Mount Faithful and created a Temple movement for Haredi Jews in Israel.

5

Haredi Messianic Activism
The Movement for the Establishment of the Temple

The Movement for the Establishment of the Temple is a small but remarkable interest group that has developed within modern-day Haredi (ultra-Orthodox) society in Israel. It is relatively unknown among the general public, and has been largely overshadowed by such figures as Yehuda Etzion from the Jewish Underground, and Gershon Salomon, leader of the Temple Mount Faithful movement. However, the anonymity of this group belies its importance. The Movement for the Establishment of the Temple is one of the most significant of the groups advocating the construction of the Third Temple, and includes most of the activists in this field. Its unique character lies in its special blend of Haredi and messianic theology.

The importance of this group lies in its revolutionary attempt to demand the rebuilding of the Temple. It argues that both the Haredi and Zionist wings of Orthodox Judaism committed a grave theological error in adopting a passive approach to the rebuilding of the Temple. In presenting this argument, the group offers an alternative Halachic and historiographic narrative, and challenges the validity of the grave Halachic prohibition against entering the Temple Mount, the punishment for which is *Karet*—the divinely imposed death penalty. In its activities and polemical arguments, it succeeded in changing attitudes on this subject among some of the rabbis of Gush Emunim. While after the Six-Day War only a small minority favored entering the Temple Mount and praying on the site, and this position was identified mainly with Rabbi Shlomo Goren (though he did not express it publicly while serving as Chief Rabbi), this position is now encountered more widely among Orthodox Zionist religious authorities, particularly those identified with Gush Emunim.

In this chapter, I will describe the mind-set of the activists in the Movement for the Establishment of the Temple; to examine their struggle to change opinions on the question of the Temple Mount among the Orthodox public; to consider the manner in which they have coped with the Oslo Process—which is founded on the desire to achieve a compromise between Israel and the PLO, including on the issue of the Temple Mount; and to show how their ideas have begun to find currency among Gush Emunim rabbis in response to the peace process.

The Movement for the Establishment of the Temple is another manifestation of the transformation that has been seen in the Orthodox world, and indeed takes this transformation one step further. Although the movement has its roots among the Haredi public in Israel, its approach represents a fundamentalist, millenarian, and activist position more radical than that of Gush Emunim. Whereas the approach of Gush Emunim leaves room for the possibility that a transcendental experience will complete the process of natural redemption, only parts of which are incumbent on humans,[1] the Movement for the Establishment of the Temple perceives the completion of the process of redemption in a totally independent manner, without Divine intervention. In common with Gush Emunim, the Movement for the Establishment of the Temple views the Zionist endeavor as an important step toward the ultimate redemption, but it does not confine itself to this, demanding progress toward the construction of the Temple, the reinstitution of the sacrifices, and the establishment of the Sanhedrin. According to its perspective, all these achievements must be secured through human means and by human endeavor, and certainly not through miracles or supernatural occurrences. Accordingly, the movement acts to prepare the vessels for the Temple, to pray on the Temple Mount and to engage in intensive study and preparations ahead of the establishment of the Temple. Its activities, however, are not without a certain passivity. It acts quietly, almost surreptitiously, and explains its actions exclusively in religious terms. It does not claim that the construction of the Temple constitutes the ultimate realization of the Zionist enterprise, neither does it see the Temple Mount as the proper place for the Israeli institutions of government, as does the Temple Mount Faithful movement. Neither does it seek to remove the mosques from the Mount. Instead, it represents a unique case of a fundamentalist movement that does not rely on passionate messianic rhetoric, and whose radical messianic arguments are presented in the ostensibly moderate demand to be enabled to observe as many commandments as possible (issues to which I will return later).

Alongside the trends to religious extremism, the fear of messianic failure must also be taken into account. Here, too, the Movement for the Establishment of the Temple provides an additional and interesting case. Over its years of activity, the movement has been forced to address dramatic political developments in the shape of the Oslo Accords, in which different Israeli governments have de facto agreed to make concessions on the Temple Mount. The present study illustrates the manner in which this political move by successive Israeli governments created a counterreaction in the form of an intensified aspiration to secure the Temple Mount and to show a higher level of commitment to the site. The fear of future changes unfavorable to their position led to further radicalization in an effort to avoid these changes. This chapter seeks to explain the manner in which this crisis led the thinking of the Movement for the Establishment of the Temple from the margins of religious life in Israel ever closer to its core. Its activities in the wake of the Oslo Accords enabled it to influence Orthodox Zionist rabbinical authority, particularly that of the Gush Emunim rabbis, weakening the force of the Halachic ban on entering the Temple Mount, which was once considered an extremely grave prohibition.

The Establishment of the Movement

The Movement for the Establishment of the Temple was founded in 1987 by a small circle of members. The initiative for the new movement came from a Belzer Hassid by the name of Yosef Elboim. Elboim broke away from Gershon Salomon's movement, the Temple Mount Faithful, and was joined by a Haredi group from Jerusalem that referred to itself as "an association comprised of God-fearing persons, including rabbis and Torah sages."[2] This group was also joined by figures identified with the Kach movement, a far-right political party in Israel founded by Rabbi Meir Kahane. The initiative reflected a feeling that the existing public bodies working to permit prayer on the Mount, particularly the Temple Mount Faithful group, were not meeting their needs. As a Haredi Jew whose life was dedicated to religious worship, Elboim believed that the claim to the Temple Mount is first and foremost a religious commandment: "Make for Me a sanctuary that I might dwell among them" (Exod. 25:8). Salomon's belief in the need for the State of Israel to impose Israeli sovereignty on the Temple Mount, and to displace the Arab Waqf, led to activities such as public demonstrations and court petitions demanding that the members of the movement be permitted to pray on the Temple Mount at specific dates during the year. Due to the public nature of these hearings, the courts generally rejected his petitions, and permits were conditioned on police authorization, based on considerations relating to public security. The police consistently refused to permit the group to pray on the Temple Mount for these reasons. To that end, the members of the Movement for the Establishment of the Temple decided to adopt a different tactic: eschewing publicity, they would hold orderly visits to the Temple Mount to pray on the site, in small groups and in coordination with the police. Elboim emphasized the differences between the movements: "In recent times, two paths to the Mount have been apparent. Path 1 is silent, difficult—and gets there. Path 2 is easy, loud—and is shattered. . . . Better for us a quiet and mournful visit to the Temple Mount than to sing at its gates and cheer at its walls."[3] Elboim believed that the physical Jewish presence on the Temple Mount, rooted in a religious commandment (and distinct from any other Jewish presence, such as tourism), was vastly more important than public gatherings and demonstrations. To "conquer" the Mount, for Elboim, was to ensure a constant presence at the site, even if this was in relatively small numbers and almost completely without publicity.

The Movement for the Establishment of the Temple decided that its principle goal was to win souls for its approach within the Haredi community, and to create change within that sector. The expectation was that a change of direction following their activities in this sector would undoubtedly have the force to spark changes among other groups. The challenge undertaken by the movement was far from simple, given the conservative tendencies of the Haredi public, who reject changes in religious behavior. As a result, the movement's activities centered mainly on informational efforts, with a particular emphasis on finding Halachic considerations supporting activities relating to the Temple Mount, such as praying on the Mount and engaging in other religious activities there.[4] After its establishment, the movement published a monthly journal entitled *Yibaneh Hamikdash* (Let the Temple Be Built), which appeared for twelve years and included discussion of Halachic aspects permitting Jews to ascend and enter the Temple Mount. The monthly became a key tool for the movement in disseminating its ideas. The journal is highly informative in terms of the opinions and methods of the movement. Another important activity was to arrange orderly and regular visits to the Temple Mount, without provocation and with virtually no public attention, to hold prayers on Tuesdays and Saturdays. These visits continued until the Temple Mount was closed to Jews following the outbreak of the Al-Aqsa Intifada in September 2000, and were reintroduced following the opening of the site in November 2003. The movement also established a religious court (Beit Din) to issue Halachic rulings; organized public activities, including petitions and lobbying; encouraged study of the religious laws relating to the Temple in various frameworks; practiced and prepared for Temple worship; and attempted to train priests and Levites and to prepare the priestly garments.

THE ARGUMENT OVER THE NAME AND GOALS OF THE MOVEMENT

The new group engaged in internal soul-searching around the question of the difference between itself and the Temple Mount Faithful, and around the methods it should adopt to promote its goals. Since the group was comprised of individuals who were reluctant to draw attention to their ideas among the sector from which they came, "due to the prohibition imposed by the rabbis" (as I will discuss at length later), one may understand the decision taken at the first gathering in August 1987 to act through interpersonal contacts and to avoid broad publicity. By contrast, members who did not come from the Haredi community, and who were more closely identified with Kach, argued that aggressive informational approaches should be adopted, including paid advertisements, in the style of the Temple Mount Faithful.[5]

An additional argument that arose among the members of the movement from the earliest stages related to the name of the group. From the outset, some members expressed the view that stating "the establishment of the Temple" as a goal of the group was presumptuous and liable to discourage others from joining the movement. Others, however, argued that concealing the true purpose of the group made it no different from the Temple Mount Faithful, whose name also avoided mentioning the establishment of the Temple.[6] Yosef Elboim suggested that the group avoid choosing any name, at least until seventy members joined—the same number as in the Great Sanhedrin.[7] However, the debate over the name was influenced by an unexpected consideration. The members' application to be registered at the Registry of Associations was rejected because of a "fear of misleading the public." It emerged that the attorney-general at the time, Meir Shamgar, issued instructions that associations to build the Temple should not be registered, arguing that it was an insult to the public to suggest that "these are the builders of the Temple." Accordingly, the formal name of the group was amended to the Association for Research and Information for the Establishment of the Temple.[8]

THE MOVEMENT FOR THE ESTABLISHMENT OF THE TEMPLE AND KACH

An important characteristic of the Movement for the Establishment of the Temple is its rejection of physical or verbal violence. From the earliest days, the members took care to avoid insults or inflammatory statements. Their writing was sometimes pained and impassioned, but they were generally careful to adopt a respectful tone and engage in civilized debate. On occasions when articles appeared in the movement's publications that included offensive remarks, this was always followed by a demand for apologies and an emphasis on the need to show respect for rabbis, publicists, and religious and political leaders, even those who were far from being supporters of the movement's approach. The members of the movement realized that the public image of activists on the issue of the Temple Mount was that of a dangerous and violent minority; accordingly, they must be seen to be balanced and dignified, and at no cost aggressive or eccentric.

These principles were tested during a heated debate with Kach, a movement that had similar ideological beliefs and from whose ranks many of the supporters of the Movement for the Establishment of the Temple came. Detailing this debate is important to understand the idea of attacking the mosques on the mount. Kach's founder and head, Meir Kahane, was a supporter of the Movement for the Establishment of the Temple, and even permitted the organization free use of printing equipment to which he had access.[9] Moreover, Yoel Lerner, the first chairman of the Movement for the Establishment of the Temple, was on close terms with Meir Kahane. After Kahane was murdered in 1989, his son, Benjamin Zeev Kahane, assumed the leadership of Kach,[10] and entered into a passionate ideological debate with the members of the Movement for the Establishment of the Temple, arguing that his father's legacy, focused on the struggle against "the Desecration of God's Name," implied a struggle against those who oppose the right of the Jews to the Land of Israel.[11] So, he believed that the focus should be on a negative campaign against the Arabs, because of their control of the Temple Mount, whereas the Movement for the Establishment of the Temple adopted a positive approach in its publicity, with the aim of changing opinions within the Orthodox community in Israel. Kahane sent an article to the editorial board of *Yibaneh Hamikdash* in which he attacked members of the movement

> who are extremely cautious to avoid creating the impression that it [the establishment of the Temple] will be "at the expense" of the Arabs. They use all kinds of ways to argue that the Arabs will not be affected, and that this supposedly does not require any conflict with them. . . . In the war against the desecration of God's name, and in the war against this national disgrace, . . . without a struggle against the *Sitra Achra* (The forces of evil of the Other Side), and without a struggle against evil, we cannot reach good and reach construction. If someone goes up to the Temple Mount and looks toward that holy place, and does not return with the awareness that we must wage a fierce war against this desecration, against this disgrace, and thereby come to construction—what is he fighting for?![12]

Another article, by Pinchas Gil from the Kahanist Yeshiva of the Jewish Idea, raised an even more radical argument: the required religious war should be not only against the Arabs, but also against

> the state that adorns itself with the name Israel. After all, this state is possibly the greatest obstacle that currently stands in the

path of the Jewish people to redemption . . . and accordingly
nothing sacred can be done on the Temple Mount without fighting those forces of the *Sitra Achra* that control it—both the Arabs
and the State of Israel.[13]

The response to the arguments presented by the writers from the
Yeshiva of the Jewish Idea emphasized and accentuated the approach of
the Movement for the Establishment of the Temple. Responding to Gil,
David Shafir, one of the founders of the movement, wrote:

> The members of the "gangs" that control the state did not seize
> control from you, they simply moved first and entered the vac-
> uum left by you and your like in your sins, so what cause have
> you to complain about them? . . . It is impossible to succeed by
> speaking loftily of the need to remove the mosques until you
> have "done well with the people" and allowed them to taste some-
> thing of the light and vision of the future Temple, which indeed
> includes the mending of the entire world to good.[14]

Benjamin Zeev Kahane was quick to respond to this argument, further
sharpening the principled argument between the two groupings. According to Kahane, the verse "avoid evil and do good" proves that the
proper order of things is to condemn the wicked (by which Kahane meant
the Israeli administration and the Arab control of the Temple Mount),
and only then to engage in positive activities in the field of information.
"Only by condemning the wicked and those who destroy, willingly or
under duress, can we reach the government in this state and this people."
In any case, while it might be possible to postpone the construction of the
Temple, as far as the mosques on the Temple Mount are concerned:

> It is obvious to me that if we do not speak of deleting the dese-
> cration of God, we have missed an essential and principal stage,
> and it is very doubtful what we have achieved. While the building
> may be postponed for a while, the deletion of the desecration
> must not be postponed.[15]

Responses to Kahane's article were published by Elitzur Segal (who
was associated with Kach and taught at a college in the settlement of
Tapuah, home to many supporters of the Kach movement) and Yosef Elboim, both key figures in the Movement for the Establishment of the
Temple. Segal explained that, as he saw it, the problem was not how to
change the system of government, since even if Kahane were to come to
power the next day, "I doubt whether he would be able to move all the

rusty machinery of government overnight." Government is a reflection of the people, and the popular objection to the idea of the Temple was widespread and found in all sections of the populace. Accordingly, Segal explained, the solution lies in slowly creating a basis of human consciousness that will eventually be able to confront the government "if it still continues with its opposition."[16] Yosef Elboim compared the activities of the Movement for the Establishment of the Temple to the First Aliyah period: "This is the way of revolution: they seek legitimacy, they struggle to increase their share, then they compete for first place and eventually they push the alien beyond the scope of the law." Commenting on Pinchas Gil's article "Down with the Occupation!" Elboim wrote:

> Were the weapon in my hand ready for action, where would I direct it? Against those who sit on the seat of executive in the government, or against those who sit on the throne of the law, or perhaps against those responsible for issuing official religious law on behalf of the authorities of state? Or maybe against the various private religious courts, or perhaps even against those unfortunates who sit on the Opposition—or maybe it would be easier to make a list of those who are not targets? In brief . . . no good will come of this for our deserted Temple. . . . Go out and realize that most of those who hear of the activities to restore our blessed Divine Presence to Zion are terrified by the idea that they must join those who blow up mosques—almost the sole association that the Temple inspires in them, since they have not yet understood the construction of the Temple—and this only leads them to avoid anything to do with the Temple.

Accordingly, Elboim concludes, there are no short cuts, and the focus must be on education and information, "and not on angry contention that leads to despair."[17]

The ideological argument with the members of Kach emphasized the character of the movement. The Movement for the Establishment of the Temple did not aim to be another grouping of "mosque busters," but rather to work through education and opinion-forming to change public consciousness regarding the need to build the Temple. The movement chose this approach from the outset, and over the years it enabled several achievements, most notably influence on Orthodox rabbinical decisions relating to the annulment of the taboo against Jews entering the Temple Mount. The movement also chose to distinguish itself from the approach taken by the Temple Mount Faithful: rather than demonstrating the claim to the Temple Mount, the Movement for the Establishment of the Temple was primarily interested in finding Halachic solutions to the prohibition against entering the site and against the reinstatement of the sacrifices. It was precisely this tactical choice that enabled it to make headway.

The Ideology of the Movement

The ideology of the Movement for the Establishment of the Temple focuses on offering a religious interpretation for historical and political reality. In this respect, it is similar to other fundamentalist religious streams that view the Scriptures as absolute truth, and seek to find allusions to current affairs in their interpretation of these sources. In many cases, fundamentalist movements believe that they know God's will, and therefore know the proper way to change the state of the world God created. This explains why fundamentalist movements are also often millenarian in nature.[18]

The rhetorical style of the Movement for the Establishment of the Temple preserves the style of Haredi exegesis, but uses this style to present an alternative historiographic narrative. Israel Bartal argues that the autonomous Haredi historiography was developed as an additional tool in the struggle against modernity, including modern historiography. Haredi historiography attacks the trend toward change in religion and the Enlightenment movement, using history as a tool.[19] The Movement for the Establishment of the Temple also uses historiography as a polemical tool, but one that is directed against Haredi historiography. Accordingly, this case study addresses the issue of how religious groups reformulate traditional religious texts and beliefs for contemporary and new purposes.

THE PROHIBITION AGAINST ENTERING THE TEMPLE MOUNT

The activists of the Movement for the Establishment of the Temple, numbering between sixty and one hundred individuals, stood firm against the general position of the Haredi community, including almost all its *poskim* (those who rule on Halachic matters), regarding one of the gravest prohibitions imposed on the public: the prohibition against entering the Temple Mount.[20]

When the members of the group began their activities, some were initially surprised that they were not attacked within their own communities for adopting a stance that contradicted such a serious prohibition. It was not long, however, before Yosef Elboim experienced such an attack. One morning in 1989, as he arrived at the synagogue where he usually attended morning prayers, he was not allowed to join the quorum of worshippers, on the grounds that, as someone who visited the Temple Mount, he was liable to *Karet*. A boycott was imposed on him, and the public were forbidden to talk to him or to accept him as a worshipper at any synagogue. His humiliation was compounded when he was forcibly removed from the minibus he regularly used to reach his place of work. The mezuzot were torn off the entrance to his home and the door was set on fire. The Beit Din Tzedek (religious court) of the Eda Haredit even published a "Torah Warning" not to assist "these sinners and corrupters." A war of wall posters erupted in the streets of the Haredi Jerusalem neighborhoods. Some posters urged the residents to condemn "those who willfully transgress against a prohibition incurring *Karet* and go up to the Temple Mount," while others (placed on Elboim's behalf) presented contrary arguments: "If we have forgone the Temple Mount, let us also forgo its exterior—the Western Wall." The episode ended after a bomb was planted in the home of Rabbi Simcha Waldenberg, head of the "Modesty Guard,"[21] which had led the boycott of Elboim. It was quietly hinted to Waldenberg that the bomb was planted by members of Kach who were on close terms with the Movement for the Establishment of the Temple.[22]

EXILE AND REDEMPTION

Jewish existence is encapsulated in two dichotic rabbinical perceptions: exile and redemption. Since the destruction of the Second Temple, the Jewish people have been in exile. Rabbinical exegesis views this exile as spiritual as well as physical. The End of Exile can come only through prophetic leadership and miracles leading to ultimate and complete redemption. The Zionist movement opposed the traditional framework that sanctified political passivity and awaited a miraculous end to the era of exile. Zionism sought to achieve the return of the Jewish people to Zion—a transition that had traditionally been considered one of the ultimate stages of the End of Exile, and to establish a political entity in the Land of Israel, through pragmatic human endeavor in the mundane world. The rejection of basic Orthodox norms regarding the perception of redemption, particularly when presented by irreligious Jews who attacked traditional values, provoked fierce opposition among the Orthodox leadership that began to emerge during the late nineteenth century and the early twentieth century. This opposition found theological expression in the argument that the establishment of the State of Israel was merely the extension of exile, albeit in the Holy Land.[23]

The Movement for the Establishment of the Temple sought to challenge this perception, and to prove to the leadership of the Haredi community that it was possible to move from exile to redemption without abandoning the religious commandments, by accepting personal responsibility and acting within the mundane world, while at the same time observing every major and minor commandment. This would be possible if there were a religious and political transformation within the State of Israel, and the force and pinnacle of this transformation lay in the demand for the Temple—a symbol powerful enough to counter and overcome what they perceived as an empty and valueless democracy.

The messianic passivity that characterized traditional Judaism in the Diaspora was justified in theological terms by the oath sworn to God by the Children of Israel in Song of Songs 2:7: "I charge you, O ye daughters of Jerusalem, by the roes, and by the hinds of the field, that ye stir not up, nor awake my love, till he please." Interpreting this verse, the Midrash comments: "He swore Israel not to rebel against the sovereigns, and not to 'force the End,' and not to reveal their mysteries to the nations, and not to ascend up the wall from Exile."[24] The practical significance of this oath for the Jewish people is the strict prohibition against rebeling against the nations that host the Jews in exile; a prohibition against calculating when exile will end; and a prohibition against collective migration to the Land of Israel. These prohibitions sanctified Jewish life in exile, and prevented Jews from associating to reinstitute Jewish sovereignty in the Land of Israel. Only God would do that, through miraculous acts.

Rabbi Yoel Teitelbaum, leader of the Satmar Hassidic sect, which is the most radical element of Haredi society, draws on theological insights to argue that Zionism is an overt case of rebellion against God. The three prohibitions previously noted are not a tactical provision intended to protect the Jews and prevent any temptation to act rashly while they were in exile. Rather, these prohibitions are a substantive manifestation of Divine leadership and the Divine providence of the Jewish people. Therefore, Zionism and the State of Israel are a rebellion against God, and must not be recognized in any circumstances. The Satmar rabbi, who sought to find reward and punishment in all human acts, viewed the Holocaust as a grave punishment for the Zionist rebellion against the ideas embodied in the oaths, which he transformed into a fundamental principle of faith. Those Zionists who "force the End," ascended "up the wall" from exile and rebeled against the familiar order of things and were guilty of the terrible Divine punishment manifested in the Holocaust. It was not exile that collapsed in the Holocaust, but Zionism that led to the abandonment and desertion of Jewish lives.[25]

It was this fundamental argument that was challenged by the members of the Movement for the Establishment of the Temple, and particularly by Yosef Elboim. According to their perspective, blame for the Holocaust lay not with the Zionist rebels against God, but rather with those who remained passive and expected the miraculous Kingdom of God to arrive from the skies. This conclusion had far-reaching consequences regarding the nature of the messianic process.

In 1917, the British foreign minister, Lord Arthur James Balfour, announced that the government of Great Britain viewed with favor the prospect of establishing a national home for the Jewish people in the

Land of Israel. This declaration was ratified by the countries that emerged victorious from World War I. The Movement for the Establishment of the Temple argued that the Balfour Declaration was tantamount to the annulment of the three traditional oaths. After the nations of the world ratified the declaration, under Divine providence, the Jews should leave their places of exile and ascend to the Land of Israel and establish their own state. In effect, this process was perceived as a new oath God required from the Jewish people: to leave exile and enter the stage of redemption. This oath was made with the approval and support of the nations of the world, so that it should not be considered rebellion against the nations or "forcing the End." According to the principle of reward and punishment, the members of the Movement for the Establishment of the Temple now interpret the Holocaust as a punishment for the failure by Orthodox Jewry in Diaspora to respond to the new Divine oath:

> It is true that we are educated to believe that the Holocaust was the fault of the Zionists, who threw off the Divine yoke and "ascended up the wall" and infringed the three oaths, but I have always been bothered by some questions. If the Holocaust was due to the Zionists, how did it transpire that the Zionists were so successful, and built us a splendid country and even absorbed the refugees of those *Zaddikim* (righteous man) who refused to participate in all these transgressions, while precisely those who had no part in the transgressions were all killed in the sanctification of His name like lambs to the slaughter? I also wonder why they speak of the three oaths and "ascending up the wall." We have all heard of a Jew by the name of Herzl, who acted and performed much in order to establish a Jewish state in the Land of Israel, and it doesn't say anywhere that he carried weapons or even a small pistol. All his work was aimed at securing permission from the Gentiles, until the Balfour Declaration came to fruition. . . . So where is the "ascending up the wall" here?[26]

Thus, Zionism has a cosmic destiny, and those who fail to see this, and who await miraculous redemption, pay an enormous price for their blindness—a blindness that is the lot not only of the Orthodox public, but also of the Zionist enterprise itself. The Zionists correctly interpreted God's new will, manifested in His intent to remove the Jews from exile and bring them into the stage of redemption. However, their redemption took the wrong course. God's intention was not to make the Jews into "a nation like any other," as the Zionist slogan promised; rather, He wished the Jewish people to remain the Chosen People. The redemption was not the establishment of a "safe haven for the Jewish people"; religious redemption entails the reestablishment of the biblical Kingdom of Israel, in which the Jewish people might worship their God in the fullest and most complete manner, by observing all 613 commandments.

This theological exegesis enables Yosef Elboim to consider himself an authentic Zionist. While the Zionists misinterpreted the Divine message they received, those who followed the true path of religious redemption, by observing all 613 commandments, were the true Zionists and agents of God. The value system of reward and punishment serves only to reinforce these theological perspectives. If God rewards those who follow His path—which explains why the Zionists have so far secured the upper hand, while Diaspora Jewry suffered the Holocaust—and if the Zionists deviate from a path that ultimately leads to the Temple Mount, they will lose their supremacy and they, too, will be punished by a further Holocaust. A further lesson drawn by Elboim and his fellows from this worldview is that the individual must be proactive. Elboim completely negates passive expectation of miracles and supernatural processes. So, if God's mission is not being realized, for whatever reason, the "man on the street" must take responsibility and remedy the situation.[27] These conclusions were formulated during the period of the Oslo Accords, when the Israeli governments entered into a process of compromise and agreed to divide the Land of Israel with the PLO as the Palestinian regime. This process was also expected to lead to a compromise on the Temple Mount, something that was perceived as a profound threat by the activists of the Movement for the Establishment of the Temple.

A further argument for the need to annul the oaths came from a Halachic obligation. It was argued that the oaths, which are drawn from the Aggadic literature, have an inferior status relative to binding Halacha, such as the commandment to build the Temple. Commandments certainly have a greater weight in the Jewish religion than legends, so that the commandment to build the Temple takes precedence over the legend of the oaths. Yosef Elboim explains: "Legends do not have the force to waive a commandment. And these can under no circumstances be a contradiction between legends . . . and a Halachic ruling relating to the commandment and obligations required of people in the present."[28] Israel Ariel, the founder of the Temple Institute reinforces this argument:

> The Torah is commandments, and commandments must be observed. Legends come to serve the commandments and to strengthen performance of the commandments. This is why the Holy One, Blessed be He, gave us intellect—to strengthen and observe the commandments. As long as the content of the world of faith increases God-fearing behavior and observance of the commandments, and the commandments of the Torah are respected

in full, then *Aggadah* (legend) serves Halacha and the sublime content invigorates the performance of the commandments. But if the world of *Aggadah* becomes a tool for providing excuses not to perform the commandments, . . . if the *Aggadah* starts to take precedence over the Halacha, this is not Torah or Halacha, this is nothing—this is devastation."[29]

APOCALYPTIC REDEMPTION AND NATURALISTIC REDEMPTION

The traditional Jewish sources reflect different perceptions of messianic redemption. Our discussion of these perceptions will adopt the definitions proposed by Dov Schwartz, which distinguish between apocalyptic and naturalistic messianisms.[30]

These differing approaches fueled the debate between the members of the Movement for the Establishment of the Temple and those members of the Haredi leadership who held the majority view. The basic position of the movement was that one should not await an overt miracle, but use human tools to accelerate redemption. They believed that this was both feasible and permissible in Halachic terms.

Maimonides devotes the last chapters of his Halachic treatise, *Mishneh Torah*, to the subject of redemption. As a rationalist, Maimonides rejects apocalyptic and miraculous expectations of redemption, which he views instead as a gradual process dependent on the actions of the public. Numerous interpretations of these two chapters have been offered. Some saw them as an attempt to neutralize and even negate the messianic idea,[31] while others drew on them as a justification for messianic activism.[32] David Hartman notes that in Maimonides's discussion of the laws relating to kings and wars the King Messiah will realize the full scope of the content of Torah, including the sacrifices and the construction of the Temple. The King is not an emissary declaring a radical change in natural order; neither does he announce the end of history. Rather, he realizes the ideal of establishing a kingdom administered in accordance with the Law of Moses. The Messiah is a tool for securing the ideal of the Torah. Accordingly, the Halacha will not be abolished in the messianic era: on the contrary, it will be realized in full. In the *Mishneh Torah*, messianism is elaborated primarily in terms of the significance of a Halachic society, rather than in the emergence of a supernatural society by means of a predetermined Divine plan. It is the commitment to the 613 commandments that creates the need for an autonomous, messianic political framework.[33]

The Movement for the Establishment of the Temple presents essentially the same argument: God gave the Jewish people the 613 commandments so that they could be observed. As long as the Jews lived in exile, objective reasons prevented their observing all the commandments.

Once they have returned to their own land, however, they have the capacity (at least theoretically) to observe all the commandments, and are obligated to do so. This is the essence of redemption, and it was for this purpose that God eliminated the exile. Those who ignored this process were punished, while those who began to implement this cosmic task were rewarded with success. However, the establishment of the State of Israel is far from the end of the process. Its zenith will come with the reconstruction of the Temple and the reinstitution of the sacrifices on the Temple Mount.

It is interesting to note that Elboim's position is close to that of Tzevi Hirsch Kalischer, one of the "harbingers of Zionism." Kalischer interpreted the emancipation of the Jews as an event of historical and mythical significance in the context of redemption. He proposed several stages for redemption: the ingathering of a small number of Jews in Israel with the permission of the nations, and the reinstitution of the Passover sacrifice on the site of the Temple. These stages, which are to be undertaken by humans, would be complemented by God, according to the principle "mundane actions cause sublime actions." In his book *Drishat Zion*, Kalischer drew on the argument relating to the observance of all 613 commandments, explaining that all the commandments form a single entity, and he who removes or annuls a single commandment also impairs the value of observing the others. Observing the specific commandments relating to the Land of Israel might bring redemption, and if it is possible to observe the commandments relating to the Land, anyone who refrains from doing so is liable to *"Gilgul"* (additional lives of the soul) to complete what was lacking.[34] An interesting comparison may be noted here with Akiva Yosef Schlesinger (1837–1922), who immigrated to the Land of Israel from Hungary and was among the founders of ultra-Orthodoxy in the 1860s. His unique theological position advocated Jewish nationalism and a return to Zion alongside the strict observance of the commandments. He viewed this process as part of a mundane and gradual messianism intended to establish an Orthodox Utopia in the Land of Israel. His position is so unique that modern-day research has attempted to consider him "the first Zionist."[35] In the light of these examples, it is hardly surprising that on several occasions Elboim compared his movement to the Zionist movement, and even hinted that he was the true Zionist.[36]

A TEMPLE OF FIRE OR A TEMPLE BUILT BY MAN?

A disagreement exists between apocalyptic and naturalistic messianic perceptions over the question of the establishment of the Temple. The miraculous approach, based mainly on the rulings of Rashi, argues that the Temple will descend ready-made from the skies. This is referred to as

Mikdash shel Esh (a Temple of fire). Adherents of the naturalistic approach prefer an approach that is ostensibly more activist, based mainly on the writing of Maimonides, according to which it is incumbent on humans to build the Temple. They argue that it is unacceptable to wait for the Temple to be built by itself in a miraculous form, and demand that every individual do all they can to construct the Temple.

Numerous commentators have engaged in theological experimentation in an effort to fuse these two apparently dichotic perceptions regarding the establishment of the Temple. Rashi's approach to the issue is rooted in the Midrashic literature, which notes that the Temple may be built instantaneously—even at night, and even on the Sabbath or a Holy Day. Thus, the construction of the Temple is expected to be a miraculous and supernatural event. The Third Temple will descend ready-made from the sky, and it is impossible that it will be built by men: "The Temple of the future that we anticipate is constructed and equipped; it will appear and come from the skies, as it is written: 'The Temple of the Lord Your hands will establish.'"[37] This position was supported by the authors of the Toseftot in the tractates Sukkah and Shavuot. A contrary position is presented in the writing of Maimonides (*Mishneh Torah: The Laws of Kings and Wars*), where it is claimed that the King Messiah will build the Temple: "The King Messiah will rise and restore the Kingdom of David to its former glory as a supreme government, and will build the Temple and ingather the far-flung of Israel and all the laws will return in his days as they were of old, and [they will] offer the sacrifices." Maimonides added this commandment to the 613 commandments, as appears in his Halachic work—*Sefer Hamitzvot* (Commandment 20) and in his essay *Hayad Hahazaka* (Laws of the Temple), and as formulated in his rulings: "It is a positive commandment to make a House for the Lord, a Temple, and to be ready to make sacrifices there and celebrate thereto three times a year."

As long as the Jewish people lived in exile, Halachic debate on this question was relatively theoretical. After the Six-Day War in 1967, however, the debate acquired new dimensions that are anything but theoretical. The tension between these two approaches was examined by numerous commentators, and formed the basis for a Halachic debate with practical ramifications.[38] This Halachic tension has also been a source of concern for the Movement for the Establishment of the Temple, as a movement based on the desire to view the miraculous perceptions of redemption as erroneous in Halachic terms. Miraculous Halachic approaches provide legitimacy for messianic passivity, which the movement seeks to overcome. In its efforts to do so, a variety of arguments are adopted.

Yosef Elboim notes that seventy-six positive commandments in the Torah are directly related to the Temple and its holy rituals. Many other commandments, such as those relating to the priesthood or to impurity and purity were indirectly related to the Temple. Accordingly, Elboim proposed a series of deductions based on Jewish beliefs:

1. No person is free to exempt himself from the obligations imposed on the public.
2. No commandment can possibly be observed, if it is dependent solely on supernatural events, or is dependent on the coming of the Messiah or the visions of a prophet. There is a sequence to the commandments, and it is sometimes possible to observe one commandment only after another commandment or action has been performed. However, Judaism does not permit a situation in which it is not even possible to begin to observe a commandment.
3. The legends of the Aggadah cannot exempt the Jew from observing the commandments. There cannot possibly be any contradiction between the content of the Aggadah and the Halacha, which describes the commandments and obligations required of humans in the present.
4. Halachic doubts cannot prevent the observance of the commandments. In a time when there is no religious court willing to rule on a Halacha, each individual is entitled and obliged to act as a religious court, examining the issue as best he can and reaching his own decision, until a greater authority comes and proves their errors.
5. It is impossible that the entire Jewish people be completely prevented from observing a commandment for "technical" reasons. It is certainly possibly that an individual may, under duress, be considered temporarily exempt from performing a commandment, but the public as a whole cannot indefinitely be exempted.

Elboim writes:

> These matters have, for the most part, been tried and tested over centuries of Jewish immigration and settlement in the Land of Israel, and anyone who knows that the Hand of God performed this, and not, God forbid, Satan [as argued by Neturei Karta and the Eda Haredit] can draw clear conclusions regarding the continuation of the process in the same track, to the Mount of the Lord, the House of the God of Jacob. More importantly still, since there is no inertia in the world, only progress in this direction can avoid retreat, God forbid, from what has already been achieved with regard to the settlement of the Land of Israel.[39]

Israel Ariel offers a complementary exegesis, neutralizing the miraculous dimension of the construction of the Temple, and concentrating on the issue of nullifying a commandment. He considers it paradoxical that in the State of Israel, which is home to rich and dynamic religious life, there has been no public uprising against the fact that such a large number of commandments relating to the Temple has been nullified without the least opposition. Ariel argues:

> We have 613 commandments in the Torah, yet without even thinking about it, we nullify every day two hundred commandments in the Torah. Two hundred out of 613 commandments are observed within the confines of the Temple Mount. We have national-religious Judaism and we even have Haredi Judaism; we have holy yeshivot, great rabbis, Kabbalists and righteous men— how can all that be reconciled with the nullification of two hundred commandments of the Torah? With the trampling of the sanctity of Israel in full view of the entire nation, every day and every hour? How have the great rabbis and righteous men seen this desecration for twenty-three years and not said a word?[40]

Thus, the Movement for the Establishment of the Temple promotes naturalistic messianic approaches that mandate human action as the key to redemption and explains that full redemption depends on the observance of all 613 commandments, and to this end the Temple must be built. This is the new oath to which God has sworn His people. Those who follow this path are rewarded, while those who deny it are punished. The full observance of the commandments is the fundamental foundation for the messianic process. God will ensure that those who observe His commandments are rewarded, and accordingly there is no need to fear the response of the Gentiles.

PIKUAH NEFESH AND PEACE

One of the principal arguments raised by the rabbis against the activities of the groups advocating on behalf of the Temple Mount relates to a pragmatic approach rooted in Halachic sources that sanctify life ("and live by them"), and thus prohibit any action that endangers human life. Since activities relating to the Temple are liable to lead to ferment in the Arab world, which will in turn lead to war, riots, and bloodshed, as well as fear of pogroms against Jews living in the Muslim countries, one reason for prohibiting activities on the Temple Mount is the argument of *pikuah nefesh* (the sanctity of life).[41] The Halacha states that pikuah nefesh overrules all the commandments of the Torah, with the exception of idol-worship, incest, and bloodshed (Sanhedrin 74a; Yoma 85a).

Spokesmen for the Movement for the Establishment of the Temple respond to this argument by asserting that not only is the construction of the Temple in accord with the principal of pikuah nefesh, but it is actually this act that will bring peace.

The traditional concept of "peace" differs from its modern usage. In the rabbinical literature, the term "shalom" generally occurs alongside the concept of perfection and absolute justice; accordingly, it is usually depicted in Utopian contexts removed from the realms of mundane history. For the sake of absolute justice, it is sometimes necessary to use the force of coercion.[42] By contrast, the modern concept of peace is generally associated with the principled rejection of the use of force, and with a recognition that compromise is the principal means for the resolution of disputes.[43]

The movement's position on the question of peace reflects these different approaches. In its traditional context, peace is associated with an era of total redemption when there shall be no wars. Accordingly, the era in which the Jewish people will secure redemption will be one in which the Temple stands, the biblical Land of Israel shall be its homeland, and the nations of the world shall be subservient to the Chosen People. In this era, peace will reign. Thus political peace, which entails the division of the Land of Israel and a territorial compromise, even ceding sovereignty over the Temple Mount to the Arabs, stands in contradiction to the traditional vision. Consequently, the prohibition against the construction of the Temple delays peace, and those who argue according to the principle of *pikuah nefesh* should actually encourage the construction of the Temple. The standing Temple is the best guarantee that there will be no more war, and the observance of the Torah is the safeguard of peace. Therefore:

> Jewish peace, true peace, is not a successful "divorce settlement" . . . As Jews . . . , we cannot consider democratic values a firm foundation for true peace . . . and hence our direct call [to the nations . . . is: If you truly and honestly desire peace . . . then if you would . . . recognize the sanctity of this place, the sanctity of this Land to the God of Israel and the spirit of Israel . . . then you shall have peace with us.[44]

Another key argument used by the movement to refute the claim of pikuah nefesh posits that the mere fact of Jewish settlement in the Land of Israel and the defense of its borders and citizens entails a struggle and the loss of life. Accordingly, the laws of pikuah nefesh do not apply to such a state of combat. The Temple Mount is no less sacred than the Land of Israel, which everyone agrees must be defended; therefore, "conquering" the Temple Mount from de facto Arab control cannot be delegitimized by this principle. A further argument raised in this context is that the Jews should not be so fearful of the reaction of the Arab world: once the Arabs see that there is a firm Jewish demand for the Temple Mount, their opposition will wane. The members of the Movement for the Establishment of the Temple cite the example of the Cave of the Patriarchs to support this argument: just as the Arab world came to terms with the Jewish presence in this site, so will be the case on the Temple Mount.[45]

The Movement for the Establishment of the Temple and the Haredi Public

In its publications, the Movement for the Establishment of the Temple rails against Haredi passivity. Passivity is the cornerstone of the Haredi approach, and the members of the movement identify this characteristic as the principal obstacle they must overcome. Equally, however, they constantly face the question as to the "permissible" borders of innovation, and the point at which innovation becomes sacrilege. Haredi society emerged against the background of the conflict with the modernist movements. The members of the Movement for the Establishment of the Temple come from within this public, and seek to change it from the inside, while accepting its basic principles; were this not the case, they could simply break their ties with this community. Accordingly, they face a serious dilemma: what are the "legitimate" limits of innovation, and at what point does innovation become "reform,"[46] with its overtones of the Reform movement, and hence intolerable and utterly prohibited in accordance with the codes of this community? To what extent can Halachic change occur without its being acknowledged as such?

This dilemma raises a further question: what justifications can be brought to legitimize innovation? Should the justification be based on a vision of the future or on illustrations from the past? In other words, should the change be justified as something new, or should it be presented as an ancient value that has been forgotten over the years for various reasons, and is now to be restored, so that the movement is doing no more than "renewing its days as of old?"

These questions become even more complex when we turn to the messianic issue. Redemption is a thing of the future; accordingly, may it be something wondrous and miraculous that extends beyond the limits of human nature? The question arises whether a conservative way of life that negates the innovations brought by the modern world and sanctifies the premodern way of life, to the point of glorifying it and viewing it as an ideal, and mandating a bitter struggle against the slightest change,[47] will be able to accept an approach that views redemption as involving man-made innovation. Is redemption to be the reconstitution of the past, maintaining the laws of modern-day society, and particularly the observance of the Halacha; or is it rather a breaking of social and legal norms, and the abandonment of the commandments at the time of redemption in an era free of sin?

These questions emphasize the profound tension that must be addressed by the members of the movement. By nature, the conservative will prefer to accept miraculous approaches to messianism that view redemption as something that goes beyond the confines of the present world. This conservatism leads him to accept a reality that he cannot personally change, since it is related to supernatural forces and the Divine will. Accordingly, he has no mundane obligation toward redemption, with the exception of his obligations relating solely to his religious behavior. From his perspective, redemption will come from God alone, through His mercy, and in accordance with His wishes and plans, which cannot be predicted, explained, or directed by mortals. Room for Jewish activism is in the field of bringing Jews to repentance. Complete redemption will come only after complete repentance, when the entire Jewish people believe in God and keep all His commandments as written in the Torah and interpreted in the Halacha. The conservative, therefore, prefers to remain within his own four walls and await the miracle that will transfer him from exile to redemption.[48]

A further tension relates to the paradox that advocates of change (such as the members of the Movement for the Establishment of the Temple) seek to explain their innovations in ostensibly conservative terms. They argue that their religious innovations are not, in fact, new, but merely the restoration of an ancient past for which the conservative believer prays each day: restoration of the Jewish monarchy, the Sanhedrin, and the sacrifices—the essence of the Second Temple period. Every Orthodox Jew yearns for the return of this era as he reads from his prayer book (in the Eighteen Benedictions, for example, he reads "Restore the worship to Your House, who restores His Divine Presence to Zion"). Presenting his argument as one of zealousness, the innovator calls on this conservative public to be innovative in the name of restoring past glory and of overcoming fragmented Jewish reality. However, he encounters an impenetrable barrier of arguments negating his approach—conservative claims founded on transcendentalism and miracles.

When the Haredi columnist Nathan Zeev Grossman (who writes for *Yated Ne'eman*, the organ of the Degel Hatorah Party) sought to delegitimize the approach of the Movement for the Establishment of the Temple, he began his arguments by stating that the movement argues that the great sages of the generation have no answer to the "proofs" presented by the movement; accordingly, the public is urged to follow the movement and make its own independent rulings. Grossman's response to this argument is simple. The public should rely on its leaders' rulings, once they have considered the issue and stated their position. The fact that they ruled as they did is enough, and the Halachic interpretations made by the great sages of each generation must be obeyed. Grossman adds that only those who have observed all the minutiae of the commandments in the Torah are permitted to discuss new commandments, and there can be no doubt that this ideal situation has not yet been reached.

> In these days, when every Jewish home is shrouded in mourning out of sorrow for the destruction of the Temple, it is proper to warn once again against the false visions of various elements who seek to raise *new* ideas that were not conveyed of by our forefathers, and which contradict the opinion of Halachic rulers and teachers. (emphasis added)[49]

Grossman's position illustrates the challenge faced by the Movement for the Establishment of the Temple in its interaction with the Haredi public. Its demand to encourage active public interest in the construction of the Temple was perceived as a religious innovation, and as such was unacceptable. Accordingly, the movement was obliged to argue that its position was not an innovation, but a return to the past—a desire to realize ancient longings.

Yonina Talmon, a researcher of religious millenarianism, argues that one axis on which millenarian movements can be typified is that of restoration versus innovation. She notes that, as a general rule, millenarian movements view the present as negative and requiring repair. *Restorative* millenarian movements seek to reinstate a lost age, and perceive the future in pseudotraditional terms. *Innovative* millenarian movements are usually antitraditional and iconoclastic, rejecting the religious value system. When the millennium is presented as a regained paradise, the motives of tradition it embodies also become elements of the new order.[50] Talmon's analysis explains the complex situation in which the Movement for the Establishment of the Temple finds itself. The members of the movement claim that their demand is not a religious innovation, but merely the restoration of a perfect past. However, the reality is less simple. In my opinion, this movement meets the definition of an "innovative" movement, since it opposes accepted tradition, breaks the taboo regarding the Temple Mount, and seeks to change the religious value system and the behavioral patterns of Orthodox Judaism. The movement's orientation negates the immediate past and the present in favor of a distant, mythological past. The movement's millennium preserves the accepted religious frameworks, but in a different context. The Orthodox religion of exile—physical or spiritual—is replaced by the ideal of an Orthodox religion in the context of redemption. Accordingly, and despite its iconoclasm and the challenge it poses to religious order, the movement is careful not to place itself outside the framework of *nomos* (religious law).

In their polemical writings, the members of the Movement for the Establishment of the Temple attempt to cope with this complex situation. David Bar Haim, an Orthodox rabbi with ties to Kach and one of the founders of the movement, wrote an article suggesting solutions for the movement along the axis from restoration to innovation. After three years of activities, Bar Haim analyzes the failure of the movement to spread its message among contemporary Jewry. He writes:

> The long exile we have undergone has caused the people to forget the way of life that was its heritage before the Destruction. This forgetfulness, combined with the force of habit, have made and continue to make anything drawn from our national past alien and new to the public eye. This phenomenon was accentuated during the period when the Hatam Sofer, of blessed memory, waged his wars against Reform Judaism, claiming that "Innovation is prohibited by Torah." All sections of the people became convinced that the true Judaism is, so to speak, "things will remain the same."
>
> This is the true reason why, when a few of the great Jewish leaders began to pay attention to the idea of settling the Land of Israel, the people, including its greatest sages, would not listen to them. The fact that this "innovation" of settling the Land eventually became the domain of those who cast off the yoke of the commandments merely provided an additional excuse. The basic question was: shall we do something that our fathers did not do? . . .
>
> Accordingly, the true path is this: To begin with small changes which, despite their limited scope and size, can disprove the perception that we cannot change anything of that which we have inherited from our fathers. Any change or innovation can help a little to break down the conventions that delay the completion of our redemption. . . .
>
> *Redemption means innovation. The Temple and monarchy mean innovation.* This is why Jeremiah ended his book of lamentations with the words "*Renew our days as of old*" (Lamentations 4:21). For the secret of redemption is for us to renew our days by ourselves, "as in the former years" (Malachi 3:4). (emphases added)[51]

Bar Haim offers a stark prescription for the approach that should be adopted by the movement. His fellow members, and particularly those who came from within the Haredi community, did not dare to express themselves in such an overt and blatant manner, preferring an alternative fabric of arguments based mainly on the claim regarding the need to bypass the "great" rabbis.

Attempts to Break the Legitimacy Barrier

Unsurprisingly, the task undertaken by the Movement for the Establishment of the Temple—to convince the Haredi public of its ideas—encountered a solid wall of opposition. By its very nature, Orthodox Judaism has always negated the concept of progress or change in religious matters.[52] Accordingly, the movement raised a series of arguments relating to the question of religious authority. However, the position presented on this question was confused and indecisive. The movement was forced to address a fundamental and difficult challenge: the dilemma of how to face the Halachic world. Should their aim be to reform this world from within, or should they remove themselves and establish a separate Halachic mechanism? Should existing Halachic law be accepted or broken? Should they obey the great sages and teachers of the generation and attempt to convince them, or should they simply rebel against their authority? Perhaps the solution to the problem of authority lay in dismantling the institution of the rabbinate and rebuilding it in the new, messianic spirit.

These key dilemmas in the life of the movement have aroused exhaustive debate and formed the basis for serious disagreements. It was not only the members of the movement themselves who faced such dilemmas. The Haredi leadership was also forced to consider whether it could continue to accept the members of the movement within its midst; at times, as already noted, the members of the movement suffered physical attacks against themselves and their families.

In addressing these dilemmas, the simplest course available is to argue that their approach is acceptable and legitimate. This argument appears repeatedly in the movement's publications; the members attempt to present their approach as acceptable to rabbis, Halachic rulers, and leaders. The problem is that rabbinical approval was not stated in public. Accordingly, the members of the movement took pains to publicize this support, so that the public could see that their approach was acceptable:

> We are well aware that one of the two chief rabbis feels that he cannot now take any action for the sake of the Mount of the House of the Lord, although before his appointment he was sympathetic to this cause.[53]
>
> My uncle once went to Rabbi Eliashiv, long may he live,[54] and *pretended* that he was in the civil guard and had been stationed on the Temple Mount, and asked how he could perform his duty. During a Halachic exchange, he instructed him exactly which area

[of the Mount] was permitted and where purification was required and where it was prohibited. Then my uncle published these comments, and he received a warning from the rabbi's house that he should not do this, since he had not received permission, and they denied the entire matter. . . .

[Question]: But there are so many rabbis, how can it be that not even one leading rabbi can openly join your position?

[Answer] A. Because that rabbi knows that if he joins us he will not be a leading rabbi any more.

B. When I go to ask a rabbi a question, I distinguish between the Halachic side and the political side. On the Halachic side, he determines, and they really do not find any serious obstacle there. . . . On the political side, where every Jew is his own master, the rabbis do not determine things. (emphasis mine)[55]

The members of the movement eagerly published articles by figures who were not involved in the movement, claiming that there were rabbis who permitted Jews to enter the Temple Mount, but refrained from announcing this publicly. One such article, written by Rabbi Yehuda Shaviv, a senior teacher at the Har Etzion yeshiva in Gush Etzion, appeared in *Nekudah*, the mouthpiece of the settlers in Judea, Samaria, and the Gaza Strip. Shaviv raised the demand to "allow what is permitted"—to permit entry to the Temple Mount for the purpose of prayer, and thus prevent the Israeli governments from transferring sovereignty over the Mount to the PLO as part of the Oslo Accords. Shaviv states that Rabbi Eliashiv personally permitted him to enter the Temple Mount as a guard during reserve duty following the occupation of the site in 1967.[56]

An additional argument raised by the movement to solve the problem of rabbinical approval for its approach is to address the general public directly, without reference to the leaders. The rationale is that the leaders will subsequently have no alternative but to assent to public demand. This approach seeks to ensure that the Movement for the Establishment of the Temple remains within the general consensus. From the outset, the movement decided to attempt to convince individuals and to address the general public, in the hope that if the "man on the street" began to demand the Temple Mount, the rabbis and great leaders of the generation would be obliged to relate to the issue and change their opinion.[57] Accordingly, the movement adopted a revolutionary and provocative position that has never enjoyed currency in the Haredi community, arguing that "the great ones should listen to the little ones"—that is, the leadership should listen to public opinion. The members of the movement who wrote in *Yibaneh Hamikdash* raised numerous arguments in support of this principle:

The rabbis—and the more senior they are, the truer this is—can hardly cope with dealing with pressing problems, and cannot possibly find time to consider an issue that is presently no more than a distant vision. . . . Accordingly, the only way is for this matter to begin with ordinary people, and only after some reasonable progress is made will it be possible to attract the attention of the great leaders.[58]

In our opinion, the behavior of the leaders of the generation in all matters relating to the "Ten Holinesses," from the holiness of the Land of Israel to the Holiness of the Holy of Holies, is a weak leadership. . . . A weakness that diverts the entire matter of the Land of Israel, and the House of the Lord at its center, into a celestial matter . . . This weakness can only be combated by action from the grassroots, which will leave the leaders able to do no more than give a priori consent.[59]

Avigdor Elboim—a Belzer Hassid and father of Yosef Elboim—raised another, contradictory argument in an article written under the name of Baruch Ben-Yosef, director of the Temple Mount yeshiva, a former Kach activist and one of the leading members of the Movement for the Establishment of the Temple. In an article published in the mouthpiece of the movement, Avigdor Elboim argued that the movement should separate itself from mainstream Orthodoxy. This article was published after the Rabin government decided (in 1994) to adopt a stricter attitude toward members of the movement who attempted to pray on the Temple Mount, after which, such activities became almost impossible. This article attracted angry replies from regular writers in the journal, as well as numerous letters from readers. Elboim's forthright tone provoked debate within the movement, accentuating its position regarding the authority of the great rabbis of the generation. Avigdor Elboim attacked various rabbinical bodies that advocate messianic activism but do not demand the establishment of the Temple; Rabbis Shlomo Aviner and Zvi Tau of the Mercaz Harav yeshiva, for rejecting the idea of prayers on the Mount; and the members of Kahane Chai (formerly Kach) under the leadership of Benjamin Zeev Kahane, whom he accused of moderating their style to curry favor with Gush Emunim. Avigdor Elboim wrote:

On the matter of the establishment of the Temple, we should not recognize the authority of the rabbinate and the Beit Din Zedek. This is unkosher and impure, this is Ahab Ben Omri and Jeroboam Ben Navat. . . . Shame on the Beit Din Zedek, which denies the commandment to build the Temple; shame on the Rabbinate, which denies the building of the Temple; shame on the Mercaz Harav yeshiva, which denies the building of the Temple; shame on the *Yeshivot Hesder*, which denies the commandment of building the Temple; shame on Ateret Cohanim Yeshiva, which denies the commandment of building the Temple; shame on Gush Emunim, which denies the commandment of building the Temple—one must not rely on their slaughtering of meat; one must not rely on their Kashrut; one must not include them in the quorum for prayer—for they are Sadducees in every respect.[60]

Avigdor Elboim's claim that those who preach messianic activism (such as Chabad, Mercaz Harav, and Kach) are acting hypocritically, and accordingly should be excluded from the Orthodox public, effectively implies that he, too, is excluded therefrom. It is hard to accept that everyone is to be excluded apart from oneself. In the sociological literature, this phenomenon is known as "basic dualism," whereby a messianic movement separates itself from the remainder of the public, which it utterly rejects, and anticipates that it alone will witness redemption, which the nonbelievers will not be privileged to see.[61] Hava Lazarus-Yafeh further explained this phenomenon by noting that fundamentalists form their own countersocieties that are separate from and opposed to modern Western society, and which ostensibly cling to the "true" tradition. From their perspective, religious institutions that fail to follow their path are no better than "infidels," and must repent.[62]

This opinion was not favorably received in the movement; readers' letters even threatened cancellation of membership in the movement and their subscription to the journal. Such a public stance as Elboim's was evidently too radical. The activists of the movement sought to achieve change from within, not to separate themselves from the community. The dilemma they faced, whereby, on the one hand, they rejected existing Halachic frameworks, while, on the other hand, they were reluctant to remove themselves from these frameworks, paradoxically led to the attempt to reestablish the Sanhedrin—an attempt led by members of the movement. This solution was reached as a compromise position within the movement. The rationale was that the Sanhedrin, as an activist body with the authority to introduce religious reforms and accepted by all sections of Orthodoxy, would be able to solve their difficulty.[63]

Before establishing the Sanhedrin, however, the members of the movement sought to propose a further solution to the problem of legitimacy. Since the members of the movement came from the Orthodox world, which accepts innovations only if these are rooted in Halachic decisions based on tradition and form part of the existing sequence of rulings and laws, the movement decided to establish its own religious court (Beit Din Zedek). The rationale for this step was that:

> [Since] the "great leaders and righteous men" of the present generation show no interest in the Temple Mount, we lesser mortals attend to a commandment that is left unattended. Since the obligation to build the Temple is a commandment from the Torah ("Make me a sanctuary that I might dwell therein" [Exod. 25:8]), and particularly in modern times, when we are independent, we are obliged to perform all that is written in Moses' Law. Any type of worship that may be performed, although the Temple is destroyed, must be undertaken.[64]

Since the members of the movement consider themselves bound by the Halacha, the establishment of a court that makes its rulings in a Halachic manner legitimizes their actions. Ostensibly, the establishment of a religious court obviates the fear that their actions might be considered tantamount to breaking the confines of Halacha. Moreover, the members of the court itself emphasize that "naturally, once God's people insist, and the ordination and Sanhedrin are restored, and the great religious court that issues instructions to Israel is revived—all the laws relating to the Temple will be discussed and clarified there."[65]

However, the establishment of such a self-appointed religious court, which engages in active initiatives and introduces laws, might actually represent the very opposite of "Halachic commitment," and might have the effect of removing the movement from the confines of consensus. The capacity to pass its own laws might amount to antinomianism and carry the movement beyond the confines of what is considered legitimate in its constituency. The movement was aware of this danger.

The movement addressed issues to its Beit Din on three occasions. Twice the court approved the movement's innovative intentions, but on the third occasion these were rejected. The movement did not turn to the court again, partly because it realized that this was a dangerous tool; if used to excess, it might lead the movement outside the Orthodox camp—something the members did not desire.

The first ruling of the Beit Din stated that it was possible to carry out the sacrifices despite the atrophy of the biblical class divisions (priests, Levites, and Israelites) in modern Jewry. The sacrifices in the Temple were carried out by the priests, and since the destruction, the priesthood is no longer strictly maintained, and it is impossible to know for certain who is or is not a priest. The movement's Beit Din ruled that this does not prevent the possibility of carrying out sacrifices. The second ruling stated that since there is no longer a priestly class in Jewry, any Jew may carry out the sacrifices on the Temple Mount.[66]

It was the third ruling that tested the direction of the entire movement. Baruch Ben-Yosef, a former member of the Jewish Defense League and a follower of Meir Kahane, asked the court to rule that the route walked on the Temple Mount should include the entire site. Ben-Yosef justified his claim on the grounds of "occupation." As already noted, the ruling for generations had been that Jews must not enter the Temple Mount to avoid the risk of entering the Kodesh Kodashim area, which must not be entered by anyone but the high priest. The penalty for entering the area was *Karet* (the divinely imposed death sentence). However, it is permissible to enter the area to occupy it, and such permission was indeed given retrospectively to the IDF soldiers who entered the area during the Six-Day War. Ben-Yosef claimed that

> Due to the opposition of the Ishmaelites to Jews ascending the Mount, and due to the police order supporting the Arab side, every Jew is obliged to go up in order to nullify the desecration of God's name that has been created. Based on the above-mentioned behavior of the Arabs, it is evident to me that this matter relates to the law of occupation. Accordingly, even those who argue that there is presently a penalty of *Karet* against those who enter areas prohibited to impure persons must agree that it is an obligation to go up due to the duty of occupation and the desecration of God's name.[67]

Before presenting the argument that emerged, it is important to clarify the movement's position regarding prayer on the Temple Mount. The followers of the movement shared the belief that the Temple has to be built by the entire public; but in a situation in which the public is not willing to rebuild the Temple, each individual has to do all he can to build it. To this end, they mandated prayer on the site. While they admitted that they did not know the location of the Holy of Holies, there were certain parts of the site where the Kodesh Kodashim could not possibly be—namely, the additional areas constructed by Herod. They ruled that it was permissible, and indeed desirable, to enter these areas. As a precautionary measure, members of the movement take additional Halachic steps before entering the area, including immersing in a mikveh and wearing cloth shoes. Prayer on the Temple Mount strengthens the longing for the Temple, and is therefore desirable. The activists believe that reinforcing attachment to the Temple will also encourage the general public to take active steps.[68]

As mentioned earlier, the discussion in the movement's Beit Din Zedek led to a fierce argument. Baruch Ben-Yosef argued that anxious to avoid

entering prohibited areas on the Temple Mount (i.e., areas other than the
additions built by Herod), the movement had adopted a fixed route for its
visits to the site, passing through areas that they believed were free from the
possibility of prohibition. When Ben-Yosef attempted on one occasion to
change his route, the police prevented him from doing so. He interpreted
this as implying that the adoption of a fixed route by the movement meant
that they might be seen to be demanding only those areas in which they
walked, rather than the entire Mount. In Halachic terms, Ben-Yosef based
his case on an interpretation of a ruling by Nachmanides stating that the
occupation of the Land of Israel nullifies prohibitions from the Torah, arguing that this ruling should be extrapolated in the case of the Temple
Mount. After extensive discussion,[69] the Beit Din ruled as follows:

> Despite the miserable situation, the court saw no possibility of
> permitting general entry to every place on the Mount, since this
> is subject to changes in reality and an evaluation of the situation.
> Equally, it is inappropriate to prohibit entry into the holy areas,
> since it is certainly possible that the reality changes from day to
> day and from one person to another.
>
> Accordingly, it was decided *to leave the decision to those in the field*,
> who are thoroughly aware of the state of affairs on a daily basis, and
> can guide their fellows who ascend *as to the situation at that time*.
>
> The court is aware of the various methods that exist regard-
> ing the [historic] position of the Temple . . . Nevertheless, it is
> the court's opinion that as long as no precise study has been un-
> dertaken within the Temple Mount, and, particularly, extensive
> archeological excavations, it is inappropriate to change the
> method adopted by the Radbaz, which identifies the "*Sakra*" with
> the Foundation Stone. . . . *Accordingly, the old route remains valid
> and unchanged*. (emphases in original)[70]

In effect, the movement's religious court did not reach a determination, choosing instead to permit every member to act as he saw fit on
this matter. In practical terms, the court permitted entry into all parts of
the Temple Mount, but without stating this in express terms, and while
adding a formal reservation. The court realized the danger that it would
exceed the limits it had set itself, and that it could not be seen to allow
everything. Even in the Movement for the Establishment of the Temple,
innovation has its limits, as this ruling made clear to the members. To deviate beyond the basic framework of Orthodox society (within which they
already found themselves on the margins), it was important to maintain
taboos and laws. As I mentioned, the movement's court was not used
again after this episode.

The Oslo Process and the Movement for the Establishment of the Temple

The underlying ideology of the Movement for the Establishment of the Temple is based on the perception that historical developments form part of a Divine plan for this world, with the objective of bringing redemption. Redemption is interpreted as the establishment of an independent political entity that acts in accordance with Jewish law, reinstating the sacrifices on the Temple Mount and rebuilding the Temple. This approach is based on an interpretation of Maimonides's rulings regarding the ideal messianic society, according to which redemption is the complete worship of God through observance of all 613 commandments—a goal that can only be met if the Temple is rebuilt. The exile was ended to permit the Chosen People to observe all the commandments in their own land. Those who ignored this process were punished, while those who began to implement this cosmic task were rewarded. However, the establishment of the State of Israel is far from the end of the process. Its zenith will come with the reconstruction of the Temple and the reinstitution of the sacrifices on the Temple Mount.

According to the movement's perspective, every human action entails reward and punishment. The Oslo Process, which culminates in the partition of the Land of Israel between two peoples, including a territorial compromise and some form of Arab sovereignty on the Temple Mount, constituted a horrifying disaster for the movement.[71]

Based on this reading of history, the refusal of the Jewish people to leave exile for redemption following the Balfour Declaration led to the horrors of the Holocaust. What, then, would be the theological ramifications of the decision by the Jewish people publicly to abandon their aspiration to rebuild the Temple? What would be the cosmic results of the abandonment of the process of redemption?

Yosef Elboim's answer was stark and simple. Abandoning the Temple Mount was tantamount to another Holocaust and to annihilation. The ongoing willingness of the public to refrain from religious worship on the Temple Mount had led, in cosmic terms, to the partition of the Land of Israel, and the transfer of sovereignty on the site to Arab rule would lead to the elimination of the State of Israel. On the eve of Rosh Hashanah 5754 (1994), an editorial comment in *Yibaneh Hamikdash* summarized the process in bleak terms:

When we willingly gave Islam the keys to the Temple Mount, it was ruled that we would have to part from Sinai—the southern Land of Israel. When we prohibited Jews from praying on the Temple Mount, we were punished by the withdrawal from South

Lebanon—the northern Land of Israel. When we equipped the Waqf with means of communication and control on the Temple Mount, we saw "autonomy" (= the loss of control) in the center of the Land of Israel, and when we finally gave up all hope of building the House of God (our Temple) on the Temple Mount, we were condemned to the final renunciation of our national home.[72]

After the emergence of the Oslo Accords, the Movement for the Establishment of the Temple began to strengthen the Jewish presence on the Temple Mount, recruiting new members to pray on the site, despite the stricter approach taken by the Israeli governments toward such activities. During this period, the movement also began to approach the supporters of Gush Emunim—an Orthodox segment of the population to which it was closer in ideological terms. The contacts with this group led to a dramatic increase in the number of participants in the movement's activities. For example, the Temple Feasts held annually to raise funds and encourage social contacts in the group were now attended by between five hundred and one thousand people.[73]

The greatest success of the movement came in 1996, during the high point of the campaign against the Oslo Process among the settlers, when the Committee of Yesha Rabbis, a body uniting the rabbis from Judea, Samaria, and Gaza (hence the term "Yesha"), most of whose members are identified with Gush Emunim and the Mercaz Harav yeshiva, issued a ruling calling on all those who believe that it is permissible to ascend the Temple Mount "to go up themselves, and to guide their congregants on how to go up in accordance with all the Halachic restrictions."[74] The Yesha rabbis announced their ruling at the Temple Feast, published it in *Yibaneh Hamikdash*, and noted that it had been made after consultation with "the rabbis of the Movement for the Establishment of the Temple." This ruling was reiterated on July 17, 2001, at a joint meeting of the Committee of Yesha Rabbis and members of the Movement for the Establishment of the Temple.

The ruling by the Yesha rabbis may, I believe, be considered the zenith of the activities of the Movement for the Establishment of the Temple, since it showed that the goal of changing Orthodox attitudes on the question of the Temple Mount was attainable. Fear of the loss of Jewish sovereignty on the Temple Mount led a committee of Orthodox rabbis to change a Halachic ruling that had been considered a complete taboo for centuries. The ruling suggests that the movement's objective of changing religious perception relating to the Temple Mount can strike roots, given particular political circumstances.

The closure of the Temple Mount to Jews in September 2000, following the outbreak of the Al-Aqsa Intifada, came as a severe blow to the movement. For a period of three years, the members were unable to enter the site or pray on the Temple Mount. This situation eroded the movement, and several key members began to direct their activities toward other groups and issues. The movement effectively ceased to function during the period, although it continued to publish a limited and irregular version of its journal.

During the same period, however, the ideas promoted by the Movement for the Establishment of the Temple began to find increasing favor among Religious Zionist rabbis. The ruling by the Yesha rabbis sparked an open debate among leading rabbis on the question of prayers on the Temple Mount. A subject that had been taboo became a burning issue, and during the three years when Jews were not permitted to enter the site (2000–2003), a number of religious publications appeared accentuating the debate over the authorization of prayers on the Temple Mount.[75] Under the influence of these trends, Member of Knesset Uri Ariel, the unofficial representative of the Yesha Council in the Knesset and its leader prior to his election to the Knesset,[76] tabled a proposed law seeking to regulate prayer by Jews on the Temple Mount. It is hard to imagine that, even a few years earlier, a Member of Knesset identified with Gush Emunim would have raised such a proposal.

A survey commissioned in 2002 by the Reform movement's Israel Religious Action Center showed that 42 percent of the public favored permitting Jews to pray on the Temple Mount, while 55 percent were opposed. The same proportions apply in the Haredi and traditional sectors. As for the question "Do you favor the establishment of the Third Temple?", 53 percent answered in the affirmative and 37 percent in the negative.

Since the reopening of the Temple Mount to Jews in November 2003, dramatic developments have occurred with regard to prayer on the site. Almost every day, Jewish groups—sometimes numbering hundreds— arrive to pray on the Mount. This outburst of enthusiasm has been led by key religious and political authorities within the Religious Zionist movement, and not only from its more extreme fringes.

It would appear that the strength of the prohibition against Jews entering the Temple Mount, or praying on the site, has weakened, and that there is increasing support for such actions among widening circles. The Movement for the Establishment of the Temple has played an important role in this change. The fear that the Temple Mount would be transferred to the Arabs, following the Oslo Process, legitimized changes in Jewish religious law that had stood for centuries, and revitalized the messianic vision of the establishment of the Temple.

6

Yitzhak Ginzburg and "Od Yosef Chai" Yeshiva
Theocratic Messianic Revolutionism

Yitzhak Ginzburg is a rabbi affiliated with the Chabad Hassidic movement (also known as Lubavitch). Chabad has faced a leadership vacuum since the death of Rabbi Menachem-Mendel Schneerson, the last Rebbe (rabbinical leader) of the movement, and Ginzburg is one of the figures who have since been drawn into leadership positions.

Ginzburg has a broad and eclectic education. Interestingly, Schneerson acquired a secular academic education before becoming a rabbi and a Hassid. Also Ginzburg did not grow up in a traditional religious background. His familiarity with the secular world enables him to identify with newly observant Jews, while his followers claim that he received his rabbinical and Hassidic education directly from his teacher: Schneerson.

Ginzburg was born in Cleveland, Ohio, in 1944, the only son of a family with liberal Zionist leanings. His father, Sylvan Ginzburg, had originally emigrated to Palestine, but after the outbreak of World War II he returned to the United States, where he married and worked as a Hebrew teacher. Yitzhak spent a year in Israel when he was fourteen; the Hebrew he acquired during his time in Israel encouraged him to take an interest in Jewish tradition, and he began a gradual process of becoming an observant Jew. At the same time, he pursued academic studies in mathematics and philosophy. In 1965, Yitzhak moved to Israel. During his first few years in the country, he studied at the Lithuanian Kamenitz yeshiva in Bnei Brak, while at the same time beginning to study with Chabad Hassidim. He later attended the Salonim Hassidic yeshiva in Tiberias, where he remained until the outbreak of the Six-Day War in 1967. After the war, he came to the Old

131

City in Jerusalem, before Jews began to resettle the Jewish Quarter. He often slept at the Tzamah Tzedek synagogue, where he met Moshe Segal, one of the founders of the Brit Hachashmonaim youth movement, which was established in 1937 and was active during the prestate period. Segal combined Revisionist Zionist ideology with a longing for religious redemption and a romantic political messianism.[1] The bond between the two men was strengthened after Ginzburg married Segal's daughter, Romamiyah. Before his marriage, Ginzburg traveled to New York to study Hassidism in the court of the Lubavitcher Rebbe (Schneerson) for three months. On his return to Israel, he began to study with Asher Freund in Jerusalem, and later was among the founders of the Or Yerushalayim yeshiva. During the same period, he developed a following of students, and moved to Kfar Chabad, where he taught his approach. Ginzburg is considered a highly popular lecturer throughout Israel in Chabad and extreme right-wing circles, and serves as the president of "Od Yosef Chai" ("Joseph Still Lives") yeshiva, which was originally based at Joseph's Tomb in Nablus. After the outbreak of the Al-Aqsa Intifada in September 2000, the site was abandoned by the IDF and the yeshiva moved to the nearby settlement of Yitzhar. Ginzburg also headed a Kollel (an institute for advanced studies of the Talmud and of rabbinic literature) at the Ancient Synagogue in Jericho, which was also abandoned by the IDF after the outbreak of the Intifada.[2]

Yitzhak Ginzburg is considered an important spiritual and ideological authority among the so-called hill dwellers, who are also sometimes known, due to their relative youth, as the Youth of the Hills. The term refers to a group of people aged nineteen to thirty who live on temporary, often unlawful, outposts established on hilltops around Judea and Samaria. They are estimated to number a few hundred activists. These groups form the fringe of the settler movement, and are perceived as a radical ideological faction that is willing to accept a hard and ascetic lifestyle.

Ginzburg became the object of widespread public interest after publishing an article entitled "Baruch Is the Man" (the name Baruch also means "blessed") in which he lavishly praised Baruch Goldstein, who murdered twenty-nine Arab worshippers at the Ibrahimi Mosque (the Cave of the Patriarchs) in Hebron in 1994. Ginzburg's publications are often brought to the attention of Israel's attorney-general, and demands are raised to prosecute him for racial incitement.[3] Ginzburg and his students are widely considered to constitute a subversive group, and have often been subject to the surveillance of the Israeli security services.

Ginzburg's circle of students—Yosef Peli (the son of Menachem Felix, one of the founders of Gush Emunim), Yitzhak Shapiro, Israel Ariel (Leibowitz), and David Dudkowitz, the rabbi of the settlement Yitzhar—plays a vital role in explaining their teacher's positions. His students discuss and develop his thoughts and render them more comprehensible (since Ginzburg often writes in mystical language) and translate his theoretical and intellectual points into practical proposals for action. The group as a whole constitutes a central ideological force influencing much wider circles inside the yeshiva and elsewhere. The circle of students presented their teacher's ideas in a newsletter published by the yeshiva under the title *Lehavah* (Flame) The newsletter, which appeared during a period of almost two years (2001–2002), focused on the study of the weekly Torah portion read in the synagogue. This chapter will discuss in detail the messages conveyed in the newsletter.

Ginzburg's students tended not to refer to the classic corpus of Halachic literature in interpreting the biblical texts. Instead, they addressed the text directly, weaving their own ideas and approaches around the biblical stories as the foundation for presenting practical messages for contemporary action. This approach is consonant with the fundamentalist tendency to return to the sacred scriptures, circumventing exegesis, and to use the Bible as a tool for understanding present-day reality and even for predicting the future.[4]

This chapter focuses on four central aspects of Ginzburg's thought. I will begin by presenting the intensive discourse developed in his writings on the subject of the supernatural characteristics of the Jews and their superiority over other humans. This issue is important in order to understand the second issue I will examine: religious zealotry. In their writings, Ginzburg and his students discuss at length the question of the relationship between normative religion and its boundaries, in an effort to develop zealous activity outside the boundaries of religious norms. This theoretical discussion is of relevance in understanding the root causes of the group's radical behavior. Thus, for example, Ginzburg was almost the only Orthodox figure of any standing that supported the act committed by Baruch Goldstein. After clarifying these aspects of Ginzburg's religious and political approaches, the foundation will be provided for examining the remaining two issues examined in this chapter: theocratic approaches and the question of the rebuilding of the Temple. Ginzburg's theocratic approach draws extensively on the worldview of political messianism, and overtly places religious law above any other political law. This also explains the legitimization of violent action against the authorities, if they fail to act in accordance with strict religious law. The fourth section of this chapter discusses the views of Ginzburg and his students regarding the construction of the Temple here and now, and their consequent activities in establishing the "Temple Guard" and in instating the "March around the Gates."

The Supernatural Character of the Jews

In traditional Jewish approach, beginning in the postbiblical literature, we can find the idea that the Divine choice of the Jewish people is a cosmic act that grants superiority to the Jews.[5] In medieval times, this concept was developed in *The Kuzari*, the essay written by Rabbi Yehuda Halevy (1075–1141) in which he argues that the Jewish people stand above nature, since it was imbued with the Divine essence that prepared it to receive the Torah. This perspective was developed extensively in the Kabbalistic literature, in which the Jews were presented not merely as distinct from the other products of Creation, but as a part of Divinity itself.[6] Within the dualistic approach of the Kabbalah, with its distinction between sanctity and impurity, the non-Jew was often presented as part of the "other side."[7] The dualistic concept of the distinction between the Divine soul of the Jews and the animal like soul of the Gentiles became a prominent element at much Hassidic discourse, and particularly in the case of Rabbi Schneur Zalman of Ladi, the founder of the Lubavitcher (Chabad) sect of Hassidism. He posited that the soul of the Gentile originates in the three shells of impurity. Even if a Gentile commits a good act, they do so for negative motives, such as the expectation of some personal benefit. By contrast, the Jewish soul is Divine, and hence its status is superior to any created being.[8]

Yitzhak Ginzburg has continued to develop these theological approaches. He argues that the Jewish people are a supreme, chosen people; as such, it includes a Divine spark and stands above nature. The Jew forms part of the Kabbalistic world of "emanation"—the uppermost of the four worlds in the Kabbalah: action, formation, creation, and emanation. The Gentile is created, but the Jew forms part of Divinity itself. These perspectives are just part of a complex construction presented at length in the article "Between Israel and the Nations," which appears in *The Dominion of Israel*, a collection of his articles.[9] This article was later elaborated into an entire book—*His Pride Is in Israel*, written by Israel Ariel (Leibowitz) on the basis of Ginzburg's classes. The book emphasizes the distinction between Jew and Gentile on the foundation of Kabbalistic theory.[10]

In his writings, Ginzburg gives prominence to Halachic and Kabbalistic approaches that emphasize the distinction between Jew and non-Jew (Gentile), imposing a clear separation and hierarchy in this respect. He claims that while the Jews are the Chosen People and were created in God's image, the Gentiles do not have this status, and are effectively considered subhuman. Accordingly, for example, the commandment "You shall not murder" does not apply to the killing of a Gentile, since "you shall not murder" relates to the murder of a human, while for him the Gentiles do not constitute humans.[11] Similarly, Ginzburg stated that, on the theoretical level, if a Jew requires a liver transplant to survive, it would be permissible to seize a Gentile and take their liver forcefully.[12] From this point only a small further step is required to actively encourage and support the killing of non-Jews, as Ginzburg did in the case of Baruch Goldstein.

Ginzburg's theological approach should not be seen merely as a continuation of certain Jewish perceptions that were popular in medieval times regarding the profound distinction between Jews and Gentiles. Rather, it centers on the presentation of a Jewish dominion that constitutes an innovative and far-reaching mutation of these perceptions. A key principle in his thought is the affinity between the unique and supernatural character of the Jews and the theocratic order he proposes. To support this claim, I will first present the argument presented by Gershon Weiler that there can be no such thing as a Jewish theocracy. Weiler claims that a central traditional approach in Judaism regarding the relations between religion and state, as formulated in particular by Don Yitzhak Abrabanel, argues that if the world includes two legal systems, one for the Gentiles and one for the Jews, then any mundane Jewish regime established according to the Gentile model will inevitably be defective, since the Jews are subject to different laws of nature than those applying to the Gentiles. Accordingly, the only worthy political condition for the Jews is that their redemption will come in the days of messiah, when God will rule over them directly, without human intermediaries liable to deviate from His path. A human regime is intended, by its very nature, to ensure compliance through the imposition of sanctions. The need for political organization shows that humans have deviated from the Divine plan. If theocracy means Divine rule, then it follows that human government is inherently illegitimate. Therefore, Abrabanel continues, the Jews must not do anything to advance their political independence; this is God's function alone. If special laws of nature apply to the Jews, and if Israel differs from the other nations, then Israel should be ruled directly by God, unlike the other nations, which may install a mundane regime. Thus, there is no place in Judaism for theocratic messianic activism.[13]

Ginzburg accepts the starting premise of this approach, but rejects its conclusion. He certainly accepts the idea of Divine election, with its sharp separation between the Jews and the Gentiles on the basis of laws of nature, so that the Jews are superior to all the other nations.[14] However, he rejects the approach that mandates messianic passivity and the expectation that Divine dominion will descend to Earth by miraculous means. In its place, Ginzburg adopts an activist interpretation of the traditional approach, arguing that agitation in the mundane world will also lead to agitation in the upper world; mundane activity can cause its own completion through the miraculous and perfect intervention of God.[15] Thus, Ginzburg presents an innovative religious perspective combining two Halachic approaches, one of which mandates messianic activism, while the other retains the concept of the unique status of the Jewish people in accordance with the laws of nature.

Religious Zealotry

In light of Ginzburg's determination that the Jews enjoy unchallenged substantive and ethereal superiority over the Gentiles, it is hardly surprising that he argues that if Gentiles attempt to harm or kill Jews, it is a commandment to stop them from doing so by all means. It is in this context that we may examine the pamphlet "Baruch Is the Man," which justified the massacre committed in the Ibrahim Mosque (the Cave of the Patriarchs) on the Jewish festival of Purim in 1994, in which twenty-nine Muslim worshippers were murdered. After this incident, radical right-wing circles justified the massacre by claiming that Goldstein's actions had been intended to prevent a major terror attack planned by Arabs against Jews.[16] It is difficult, however, to find any corroboration for this claim, which appears to have been invented post factum.[17] Ginzburg's pamphlet created a public fury; he was investigated by the police but not indicted. Further editions of the booklet were published in 1995 and 1996 and gained popularity in some circles; again, no legal action was taken against Ginzburg, although some sources in the State Prosecutor's Office believed that sections of the publication constituted a criminal offense under Israeli law.[18]

The article begins by praising and adulating Goldstein. Five justifications are presented for his actions:

1. *The Sanctification of God's Name.* In the Halacha, this concept refers to the willingness of an individual to sacrifice their life rather than violate three key prohibitions—against idol worship, incest, and bloodshed.[19] This concept permits Jews to consider committing suicide in certain defined instances, in order to "sanctify God's name." It does not, however, constitute a permit to take the lives of others as Goldstein did.

Despite this, Ginzburg alters the religious meaning of the concept, arguing that since Goldstein's actions were ostensibly intended to prevent a planned massacre of Jews by the Arabs, they may be considered the sanctification of God's name. Ginzburg further argued that "almost all the religious sages of the Arabs who live here beside us believe that it is a religious commandment for them to shed Jewish blood." Accordingly, they are considered to have violated one of the seven Noahide commandments (the prohibition against murder) that apply to all non-Jews, and hence, he claims, they fall under the definition of the sanctification of God's name.[20]

2. *Saving Life.* Ginzburg argues that the killing was the product of the anticipation of future events, rather than a response to an immediate and unequivocal threat. In the short term, he explains, "the action prevented a pogrom that was just about to be committed." Goldstein's willingness to ignore the complexities of reality and do what he felt must be

done, on the strength of his inner instinct, is in itself "a positive action produced by the action itself, outweighing the results that those who engage in account-keeping imposed on this action." On the basis of his perception of the distinction between Jew and Gentile, and on the basis of "care for our fellow, care for Jewish life," Goldstein negated himself for the sake of his fellow Jews. Ginzburg comments:

> Regarding the sanctity of Jewish life, we can see simply that a Jewish life is superior to a Gentile life; and even if a Gentile does not wish the Jews any ill, it is permitted to kill a Gentile in order to save a Jew . . .
>
> All this is indeed true in a situation when a Gentile is not threatening the Jews; but when there is fear (however remote) that the Gentile may act (even indirectly) to kill Jews, then no consideration at all is to be given to the life of the Gentile; on the contrary—"the best of the Gentiles are to be killed."[21]

3. *Revenge.* This is the crux of the matter. According to the medieval Ashkenazi perception of messianism, as presented by Israel Yuval, there is a close connection between martyrdom and revenge. The death of martyrs who sanctified God's name obliges God to wreak vengeance. Revenge is the punishment for bloodshed; it is not merely revenge, but blood vengeance. The death of martyrs is intended to encourage redemption. This was the argument used to justify the phenomenon of mass suicide, which was relatively common among German Jews in 1096 during the Crusades.[22]

Yitzhak Ginzburg employs a similar line of argument: Revenge is a manifestation of inner emotions that conveys a message of national pride, and tells the world at large that Jews will not agree to be maltreated. If a Gentile harms a Jew (or, as was deduced in this case, plans to do so), the Jew should take revenge. Accordingly, this type of revenge includes an element of doing justice. In the eschatological struggle between good and evil, as described in the Kabbalistic thought of the Ari (Rabbi Isaac Luria), the victory of good is also a cosmic victory. Moreover, the act of sanctification of God's name leads to a state of "holy terror," whereby the believer who commits suicide forces God, as it were, to intervene and bring redemption to avenge their blood. This is an act of provocation and incitement toward God to ensure an absolute determination in favor of messianic justice:[23]

> The individual and the people that take the risk of committing an act of revenge put God to the test, as it were, as if saying, "Let's see who will survive and who will be annihilated," and by so doing they expedite the determination. This is a plea to God to instigate the

day of vengeance in His heart and, in this respect, there is a demand and invitation here for redemption (in the form of the redemption of blood) which, as we know, will come through agitation from below, through the distress of the lower beings who sense that the appearance of God is already an absolute imperative that cannot be done without.[24]

Furthermore, revenge embodies an element of social Darwinism: Revenge is the law of nature, in which "viable good" must vanquish "flimsy evil that will yet be ejected by nature."[25]

Ginzburg justifies the act of revenge by reference to the biblical story of the vengeance wrought by Shimon and Levy against the inhabitants of Nablus following the rape of their sister Dina. The Book of Genesis (chap. 34) relates that Shechem (a personal name and also the Hebrew name for the city of Nablus) took Dina, the daughter of Jacob, and raped and tortured her, and then asked to marry her. By way of a condition for the marriage, Dina's brothers demanded that all the men of Nablus be circumcised. The residents agreed and, on the third day, when the men were in pain and at their weakest, Shimon and Levy entered the city, killed all its male inhabitants, looted their property, and took the wives and children prisoners, all in revenge for the attack on their sister. Their behavior has been the subject of debate. In the Bible, Jacob sharply criticized his sons' actions. A Halachic discussion developed asking whether it is permissible to harm innocents (since only one of the residents of the city raped Dina). The solution offered by the Maharal is that the case involves "two peoples," and the relations between peoples are gauged not on the individual level but on the collective level. Accordingly, either side participating in a war may attack any of the members of the opposing nation. The fact that not all the residents of Nablus took part in the rape is irrelevant for the purpose of defining the extent of violence against them that may be permitted.[26]

On the basis of the Maharal's interpretation, Ginzburg states: "We may learn from this instance that the essence of revenge is that the injured party stands up straight, without particular interest in the enemy and its motives. The motive for revenge is the uprightness of the 'self' and not criticism of evil; after all, the vast majority of the people of Nablus had committed no sin."[27] Another pamphlet published by his students Yosef Peli and Yitzhak Brand reinforces the claim that in war people who are not directly involved in the fighting are also harmed, even young children. They argue that a population that supports the enemy is considered "a pursuer coming to kill us," including young children, "and hence we say in any case that, since this is about war, even if 'innocent people' are injured, we should not refrain from bellicose actions because of this."[28]

Ginzburg's interpretation of the action of Baruch Goldstein inverts the sequence of actions and exchanges the assailant and his victims. Goldstein the aggressor is transmuted into a victim, while his victims become enemies who are in a state of war, and must therefore be attacked without consideration. Only Goldstein's blood continues to cry out from the ground, demanding messianic vengeance in the End of Days.[29]

4. *Eradicating the Seed of Amalek*. Ginzburg argues that in every generation there are "evil ones" who seek to annihilate the Jews or to thwart Jewish redemption. The Gentiles still fail to negate themselves before the Jews, and show signs of anti-Semitism and hatred of Israel. Accordingly, all those who wish Israel ill are considered to form part of the "seed of Amalek." Ginzburg states that the Torah commanded that all the coming generations wage war against Amalek.[30] Although Ginzburg does not complete the argument, the inevitable conclusion is clear: The Palestinians are to be seen as Amalek, and hence their males are to be annihilated. His argument requires no exegesis.

5. *War*. A key component in Ginzburg's theological approach relates to the commandment to seize the Land of Israel. According to Nachmanides, who bases his position on the Talmudic tractate of Sanhedrin (20b), the entry of the people of Israel into the Land comprises three stages: the coronation of a king, the annihilation of the seed of Amalek, and the construction of the Temple. A further commandment associated with this process is the seizure of the Land, on the basis of the Book of Numbers (chap. 33). This commandment mandates the expulsion of all the residents of the Land as the people of Israel enter and conquer it. I attended a lecture by Ginzburg in which he explicitly stated that he believes that all the difficulties in contemporary Israel between the Jews and the Palestinians are the result of the failure to comply with this commandment when the Jews returned to the Land at the end of exile. Goldstein's actions are also justified in accordance with this principle.

To summarize the message of the pamphlet, the arguments Ginzburg presents clearly reflect his strong admiration for the action of Baruch Goldstein. As he sees it, Goldstein not only saved Jewish lives, thus justifying his act of zealotry (the sanctification of God's name); he also performed a kind of pure and purifying vengeance—a vengeance accompanied by a spiritual value that advances redemption. His mundane actions call out to the Heavens for their completion and for Divine intervention on the "great day of vengeance" at the End of Days.

Another important issue in understanding the ideological approach of Ginzburg may illuminate his position regarding the actions of Baruch Goldstein from a different angle. This issue is the question of the "emergency provision." Although his comments on this issue are somewhat opaque, deciphering his position can reveal one of the most radical aspects of his thought.

The historian Elchanan Reiner reports that he was present at a sermon given by Ginzburg at Yeshurun Synagogue in Jerusalem at which Ginzburg stated that, in certain cases, it may be permissible to disobey the spiritual leadership, in keeping with the spirit of the verse:[31] "It is time to work for the Lord; they have made void Your Torah" (Ps. 119:126).[32] I would reinforce Reiner's claim, and add comments of a similar nature that reveal an approach that lies on the seam between hypernomism and antinomianism. The interpretation of the concept of religious zealotry as offered by the "Od Yosef Chai" circle constitutes a dialectical junction; a point at which the desire to amplify one's worship of God may actually lead to the transgression of religious law. In precisely the same way, actions that are contrary to the Halacha may be considered the sublime manifestation of religious faith.[33]

In his book *The Dominion of Israel*, Ginzburg argues that actions to "expedite the end" are forbidden unless they are executed in accordance with the rules of the Torah. Therefore, actions to expedite the end should be undertaken in accordance with the rules and laws of the Torah. As an aside, he emphasizes that action to expedite the end through the transgression of the rules of the Torah is indeed proper in accordance with Kabbalistic theory; however, in light of current reality, it must be considered forbidden. Nevertheless, he does not establish this by way of a categorical fact, stating in a somewhat obscure manner that, on some occasions, it is permissible to violate religious law.[34] He argues that such violation of religious law might occur by way of a "temporary provision." Such a provision must be a one-time act and must reflect the utmost devotion, in keeping with internal feelings and the instincts that drive the individual to action. The transgression of the Torah on a systematical basis, however, is forbidden. In response to my question requesting a clarification of the term "temporary provision," the rabbi replied:

> The term "temporary provision" (*hora'at hasha'ah*) has been discussed extensively in Halacha and in Hassidism. In brief, its significance is that although the Halacha never undergoes an eternal change, there are points in time at which it is appropriate to make a temporary change in accordance with the words of a prophet or a true scholar. In the future, too, the Halacha shall not change, but it may be that during the process of redemption certain temporary provisions shall be required. In Hassidism, it is explained at length that a temporary provision reflects the most sublime manifestation of the human soul, and the works of the Izhbitze sect of Hassidism (*Mei Hashilo'ach, Beit Ya'akov,* and

Sod Yesharim) place a strong emphasis on worshipping God through temporary provisions. It should be noted that the perception of the temporary provision as a special Divine revelation in the soul does not apply only to temporary provisions that contradict the Halacha, but also to the historical perception that *a given generation, or a given individual, must act in an exceptional manner and emphasize in their action a given aspect of Divine worship.* Another important point is that true temporary provisions, stemming from the inner soul of the Jewish people, are often, as time passes, established as part of the permanent Halacha. (emphasis added)[35]

The term "temporary provision" as used by Ginzburg seems to have been developed on the basis of the writings of the Izhbitze Rebbe, Mordechai Yosef Leiner (1800–1854), whose works are mentioned in Ginzburg's reply to me. It is worth noting that Leiner is a controversial figure in the world of Hassidism. His approach is based on the existence of a gap between the Creator's intention and the letter of the religious law, thus creating an inability to fathom the intention of God. Leiner argues that the starting point for human endeavor is the uncertainty and the doubts that underpin reality. Accordingly, the human has the potential to receive direct enlightenment from the Creator ("temporary provisions") since the will of God is a changing concept. Joseph Weiss identified an antinomist tendency in this position, which creates the potential for religious anarchy. He argues that this approach originated with Sabbateanism and was adopted by Hassidism.[36]

The element of doubt regarding religious law that is apparent in Ginzburg's theoretical discussion of the temporary provision in his reply to me is still not entirely clear. Thus arises the question, When Ginzburg lauded the action of Baruch Goldstein, who committed a massacre, justifying this on the grounds of the sanctification of God's name, did he see this as an example of a temporary provision?

To clarify this question, I will present the interpretation offered by Ginzburg's students regarding the question of the zealotry of Pinchas. The discussion of the concept of zealotry as just presented was not written by way of an interpretation of the concept of the temporary provision. Nevertheless, in my opinion, it stems from the internalization of the idea that the laws of the Torah may be contravened, at specific points in time, to glorify God's name. The students deliberately obscure their interpretation and address the issue on a purely theoretical level. However, I will seek to argue that their intention in this respect is to justify zealous action, including spontaneous acts of murder, without obtaining religious sanction for such steps.

The story of Pinchas (Num. 25–26) presents the reader with a theological dilemma relating to the status of mundane law (represented here by the leadership of Moses) and Divine law. The story highlights some difficult questions: May an individual violate earthly law in the name of an "inner truth" that stems from truth of Divine origin? Can human orgin law stand up against Divine law, or does the latter subordinate the former?

The story of Pinchas focuses on the following drama: The people of Israel, camped at Hittin on their way to the Land of Israel, meet Moabite women and the menfolk begin to pursue them. The sexual act this involves constitutes part of the Baalite ritual of the Moabites. God is furious with the Children of Israel and imposes a plague that leaves twenty-four thousand dead. Moses summons the leaders of the people to the Tent of Meeting (*ohel mo'ed*) and demands that they stop their evil acts. While they are discussing the matter, Zimri Ben Salu, prince of the tribe of Shimon, appears on the scene together with a Moabite woman by the name of Kazvi Bat Zur. The Bible does not tell us clearly what happened next, but it was enough to cause great weeping among all those gathered at the scene.

Zimri's appearance was clearly a challenge to Moses—just as he demands that the men of Israel stop fraternizing with Moabite women, one of the leading members of the tribe of Shimon appears together with a Moabite woman. Although the text is ambiguous, it seems clear that what took place in the tent was an act of sexual intercourse in public, observed by the entire people, as part of the Baalite ritual.

Pinchas Ben Eliezer sees this act, seizes his spear, and promptly stabs both Zimri and Kazvi with a single strike of his weapon. They die instantaneously, and at the same moment the plague ends. Moreover, God speaks to Moses:

> Pinchas, the son of Eleazar, the son of Aaron the priest, has turned My wrath away from the children of Israel, in that he was very jealous for My sake among them, so that I consumed not the children of Israel in My jealousy. Wherefore say: Behold, I give unto him My covenant of peace; and it shall be unto him, and to his seed after him, the covenant of an everlasting priesthood; because he was jealous for his God, and made atonement for the children of Israel. (Num. 25:11–13)

Thus we see that not only does Pinchas kill two people without any trial, in violation of the explicit commandment "You shall not murder," but he is not punished for this act. On the contrary, his descendents are awarded an everlasting priesthood. It is also notable that it is not Moses or the tribal elders who act as zealots; Pinchas operates on his own, with no need for court or law. He feels internally that he knows what is zealotry to God and what is God's will, and he acts at that precise moment in accordance with the command of his conscience.

The Sages added their own interpretations to the story of Pinchas in an effort to dilute its potentially anarchist message. The Babylonian Talmud states that had Zimri turned around and killed Pinchas, rather than vice versa, he would have been found innocent, since Pinchas had the status of a "persecutor" (Sanhedrin 71b–72a).[37] In the Mishnah, we learn that before a person is executed they are entitled to a fair trial; two witnesses must be questioned. A Sanhedrin that sentenced one person to death in seventy years was considered a "murderous" court. Rabbi Akiva and Rabbi Tarfon said, "Had we been on the Sanhedrin, no one would ever have been executed" (Babylonian Talmud, Makot, 7a). Yet in the biblical story, Pinchas implements a "sentence" without any such niceties, and rather than punishment he receives a dramatic reward.

The lesson that Ginzburg's circle learns from the story of Pinchas is that at certain points it is permissible to act in a manner that is contrary to normal rules to perform an act of zealotry to the Lord. The logical conclusion drawn from the story is that Divine truth stands above mundane law. This is proved by the fact that the killing of Zimri led to the end of the plague, the awarding of a prize, and a Divine blessing for the murderer.

This story reveals the inherently anarchic element of religious zealotry. The zealot acts beyond the Halachic framework, while believing that they are implementing God's will and that of the community. The justification for their acts is retrospective, not ab initio. This approach weakens the status of the ruling institutions and the leaders of the community.[38]

Such anarchist perspectives are certainly to be found among Ginzburg's students:

> In a fit of zealotry, Pinchas murders sinners, thus saving Israel from a plague. Is this Pinchas' role? . . . In this situation, there is one individual who knows what he should do—but is he charged with implementing this? . . . Pinchas sees that he is in a place where "there are no men" and he decides "to be a man," and the act he performs brings a blessing on the entire people of Israel. We should learn from this act that each individual must always sense the responsibility they bear for the collective.[39]

The students' theological position on this matter is so exceptional that they are even willing to justify the actions of Nadav and Aviyahu who, the Bible informs us, were killed by God because of their excessive zeal for Divine worship. The *Shemini* Torah portion (Lev. 10:1–3) relates the story of Nadav and Aviyahu, the sons of Aharon the Priest, who were engaged in building the Tabernacle. In their enthusiasm to worship the Lord, they performed more than they were required to in their work: "[They] offered strange fire before the Lord, which He had not commanded them." Their punishment was immediate—God brought forth a fire that consumed them on the spot.

It might be presumed that this story shows that excessive enthusiasm for Divine worship is prohibited. Ginzburg's circle, however, draws the opposite conclusion, claiming that the presence of people such as Nadav and Aviyahu is a credit to the nation. If there had not been people who sought to worship God more than they are commanded, Moses would have been profoundly disappointed. There is a place for Divine worship even if it deviates from the borders of what is permissible; and particularly when its intention is to strengthen rather than weaken faith. They explain:

> True leadership is one that knows how to give a place of honor to the outbreaks of individuals. A leader who is terrified by any outbreak that is not "according to the rules" and immediately and categorically rejects it is not a true leader. Such a leader believes that it is only the dry legal system that maintains the people, and does not realize that without the inner burning, the engine that drives the people forward will be lacking. A true leader can appreciate the positive impulse that drives people to action. Such a leader must also know and admit that, in this respect, these people are greater than himself, and sometimes precisely because of their actions truly great things may be accomplished.[40]

The license granted by this circle to commit violent acts of zealotry requires the adoption of a perspective that permits individuals to take the law into their own hands. The zealot challenges the Halachic framework; while the latter must respond to changing circumstances rationally and act in the interests of the public as a whole, the zealot acts only in the name of a Divine truth as they themselves interpret this. An understanding of this aspect explains Ginzburg's admiration for the actions of Baruch Goldstein—a man responsible for murdering innocent people and who is perceived as having overcome pragmatic considerations to commit an act of zealotry that he believed was essential.[41] Goldstein did not consult with anyone; a person truly zealous to God service has no need for consultation—on the contrary, zealotry is a spontaneous and impulsive quality. A zealot claims to know best what is proper and just; he does not shy away from committing acts that violate formal religious law, and his violent mission stems from a burning faith. Whereas the Sages sought to restrict and delineate zealotry,[42] Ginzburg's students encourage it and praise zealous actions. This zealous approach may encourage and lead individuals to commit acts of terror in the name of "Divine truth" on the basis of personal considerations. The issue lies on the seam between what is permitted and what is forbidden within religious law, and may indicate the emergence of antinomist tendencies.

The Theocratic Approaches of the "Od Yosef Chai" Circle

Having examined the question of the supernatural status of the Jews and the issue of zealotry, I now turn to presenting Ginzburg's thoughts on the subject of the state and the role of the Temple.

Ginzburg begins his discussions on the question of the ideal regime for the people of Israel by presenting the assumption that there are two types of regimes; one prefers to emphasize the good of the individual, while the other prefers the good of the nation as a whole. These are the democratic and the monarchist regimes, respectively. The democratic regime emphasizes the importance and choice of each individual; accordingly, it stresses minority rights and basic civil rights. In a monarchy, however, the king enjoys absolute rule, and is not obliged to take into account the personal opinion of each individual. The natural function of the king is to maintain the rights of the people, and not necessarily the rights of its constituent individuals.

These two types of regimes are ostensibly contradictory: democracy is perceived as an extreme form of nihilism that does not enable the nation to address collective goals, while monarchy is a form of dictatorship that tramples on individual rights. From a different perspective, however, Ginzburg argues that the monarchy actually represents the will of the individual—the will of the king as an individual. To understand this point, it is vital to understand the profound concept of the monarch of Israel. This king represents the will of God; as such, he cannot be a ruthless dictator. A true king takes account of all the individuals who comprise the public, is sensitive to their needs, and is capable of meeting their needs. [43]

Therefore, according to Ginzburg there are three types of regimes: democracy, national regime, and monarchy. A monarchist regime does not differ in practical terms from a national regime. However, the basic difference between the king and a national regime, described as a "military junta," is that the king's rule reflects the will of individuals, from a collective perspective, whereas the junta is a completely tyrannical regime. However, the monarchist system is appropriate only for Israel, since the Torah and the Jewish collective are unique entities. Ginzburg explains that a three-phase process is responsible for leading Jews to see themselves as part of the greater whole, and for sensing the manner in which the collective is reflected within themselves. First, the individual must ignore and repress his own ego to become part of the whole. In the second phase, he must focus on his ego and find the whole within himself. A complete unity already exists between the individual and the collective, and the collective is reflected in each individual. In this situation, the individual becomes part of the collective, devoid of their individual will and ego, combining in perfect unity the individual and collective will, with no contradiction between the two.[44]

Consequently, the search for the collective goal will bring liberty, and the realization of this goal will ensure the liberty of the individual. The individual strives to realize the collective goal—the redemption of Israel—since this is the only way to be free. The commitment to this idea negates the need to impose ideas on the individual by force, since they will emerge internally.

The complete integration of the individual and the collective, ostensibly on the basis of the individual will of each person to become part of the great machine of the nation, is one of the founding concepts of totalitarian thought. It is in this field that the influence of nationalist rhetoric on Ginzburg may be seen. His definition of the ideal monarchy is consonant with the definition of the "general will" as presented by Jean-Jacques Rousseau. According to Rousseau, the proper thing to do is enter into the social contract and act in coordination with the general will of the nation. Accordingly, the purpose of political life is to prepare individuals to accept the general will without feeling that they are being subjected to coercion. This foundation underpins Jacob Talmon's definition of "totalitarian democracy." According to Talmon, a totalitarian democracy is based on the assumption that there is only one truth in politics. This approach may be considered a form of "political messianism," insofar as it is guided by a perfect, harmonious order—a type of End of Days destiny that people long for and will eventually attain, despite themselves.[45]

Ginzburg argues that the principle objectives Israel should aspire to are the coming of messiah and the resurrection of the dead—both of which appear in the Thirteen Principles of Faith articulated by Maimonides. The only difference between the messianic era and the current world is the subjugation of the nations, interpreted as "the success of Israel in the world as a collective; in terms of the individual life there is no substantial change." In other words, this is a perspective based on naturalistic messianism. Messiah reflects the national will of the Jewish collective, subjugating any private and individual will, and leading to the realization of the eternal character of the Jewish people. As each dead person rises from their grave in the resurrection of the dead, the very character of nature changes in the Jews' favor. Now we are in the domain of apocalyptic messianism. Then "the entire collective will be manifested in each individual Jew, as this quality is inculcated from the Messiah King to each and every Jew."[46]

According to Ginzburg, this absolute truth is present in theocracy, and the advantages of this system over parliamentary democracy are therefore obvious. This idea is central to an understanding of the philosophy of Yitzhak Ginzburg and his students. Individual will cannot possibly contradict the words of God, and a regime manifesting individualism cannot overcome a regime that represents God's word on Earth. Thus, this circle develops an ideology that emphasizes this dilemma and seeks ways to remedy the evident distortion. Such an ideology is subversive with regard to the state and its institutions and encourages manifestations of religious zealotry.

A journalist once asked Ginzburg whether it was right for an individual to take the law into their own hands and commit acts of revenge against Arabs. He replied:

> I would support actions that are not within the framework of the army only if they enjoy broad public support. What is needed is for a serious body of publicly-recognized figures to take responsibility—a group comprising rabbis and other public figures. The leaders of this body, the rabbis, should determine how to act, what is permitted and what the Torah law says, and it is evident to anyone who believes in Torah that Divine law takes precedence over all else. If human law is not in contradiction to this, that's all well and good, but when the two clash, naturally it is Divine law that prevails. [47]

It is worth noting that after his release from prison in 1989, Yehuda Etzion also argued that there was a need for a larger critical mass to revolt against the state authorities.

During the struggle surrounding the eviction of the illegal settlement of Chavat Maon in 2004, Ginzburg wrote: "Anyone who comes to uproot Jews from sections of their Land thereby loses their right to speak on behalf of the Jewish people . . . On behalf of the residents of the hills in the settlements of Judea, Samaria, and the Gaza Strip, we turn firstly to our fellow Jews—any Jew wherever they may be, civilian, soldier, or policeman: do not cooperate with actions that harm the Jewish people." Regarding negotiations for the granting of territory in exchange for peace, he stated: "Any agreement made by the representatives of the people of Israel contrary to the Torah of Israel is inherently null and void, unbinding and invalid."[48] In an open letter to Israeli Prime Minister Ehud Barak in 2000, after he proposed a referendum to ratify the peace accords with the PLO, Ginzburg stated that the demand of the Torah for the integrity of the Land of Israel could not be challenged in a referendum. In particular, he opposed the fact that Arab citizens would also be able to participate in such a referendum.[49]

In light of the rejection of the concept of democracy as an "alien presence" in Jewish thought, it is interesting to examine the position of Ginzburg's circle on the question regarding "Gentile wisdom." As I have explained, their approach is based in long-standing Jewish traditions that place the Jews above nature. Accordingly, it is inappropriate to learn from those who have an inferior status. Theories of non-Jewish origin should be rejected, as should alien culture and ideals; Jews should adhere exclusively to the Torah:

> Along all our paths and through all our generations, we find ourselves at new junctions. Time and time again we must emphasize and accentuate our insistence on our own inner essence and choose our Father. Through all our searches, we encounter the possibility of adhering to substitutes that come from the nations—alien cultures and beliefs, strange gods, Gentile ideals, and different ways of life—but we know that no alien can ever know our Father as we do . . . One thing is engraved in our soul for eternity: We know what we are looking for, and we will never be tempted to accept a substitute![50]

Ginzburg's position is less monolithic than this quote implies, however. If it is found that science can corroborate the truths contained in the Torah, it is permissible to use it. Ginzburg proposes that "Gentile wisdom" should be carefully sifted, and should be "included in pure faith, the faith of Israel, after it has undergone a 'Halachic conversion.'"[51] It is also important to note that despite the condemnation of modern science, there is no objection to the use of modern technology to disseminate their religious doctrine; accordingly, although Ginzburg and his students depict themselves as the defenders of "traditional religion" against scientific intrusion, they also adopt scientific methods.[52] In this respect, Ginzburg follows the approach of Chabad, which is willing to use modern technology to disseminate its ideas.[53]

Ginzburg often quotes the commandment "You shall make no covenant with them" (Deut. 7:2), which was interpreted by the Talmud as meaning that non-Jews should not be permitted to reside in the Land of Israel (Babylonian Talmud, Avodah Zarah, 20a). Maimonides interpreted the commandment as meaning that non-Jews should not be permitted to live or reside in the Land of Israel, with the exception of those who are considered "resident strangers" (Hilchot Avodah Zarah 10:6). Accordingly, Ginzburg argues that given security considerations and given the fact that the presence of the alien among Israel "corrupts ('consciously' or 'subconsciously') our spirit, and particularly the spirit of our youth, influencing them to be 'like all the nations,' no Gentiles should not be permitted to live in the Land of Israel."[54]

The newsletter of the yeshiva explains:

Those Gentiles whom the Torah states have no place in the Land
of Israel constitute a significant obstacle to the bond that should
emerge here between Israel and their heavenly Father. The contacts and alliance between Israel and these nations violate the alliance [also: "covenant"] between Israel and the Holy One,
blessed be He. Accordingly, our aspiration from the outset
should be to expel them so that "they shall not dwell in Your
land." Only in this way can we fight the damaging cultural and
spiritual influence. Recognition of our responsibility to expel the
peoples of Canaan—as a task imposed on us—is a "precondition"
for creating "a kingdom of priests and a holy nation'" in the Land
of Israel.[55]

One of the ways in which this task may be accomplished is by removing Arabs from the labor market. Accordingly, Ginzburg encourages
"Hebrew labor," implying the boycotting of non-Jewish workers and produce, to deny the workers a livelihood and thus force them to leave the
country. He writes:

According to the ruling of Maimonides, may his memory be a
blessing, it is currently prohibited for a non-Jew to dwell in our
holy Land (or even to pass through). Accordingly, we must make
an effort, through devotion of the soul, body, and finances, to
avoid, as far as possible, any action (employment, purchase, etc.)
that maintains the residence of a non-Jew in the Land.[56]

Hebrew labor also meets other objectives, such as strict attention to Sabbath observance; financial help "through selling and buying with your
fellow Jews"; and support for the needy, since employing Jews gives them
a livelihood.[57]

I end the discussion of Ginzburg's theory of theocracy by examining
how he believes it is possible to move from the current damaged condition of the State of Israel, as he sees it, to the desired condition of mundane, naturalistic redemption, which he believes will be followed by
miraculous and apocalyptic redemption.

Ginzburg emphasizes that the study of his approach is not a theoretical game, but a program for implementation that will eventually lead to
the overthrowing of the current regime. The starting point for the transition to a theocracy—the dominion of Israel—lies in disgust with the existing regime: "The aspiration for dominion comes from digust with the
wallowing in limited, private rights and desires, and the wish to find a

king who will rise above individual objectives to address public objectives, even if these reject individual objectives and complicate the standard of living of the individual."[58] Ginzburg rejects the approach of Mercaz Harav yeshiva, which sees Zionist Jewish sovereignty as a sacred religious value in its own right.[59] He refers to this approach as a "sacred cow,"[60] arguing that the destiny of the kingdom of Israel, as the dominion of God, should be advanced by "natural means."

These principles are based on the concept of a partial withdrawal from general society and influence over government to gain strength as an independent force. The recommended withdrawal relates at least to a spiritual disconnection, if not a physical one. This disconnection includes the abandoning of Western ideology and rejection of the current regime and of democracy. Such approaches are a key component in the approach of fundamentalist movements in general.[61]

In a series of articles published in *Lekhatchilah*, the journal of the Jewish Leadership movement (the articles were later republished in Ginzburg's book *The Immediate Imperative*), Ginzburg proposed a series of actions designed to secure this transition. First, he wrote that it is vital to disconnect from the authority of the state and to adopt an exclusive commitment to the authority of the Torah. The next stage focuses on a recognition that only by obeying the Torah is it possible to live, on both the individual and the collective levels. Accordingly, the aspiration should be to observe all the commandments of the Torah in full, even those that were not observed in exile (this includes the commandments relating to the Temple). The same applies to the integrity of the Land of Israel, all of which must be under full Jewish sovereignty. The next stage is the recognition of the distinction "between Israel and the nations;" the final goal of this is the conversion of the Gentiles in the age of redemption. After sovereignty is declared over all parts of the Land of Israel, the Land should be settled by Jews. If the Gentiles threaten Jewish life and the Jewish presence in the Land, "the source of the threat is to be eliminated." A further, subsequent stage will encourage Jews to immigrate to Israel, which by now may justly be called a truly Jewish state. This situation will lead to the deterministic process of the elimination of the Diaspora, since there will be "a fervent desire and true passion to ascend to our Land." Encouragement of Jewish immigration will be accompanied by a process of "expelling and rejecting undesirable elements from the Land." A Gentile who resides in Israel and who shows a willingness to become "righteous of the nations" may remain; there is no place for those who do not share this aspiration. The next stage will include the unification of science and the Torah, so that science may "confirm and verify the Torah." All these stages will lead to the age of the Josephite Messiah—the stage preceding the miraculous age of redemption under the leadership of the Davidic Messiah.[62]

Additional principles presented by Ginzburg include:

1. The faction must attempt to be "independent" and to refrain from seeking benefits and funds from the authorities if this will cause enslavement to the deviant culture. Ginzburg did not comply with this recommendation; however, the Gal Eini association, which disseminates his writings, enjoyed generous state support in 2002–2003 in an amount exceeding NIS 600,000 (about US $150,000).[63]

2. "Despite all the defects and distortions of the existing establishment, we must identify with the rules of the nation that empower the establishment, for the present, to speak and act in its name. We must not ignore the fact that the establishment draws from the collective strength, and we must not detach ourselves from the public (even in thought)." Ginzburg claims that it is important to protest against the violation of God's commandments. Accordingly, action should take place from within the public, and a struggle should be waged against those who do not act in accordance with the religious perspectives of Ginzburg and his circle.[64]

Redemption and the Rebuilding of the Temple

Since the early 1990s, the Chabad Hassidic movement has been characterized by a high level of messianic tension relating to the status of its leader, Rabbi Menachem-Mendel Schneerson. Since Schneerson's death in 1994, a messianic crisis has developed. Some sections of the movement still argue that he is the messiah (and deny or reinterpret his death). As a Chabad rabbi, Ginzburg is bound by the common principle shared by all members of the movement that the current generation is the generation of redemption. He believes that the traditional restraints prohibiting Jews from seeking actively to expedite the coming of messiah are no longer valid; the age of redemption has begun. In his writings, Ginzburg evades discussion of the specific identity of the messiah; by so doing, he distances himself from that stream within the movement that identifies the messiah with the late Schneerson:[65] "We should not discuss the identity of messiah. However, we should strengthen our faith that messiah will come very soon"; "in each generation and at all times, there must be one person living who, if the generation is found worthy, will be revealed as messiah."[66]

Ginzburg rejects the passive messianic stance that has traditionally characterized Judaism. He also rejects the Religious Zionist view that interprets Israeli reality as an ongoing process of redemption. He is particularly critical of the approach that sees redemption as a slow, gradual process demanding that the Jews wait patiently and quietly for messiah. Such an approach, he argues, is completely invalid. Active and fervent efforts must be made to "expedite the end," and there is no justification to rely on processes that may be interpreted as part of redemption even if they embody no element of sanctity. Although Ginzburg agrees that God sets the pace of redemption, he argues that the public must not be weak-willed in this respect or assume that humans should not bear responsibility for the process.

Ginzburg's messianic approach combines two approaches. The first is embodied in the traditional midrash on the verse "I the Lord will hasten it in its time" (Isa. 60:22). This phrase is parsed as meaning "if they are found worthy—I shall hasten it; if they are not—it shall be in its time" (Sanhedrin 98a). The second is the Kabbalistic formula "upper awakening depends on lower awakening." The midrash explains that redemption may come in two manners: if the people are found worthy, it will come rapidly, without the suffering of the "birth pangs of messiah" that accompany the messianic age. Effectively, then, this is a naturalistic form of redemption. If the people are not found worthy, however, due to their poor religious behavior, redemption will come "in its time," including all the prophesized events relating to the Great Day of God; this is apocalyptic redemption.

The second principle is that mundane acts awaken complementary Divine action. According to Ginzburg, a naturally induced "end" depends on mundane action:

> The truth is that we must not leave anything to the Holy One, blessed be He, regarding the stages leading to the coming of messiah, the building of the Temple, and the repair of the entire world through God's dominion. The resurrection of the dead and the renewal of the coming world are matters for the Holy One, blessed be He. The coming of messiah and the building of the Temple depend totally on us![67]

Thus it can be seen that Ginzburg's circle presents a rather unusual approach. Traditional Jewish teachings argue that redemption would come as the result of repentance by the Jews; the purpose of exile was to prepare the Jews for the ultimate redemption, which would come after every last individual had repented. Therefore, redemption is the product of religious action by the people, and all that is necessary is for people to observe the commandments. Complete redemption is preceded by complete repentance—when all Jews believe in their God and keep all His commandments as written in the Torah and interpreted in the Halacha.[68]

However, in the Rosh Hashanah 5763 (2002) edition of the newsletter of "Od Yosef Chai" yeshiva, the argument was presented that advancing physical redemption would automatically lead to repentance. More precisely, the formula presented was that redemption and repentance are synonymous, and this is a mutual process: "When we return to God, God returns to us." Hence, redemption cannot be described without repentance. The assumption here is that all the Jews want to repent, but that external delays restrict this process. "Accordingly, it is not good to address repentance alone and to present Jews with the demand to return to the fold, since this desire already exists inside us."[69] It is better, therefore, to begin from the converse side of the coin—from redemption—to reach the same goal: "We must talk about the certain, promised destiny; we must tell Israel of the redemption that shall surely come." Ensuring redemption will ensure repentance; accordingly, and in keeping with the requirement to engage in mundane action, "We need only make an opening the size of a needle, to want repentance and to 'return to our hearts,' and the Holy One, blessed be He, will make an opening the size of a hall for full repentance and full redemption."[70]

This discussion leads to the question of the building of the Temple. Whereas the accepted position, such as that presented by Mercaz Harav yeshiva, is that spiritual elevation is essential before attention turns to building the Temple,[71] "Od Yosef Chai" yeshiva takes the opposite approach, arguing that the construction of the Temple will lead to spiritual elevation:

> We must only know that on that holy path that ascends to the Temple Mount, full acceptance of the heavenly yoke is expected of us, and the understanding that we are "emissaries of the Merciful one" acting solely on His behalf . . . The main transformation that will take place in reality in the time of the Temple is that we will simply begin to believe.[72]

The image of the Temple descending ready-made from the heavens (apocalyptic messianism) is indeed a manifestation of God's strength, However, the theological expectation of such a development weakens religious faith and practice.[73] According to the "Od Yosef Chai" circle, the achievement of redemption is a mundane matter and is incumbent on humans; thus, there is an obligation to prepare the foundations for the building of the Temple. According to the principle that human action will stimulate complementary action by God, Ginzburg's circle argues that painstaking preparations by humans will eventually oblige God to intervene and complete the task:

> The preparations for the building of the Sanctuary cannot remain solely on the "principled level." We cannot make do merely with "mental preparation" and general explanations about what

is to be built. Planning must address the practical work, down to its very smallest detail, and nothing must be left unresolved. Prior planning means not assuming that all the problems will be solved during the work of construction. We must present a complete vision in which every plank of wood and every piece of fabric find their rightful place, and every hand finds its special function.

. . . Indeed, after we have done all that is required of us; after all our investment and precision in planning and action; after leaving no detail to chance or improvisation—then the Divine Help shall appear to complete our work.[74]

The attitude toward the question of Jewish prayer on the Temple Mount in the present era is naturally influenced by this perspective. Ginzburg's personal position on this question seems, at first glance, to be inconsistent. In his book *Dominion of Israel*, he writes: "We bear a holy obligation to cleanse the Temple Mount and the site of the Temple and, even now, to visit the permitted areas on the Mount."[75] Yet in his essay "The Immediate Imperative: Root Treatment," published just two years later, he presents a different and apparently contrary position. In this essay, Ginzburg urges careful study of all the questions relating to the building of the Temple and the associated rituals; this includes study of the relevant Halachic laws and of the Kabbalah. He adds that it must be ensured that there is no desecration of God's name on the site; for this reason, Arabs must not be permitted to enter. Ginzburg claims that Schneerson urged the leading rabbis of the generation to determine which parts of the Temple Mount area must not be entered by Jews. The rabbis failed to meet this challenge and, accordingly,

in our generation, even if the Mount is cleansed of all the filth and impurity that are present there, it will only be possible for any Jew to ascend the Mount in purity after the King is anointed. I turn now to the best of our people, who long for the salvation of the Jewish people and are doing all they can to expedite redemption, including through the question of actual visits to the Temple Mount— I urge them here to devote their energies mainly to the more burning and topical subject: The question of anointing the King.[76]

The solution to the apparent contradiction between these two positions may be found in the minutes of a colloquy held at "Od Yosef Chai" yeshiva some ten years before both the book and the essay in question were published. During the discussion, Ginzburg claimed that, in principle, he supports the position that Jews should enter the Temple Mount in present times; however, due to a personal instruction from Rabbi Schneerson, he is not permitted to do so himself. He added that his brother-in-law Moshe Segal was in the custom of visiting the Temple Mount. As a loyal Chabad Hassid, he made sure that the Rebbe was aware of his actions, and he never received any comment on this matter. Ginzburg adopted the same approach, until he received a notice from the secretariat of the movement informing him that he was to stop doing so; he never received any letter explaining the grounds for this, and cannot, therefore, explain the reasons for the prohibition. "If it were up to me, I would go up. My mind is totally in line with Rabbi [Yosef] Elboim and Oded [Kitov, members of the Movement for the Establishment of the Temple], but I am subject and submit myself to what my guide tells me; he has a broader and more public viewpoint." Ginzburg inferred that the Rebbe did not wish the issue of Jews visiting the Temple Mount to become identified with the Chabad movement, since his focus was not on this issue, but on glorifying Judaism. Moreover, the Rebbe was facing criticism from other sections of the Haredi world, and particularly from Rabbi Eliezer Menachem Shach, and did not want to provide his adversaries with further ammunition. However, the Rebbe supported the activities of bodies directly identified with the demand to visit the Temple Mount, such as the Temple Mount Faithful. Gershon Salomon visited the Rebbe and received his blessing along with the traditional dollar bill.[77]

Corroboration for Ginzburg's interpretation of Schneerson's position regarding prayers on the Temple Mount in the present time may be gained from a further source. On the second evening of Sukkot in 1991, the Lubavitcher Rebbe made a speech at a "special conclave." The main points of his speech were faxed to Israel and disseminated in the Chabad centers. The Rebbe was quoted as saying that he urged all his followers to enter en masse, "in the greatest entirety," those areas "that are permitted on the Mount," to hold the water libation ceremony. The notice read as follows: "The water libation ceremony is to be held with the greatest of joy, and the site of the Temple—in the permitted places—is to be entered, and the water libation ceremony held there in the greatest entirety. Through this matter we shall be privileged to dance in Jerusalem, at the Third Temple, when our just Messiah comes, very soon."[78]

To understand the background of this groundbreaking announcement, it is important to appreciate the intensity of the messianic emotions rife in the Chabad movement at the time. The collapse of the Soviet bloc and the exodus of the Soviet Jews to Israel, alongside concern that the looming Gulf War would lead to the use of weapons of mass destruction, created messianic tension of an immediate and topical nature. These world events were interpreted within a classic messianic structure.[79]

The Chabad movement subsequently backed down from its announcement that the water libation ceremony was to be held on the Temple Mount. The Rebbe's comments were moderated by an interpretation explaining that his intention had been that the prayers would be held in the Western Wall plaza, and not on the Mount itself. I cannot explain this retreat; perhaps the Rebbe's original comments were intended allegorically. In any case, tens of thousands of Chabad followers attended the event at the Western Wall.

This incident can inform our understanding of the ambivalence in the Chabad movement regarding the Temple Mount. On the one hand, the special announcement acknowledged that there are areas on the Temple Mount that Jews are permitted to enter, and there is no reason why they should not do so. The movement was at a state of intense and growing messianic fervor, and the planned event on the Halac Mount could have been seen as a sublime manifestation of this anticipation. On the other hand, though, we have the later, moderate message from the Rebbe's court effectively canceling the original announcement. It seems probable that the Chabad movement did not wish to be associated with the subject of entering the Temple Mount due to the Halachic problems this subject raises. This may explain why the movement has preferred to advance this subject through agents who are not directly associated with Chabad. The same logic may explain why Ginzburg was instructed not to enter the Temple Mount. However, the prohibition does not bind the students at "Od Yosef Chai" yeshiva who are not directly affiliated to Chabad; their visits to the Temple Mount are permitted and even recommended.

The teachers at "Od Yosef Chai" yeshiva have continued to apply Ginzburg's approach, encouraging prayer on the Temple Mount and calling for the construction of the Temple. Considerable academic attention is devoted to this theme. To this end, the "El Har Hamor" association[80] was established on the initiative of "Od Yosef Chai" yeshiva to write and publish ideological works on this subject.[81] The association's publications address a wide range of theoretical issues relating to the Temple worship and methods of purification, as well as discussion of the topical issue of the permission to enter the Temple Mount in present times and engage in ritual on the site.

The association's activities are indicative of the relations between Chabad, Ginzburg, and the teachers and students of "Od Yosef Chai" yeshiva. The Chabad movement is gripped by messianic expectation relating to the character of its late leader,[82] but is not involved in activist messianic action to "expedite the end." Ginzburg is exceptional in this respect; his support for activist steps is illustrated by his position that Jews should enter the Temple Mount now. As an integral part of the movement, though, he has prevented himself from engaging in any such activities. However, his students are not affiliated to Chabad or identified with the movement; they act in accordance with Ginzburg's activist principles, free from the restrictions Chabad imposes on its supporters.

One of the most significant activities initiated by the El Har Hamor association was the establishment of the Temple Guard (*Mishmar Hamikdash*). The guard operates as a quasi-military, uniformed unit, though it has no legal authority. Ginzburg attaches symbolic importance to the Temple Guard as the vanguard of a messianic army: "Lower agitation and the first organization of the Lord's armies—an army that will serve the Righteous King who shall soon rise up."[83]

The commandment of guarding the Temple appears twice in the Bible (in chaps. 3 and 18 of the Book of Numbers). Maimonides explains that the purpose of guarding the Temple is to honor God and uplift the standing of the site. The guard also prevents strangers from entering the Tabernacle. During the Second Temple times, the priests and Levites were charged with obeying this commandment.[84]

The establishment of the Temple Guard did not meet with any objection from the rabbinical authorities. Indeed, Chief Rabbi Eliyahu Bakshi-Doron published an article in the newspaper *Hatzofeh* in which he expressed in-principle support for the establishment of a Temple guard: "Would that we had the strength to observe the commandment of guarding the Temple, and Israeli soldiers would stand like the Levites around the entire Mount as a guard of honor testifying to its sanctity."[85] According to most authorities, guarding the Temple is not part of the worship in the Temple; consequently, it is permitted even in a state of ritual impurity, without the special process of purification required for the Temple worship itself. Moreover, the activity takes place outside the actual Temple Mount.[86]

In the year 2000, the self-styled Temple Guard began its operations. The guard recruited students from "Od Yosef Chai" yeshiva, sometimes before their military service. According to publications, three years after its establishment the number of volunteers was in excess of two thousand. Each volunteer undertakes to serve at least one day a year.[87] According to the instruction sheet given to the guard, the purpose of the activities is as follows:

1. To prevent Jews entering the Temple Mount area in a state of ritual impurity, that is, without prior purification in the Mikveh, or wearing leather shoes (which are prohibited in the Temple area). This goal is to be achieved through explanations, not coercion, and is intended to prevent offenses and maintain the dignity of the site.
2. Awe of the Temple—the guarding of the Temple Mount is intended to encourage respect for the sight, and to allude to the guarding of the Mount during Second Temple times.
3. Through its mere presence and through its educational efforts, the Temple Guard emphasizes that the most sacred site of the

Jewish people is the Temple Mount and not the Western Wall. "Without the Temple Mount, walls have no special sanctity. Even those who currently only visit the Western Wall plaza must realize that they come to the Western Wall only in order to be as close as possible to the place beyond the wall."

4. Through their actions, the Guard demands "the restoration of the usurped property to its owners, and the application of the sovereignty of the Jewish people to the place David purchased for a full price thousands of years ago."[88]

The instruction sheet emphasizes that all guards must wear the special uniform and hat with a distinctive label. The guards must be dressed neatly and wear shoes, not sandals. The aim of these instructions is to ensure that the guard has an authoritative appearance. "While we do not force anyone to obey us, the message of removing impurity and of the awe of the Temple should be presented in an authoritative manner." Further instruction states that the guards may not carry weapons, and must not enter into verbal or physical confrontations with any person. The guards are not to enter the Temple Mount site itself in their uniform.[89]

The Movement for the Establishment of the Temple rented a building in the Jewish Quarter of the Old City as a preparatory base for visits to the Temple Mount. The premises were used as the headquarters of the Temple Guard. After the Temple Mount was closed to Jewish visitors (in September 2000), and due to budgetary difficulties, the center was closed. A year later, an alternative site was found for the activities on Chabad Street in the Jewish Quarter. The center also includes a model of the Third Temple built by artist Chaim Klorfin.[90]

Once a month, the El Har Hamor association organizes the large-scale "March around the Gates" together with the Temple Guard. This event does not arouse any rabbinical opposition. The opposite is the case; the decision of the El Har Hamor association to initiate this activity was precisely because of its uncontroversial nature. Standing by the gates symbolizes yearning, but without any active intervention.[91] This event enjoys widespread rabbinical support. Some of the leading Religious Zionist rabbis signed a declaration encouraging people to join the Temple Guard.[92] Chaim Druckman, the head of the Bnei Akiva yeshivot, urged his institutions to send their students to the "March around the Gates." Thousands of youngsters come to the event every month. The activities include dancing (with strict separation between men and women), prayers, and speeches by Religious Zionist leaders. I have been told informally that the Yesha Council covers most of the costs of these events, although it does not publicize this fact. The weekly newspaper *Besheva*, which belongs to the settlers' radio station *Arutz Sheva* (Channel Seven), stated that the event has been supported by the Yesha Council since 2001.[93] The Temple Guard volunteers organize these events and distribute publicity material. A smaller weekly march is also held every Tuesday; the participants walk around the gates of the Temple Mount and recite Psalms.

The activities of the Temple Guard fall well within the confines of Halachic legitimacy relating to the Temple Mount and the encouragement of longing for the construction of the Temple. The organization's activities are ostensibly inoffensive and beyond reproach, and it has not encountered any opposition. The Temple Guard has managed to locate an activity relating to the Temple Mount that promotes the issue among the religious public while avoiding controversy. At the same time, it must be noted that from the standpoint of the "Od Yosef Chai" yeshiva circle, this activity constitutes the beginning of a full-fledged military organization—a step that clearly challenges the status and legitimacy of the institutions of state.

Conclusion

A systematic examination of the program presented by Yitzhak Ginzburg and his immediate circle reveals an approach that seeks to undermine the institutions of the Israeli regime, and expresses sympathy for zealous actions that are contrary to religious law and could be considered to constitute terror. This group also operates a pseudomilitary unit that operates around the gates of the Temple Mount.

The popularity of this circle is particularly notable among a disaffected section of the settler public who are facing a crisis of identity on the national and religious levels, and which is tempted to adopt an independent approach without regard for the conventional rabbinical authorities of Religious Zionism. This group has been augmented by Chabad Hassidim who, since the death of the last Rebbe, have fragmented into a number of groups and factions. Menachem Friedman believes that the messianic tension created in Chabad following the death of the movement's leader cannot be considered static, since messianic movements can never remain in one place.[94] Ginzburg's approach clearly has the potential to attract these Hassidim, and this has been seen in practice. The combination of messianic activism and radical nationalism, as manifested in Ginzburg's writings and activities, is an appealing blend for Chabad Hassidim. The late Rebbe also tended to embody this combination, though Ginzburg's approach is markedly more activist and forceful. The result is the establishment of a bridge between two groups, Chabad Hassidim on the one side, and the ideological hardcore of the settler movement on the other. Members of these two groups can easily be identified sitting alongside each other in Ginzburg's classes. The same phenomenon was seen in 2004, when Chabad followers joined the protest by the "residents of the hills" against the eviction of the Chavat Maon settlement. This combination has created a fundamentalist potential that, in certain circumstances and after further development, could form the vanguard for a theocratic revolution.

In light of Ginzburg's involvement in "problematic" issues such as entering the Temple Mount at the present time; preparations for the building of the Temple; and his support for extreme acts of violence such as that committed by Baruch Goldstein, together with his unequivocally anti-Arab positions, it is reasonable to ask how such a figure has gained such broad support. With the exception of Yoel Bin-Nun, almost no notable authority has challenged Ginzburg's views,[95] and students from the national religious yeshivot attend his classes. Once again, the answer lies in the dilemma faced by the mainstream religious establishment in coping with zealous figures who express in public what many of their followers feel in private. This explains how Ginzburg's association can secure substantial state funds, and it explains why even his most extreme comments do not meet with any public opposition among the religious population. Even the state authorities seem to have preferred to take a laissez-faire approach to his comments—even when he was prosecuted for some of his writings, the state chose to reach a compromise and the case ended in a plea bargain.[96]

Ginzburg's attempt to create a theocratic messianic activism obliges him to seek ways to overcome the obstacle of messianic passivity as established in the Halacha. Judaism is characterized by an internal theological tension between its fundamental component of messianic anticipation and the restrictions it imposes on itself to prevent the realization of this ideal. Growing tension has forced radical ideological circles to break this pattern. The solution they have found is based on radical nationalism, and on the introduction of a narrative reminiscent of that of totalitarian regimes. Ginzburg and his students and supporters may be seen as a vanguard for the proposed fundamentalist revolution.

Concluding Remarks

In his book *Between Routine and Renewal* (1973), Yaakov Levinger (the brother of Moshe Levinger, one of the founders of Gush Emunim) discussed the question of the renewal of the sacrifices on the Temple Mount. He described the discussions that took place within the Orthodox world during the nineteenth and twentieth centuries, and examined the Halachic problems regarding the site. Levinger emphasized his dissatisfaction with the prevailing agreement among all the religious authorities—from the yeshiva circles to the university circles, from Chief Rabbi Isser Yehuda Unterman to Isaiah Leibovitch—that the renewal of the sacrificial work is currently out of question. In response, he chose to sharpen the dilemma and to reduce it into two major decisions:

> We cannot under any circumstances avoid this question of the renewal of the sacrifices. If we do avoid it, our children will not again ask "what is this work for you,"[1] but on the contrary—"what isn't this work for you?" They will ask, rightfully, why we ignore all the commandments that are written in the Bible and in the Oral Law relating to the priestly work, and we shall not know how to answer. It is time for us to decide between two alternatives: Should we see the Temple work as an integral part of the Jewish faith throughout the generations, and hence also for future generations, or should we see it as part of an ancient past—faithful to cultural conditions that are no longer valid? If we take the former approach, we should integrate this subject in our programmatic ideology and strive with all our force to study the sacrificial law, and to make religious decisions on all the questions we will encounter in our way. If we prefer the latter course, we should openly confess that our requests for

161

the renewal of the sacrifices were no more than "the whisper of the starling" and it is about time to stop expressing them.[2]

For many years, Religious Zionist society in Israel indeed chose to evade discussion of the role of the Temple in the State of Israel; as Levinger notes, this debate was postponed to a distant future beyond real time. Twenty years after the publication of *Between Routine and Renewal*, however, a mood of change was starting to develop, and growing circles started to integrate the question of entering into the Temple Mount into their religious agenda. A sign of this change may be seen in the ruling of the Council of Yesha Rabbis in 1996 permitting Jews to enter the Temple Mount; as Levinger predicted, it was the younger generation that led this renewed enthusiasm. Since the reopening of the site in 2003, thousands of students from the nationalist yeshivot have visited the Mount.

This process was due in part to the intensive activities of the movements examined in the present study, whose narrative has become more dominant among Religious Zionist circles. The demand for the Temple and the demand to pray on the Mount were indeed raised immediately after the site was taken by the Israeli Defense Forces in 1967, but at the time these demands were confined to the discourse of minority groups. The political process initiated by the Israeli governments with the Arab neighbors and the Palestine Liberation Organization, and the willingness of Israel to give up land for peace, created a theological shock wave. Only then were broad circles within the religious world willing to accept the claims of the Temple Mount activists.

I will now discuss another angle of the influence of the narrative of the Temple Mount movements in society at large: to what extent have their theocratic and revolutionary approaches penetrated wider audiences? This question is particularly significant given the reality that, from their perspective, the crisis situation facing the settlement movement has grown worse. During the summer of 2005, Gush Emunim was forced to witness the evacuation of the settlements from the Gaza Strip, as well as four settlements in northern Samaria, as part of Israel's Disengagement Plan. This study has argued that a crisis situation due to a political process can create a counterreaction of messianic radicalization. Has the Disengagement strengthened revolutionary trends in response? A follow-up question may also be posed: what leads a fundamentalist movement that has accepted that state and its institutions and worked under the cover of state power to stand against it and to become rebellious?

All fundamentalist movements interact with the outside world: some retreat from society to avoid the influence of secularity; others attempt to take over the secular regime. The study *Strong Religion* by Gabriel A. Almond, Scott R. Appleby, and Emmanuel Sivan attempts to define fundamentalists' interactions with the world in four categories: world conqueror, world transformer, world creator, and world renouncer.[3]

The world creators and the world renouncers focus mainly on strengthening their own enclaves. World renouncers build high walls that separate them from the rest of society. They do not want to transform or to conquer the world; they just want to be left alone. The world creators also focus on their own enclaves, but they show some interest in changing the secular world—at least for their own benefit. Accordingly, the world creators act to recruit more followers of their lifestyle from the secular world.

It is tempting to argue that all fundamentalist movements hold a desire to conquer the world. But the desire to rule society can be moderated. Fundamentalist world transformer movements know that they must act in a specific time and place, and if they do not hold enough power, they may lose their battle. Therefore, fundamentalist movements may adjust themselves to the secular regime and be part of it, while at the same time rejecting the values of the secular world. To pursue their goals, they may enter the political arena and try to influence the institutions, structures, laws, and customs of their society.

This analysis can help us understand Israeli Orthodoxy. The Haredi community in Israel may fit the model of *world renouncer*. This community lives within its own enclave, separating itself from the rest of the society geographically and physically. The Haredim have their own neighborhoods and towns, and are also separated by virtue of their distinctive dress. This community has its own alternative institutions and does not use the power of the state to control its members. All these features are designed to ensure its segregation from the secular world.[4]

The Shas movement may be considered a *world transformer*. Shas is an ethnic religious political party representing the interests of religious Mizrachi Jews in Israel. Their leaders are part of Israel's political structure, using the political system to achieve their religious goals.[5] Similarly, Gush Emunim may also be considered a world transformer movement; its theological framework views redemption as a gradual process that may take centuries, so that their mission is protracted. When the movement was established, it encountered some opposition from government circles, but following the victory of the Likud Party in the 1977 elections, there was an increase in support for the movement's goals. The fact that today two hundred fifty thousand Israelis live in the West Bank is a direct result of the movement's ongoing political campaign over the past three decades. This movement is an effective extraparliamentary power that knows how to manipulate the political system for its own goals. Therefore, the religious ideal of a Jewish theocracy and the construction of the Third Temple was postponed to the end of the messianic process, and only after a profound process of repentance among the secular society was achieved. The movement's immediate goals were in settling in the land and in the hearts of the greater population.

The followers of the Temple Mount movements disagree with this approach, demanding proactive efforts to build a Torah state and to build the Temple. They claim that these actions are essential to create the process of repentance; only after the achievement of the sublime goal of redemption—the construction of the Temple—will the masses find their way to faith, so the theocracy should come before the educational process. In this sense, they may fit the *world conqueror* model. Their sense of urgency distinguishes them from the mainstream of Gush Emunim, as a result of their fear of messianic failure. This is the reason for their protest against the "tranquility" of the mainstream religious society.

We may then wonder what creates a change in the behavior of a fundamentalism movement, pushing it from a world transformer stance into the role of a world conqueror. In what circumstances can the movement no longer maintain its position of reconciliation vis-à-vis the world and must it move to a mode of assault? In what conditions can the movement no longer conform to the secular regime?

I attempt to answer this question by reference to several similar processes that have been seen in the Middle East. The Society of Muslim Brothers in Egypt underwent an analogous process of development. The movement was established by Hassan Al-Banna in 1928 to correct the flaws of the Egyptian society, which were perceived as the result of the penetration of modernization and Western values into Egyptian society. Al-Banna saw the establishment of a theocratic regime as the sublime goal of his movement, but the way to achieve it was through mass education and re-Islamization of the society. The movement was persecuted by the Egyptian regime and Al-Banna was assassinated (1949). This situation stayed the same after the change of regimes in Egypt, and the rise of Gamal Abed Al-Nasser to power (1952), with the help of the Muslim Brothers. The new regime continued to persecute its followers. As a result, the movement underwent a period of radicalization, and some of its followers turned to terrorism. Followers of the Muslim Brothers were responsible for the assassination of Egyptian president Anwar Saadat (1981).[6]

Shiite revolutionaries in Iran learned the lesson of the Society of Muslim Brothers. Due to the ongoing failure of the Muslim Brothers to win the hearts of the masses in Egypt, a new tactical approach was taken. The conclusion the Shiites reached was that they must first take control of the state powers, and only then restore the rule of Islam over the populace. This conclusion was also the result of the severe government persecution of religious leaders in Iran. All those pushed the religious establishment into the revolution that took place in 1979.[7]

Accordingly, the feelings of persecution and siege led Muslim fundamentalists toward patterns of revolution and violence. I argue that the Gush Emunim establishment is also undergoing a religious crisis due to the government's decision to uproot settlements. As a result, theocratic and revolutionary sentiments can find roots within the hearts of many followers. The Disengagement put the main stream of the Gush followers in front a theological dilemma—how can they continue their bond and their partnership with a state that "betrays" her destiny for the full redemption, giving up holy lands and dismantling settlements?

Therefore, the Disengagement Plan presented the rabbis of Gush Emunim with a religious dilemma. How could it be that, despite their devotion and intense efforts, a plan had emerged that was contrary to the Divine promise for the Land of Israel? Accordingly, they almost unanimously opposed the Disengagement Plan and the eviction of settlements, and the Religious Zionist public was also virtually united in its campaign against the plan.[8]

Although the struggle against the Disengagement did not lead to an open rebellion against the army and the state institutions, it seems that during the period of the struggle the theocratic narrative penetrated into the discourses of the mainstream of Gush Emunim rabbis. Thus, Avraham Shapira, who formerly served as a Chief Rabbi of Israel (1983–1993), and who, at the time of his declaration, headed the prestigious Mercaz Harav yeshiva, stated that he supported the idea of soldiers refusing to obey the eviction orders. Some seventy rabbis joined Shapira's statement urging soldiers not to participate in the uprooting of Jews.[9]

After the implementation of the Disengagement, many of the religious leaders of Gush Emunim called more assertively to replace the secular state with a theocracy. By way of example, the weekly broadsheet *Ma'ayanei Hayeshu'ah*, of which seventy thousand copies are distributed at Religious Zionist synagogues, abandoned its usual format on the weekend following the completion of the withdrawal. In place of discussions on the weekly Torah portion and regular opinion columns, the broadsheet presented a manifesto in shades of black and white. The main content of this manifesto was as follows:

> We shall not forget—We shall not forgive
> The anger and offense within us,
> The tremendous sense of frustration,
> Must be channeled in one single direction: working among the
>   masses.
> We must seize control of the mechanisms of government, gradually
>   seize control of the State of Israel. We must transform it from "the
>   first step of our redemption" to our actual, real redemption;

From "the foundation of God's throne in the world" to God's actual,
real throne in the world.
We will remember the adage "little by little,"[10] in order not to fall into
"End calculating,"
Yet we will demand of ourselves a full effort to observe "in its time—
I shall expedite."[11] ...
With God's help, we shall live to see the building of the Temple and
the actual return of the Divine Presence to Zion.[12]

A similar message was offered by Rabbi Hanan Porat, one of the
founders of Gush Emunim and, for many years, a Member of Knesset for
right-wing parties (1981–2003). He presented his thoughts on the failure
of the struggle against the Disengagement Plan in the opening column
in *Me'at Min Ha'or*, another weekly broadsheet distributed in Religious
Zionist synagogues. Porat's conclusion was that the failure of the struggle
against the Disengagement demanded the development of new horizons
relating to government and power. Porat urged all the religious streams—
Haredim, Orthodox, and "traditional"—to present an agreed-upon leader
who could compete for power:

> And now, dear friends, let us ask ourselves whether the time has
> not come for all those who adhere to the faith of Israel to make
> a great effort to seek a worthy candidate to lead the nation, of
> whom we might say, to quote Maimonides: "Whom the Lord your
> God shall choose.".... Given the great crisis we have reached, has
> the time not, at least, come to overcome all the disagreements
> and personal rivalries, to join forces and parties, and to present
> the most appropriate person, in the present circumstances, as
> candidate for prime minister?[13]

It seems that the crisis of the evacuation opened a space for the theocratic post-Zionist narrative as a counterreaction, and it strengthened the
feelings of despair from the secular state. After the failure of the struggle
led by the Yesha Council that supported nonviolent disobedience and resistance to violence,[14] more voices claimed that if in the future the religious system will have to get into a braking battle, it should be much more
aggressive. We can assume that further political plans that hold a vast settlements evacuation plans to determine the final borders of the state will
be addressed in a more proactive approach from the settlers.

An example for that assumption came only half a year after the implementation of the Disengagement. It was when the Israeli government
evicted a further settlement, Amona, after the High Court of Justice ruled
that this was located on private Palestinian land and was therefore

unlawful (February 2006). During this eviction, a fiercer and more violent clash was seen between the police forces and the settlers, and the approach advocating a militant struggle apparently gained strength. The violent incidents during the evacuation of Amona were not similar to the passive struggle of the Disengagement. The question that was raised from the event was whether this incident is a preview to much extreme occurrences in trying to evacuate the established settlements in the West Bank.

Those trends are the result of ongoing activities of the Temple Mount followers among the Religious Zionist camp, and the changes that are being held in it allows major ideological modifications. This is the moral power of the Temple Mount movements and this is their importance. The theocratic discourse and the demand for immanent redemption made by a political act penetrated deep into the heart of the religious establishment. It was caused by identity crisis and a growing fear of prophetic failure. Those sentiments, which were related to a minority group, became over the year a sentiment of a much greater population. The solutions that were developed by the Temple followers over two decades ago are now being adopted by the core of the Religious Zionist religious establishment.

I will end with the "prophecy" of the historian Jacob Katz. Katz argued that quasi-messianic Zionist rhetoric encouraged and promoted the identification of the Zionist endeavor as a messianic process, providing the energy for the establishment of the State of Israel. However, "the messianic tradition does not contain a blueprint for the conduct of the state. Upon the realization of this fact the future of Israel may depend."[15] It is important to internalize the words of this great historian.

Notes

Introduction

1. This was illustrated dramatically in the outbreak of the second Intifada, which erupted after the visit by Ariel Sharon to the Temple Mount in September 2000, although the demonstrations were probably planned at an earlier stage.

2. *Decision of the Committee of Yesha Rabbis*, 18 Shevat 5756 (February 7, 1996) (in Hebrew).

3. The status quo on the Temple Mount dictates that the Mount itself is a Muslim place of worship, whereas the Western Wall is a Jewish place of worship. Accordingly, Jewish prayer is forbidden on the Temple Mount. The only Jewish ritual activity possible on the Temple Mount is silent, solitary prayer. See Shmuel Berkovits, *The Temple Mount and the Western Wall in Israeli Law* (Jerusalem: Jerusalem Institute for the Study of Israel), 2001.

4. This figure is mentioned in a letter from Minister Tzahi Hanegbi published in *Yibaneh Hamikdash*, 206/7 (5765 - 2005): 9 (in Hebrew). It may be assumed that most of those who visit the Temple Mount do so for religious reasons, since there has not been any dramatic resurgence of Jewish tourism to the site.

5. For further discussion of the prohibition of *Karet*, see *The Talmudic Encyclopedia* (5733 - 1972): 7, 14:553 (in Hebrew). On the Halachic debate concerning entering the Temple Mount, see *The Oral Law*, 10 (5728 - 1967) (in Hebrew); Shaul Sheffer, *The Temple Mount: Crown of Our Glory* (Jerusalem: Yefe Nof, 5729 - 1968) 61–68 (in Hebrew). A list of thirty Halachic rulings prohibiting Jews from entering the Temple Mount was collected by scholars at Ateret Cohanim yeshiva and collated in the booklet *Iturei Kohanim*, 16 (5746 - 1985) (in Hebrew). The list includes the ruling issued by the Chief Rabbinate in 1967. In a groundbreaking step, the leaders of the Haredi public at the time added their names to this ruling, as did Rabbi Zvi Yehudah Hacohen Kook, head of Mercaz Harav yeshiva.

6. Michael Avi-Yonah, *Jerusalem the Holy* (New York: Schoken Books), 1976.

7. Ibid.

8. Shmuel Berkowits, *The Wars of the Holy Places: The Struggle for Jerusalem and the Holy Sites in Israel, Judea, Samaria and the Gaza Strip* (Or Yehuda: Hed Artzi, 2000), 11–13 (in Hebrew); for a detailed bibliography on the subject, see nn. 27–29 and n. 43 therein.

9. Berkovits, *The Temple Mount.*

10. Jody Elizabeth Myers, *Seeking Zion: Modernity and Messianic Activism in the Writings of Tsevi Hirsch Kalischer* (Oxford: Littman Library of Jewish Civilization), 2003.

11. David Zohar, *Jewish Commitment in a Modern World: R. Hayyim Hirschensohn and His Attitude towards Modernity* (Jerusalem: Shalom Hartman Institute, 2003) (in Hebrew).

12. Hayyim Hirschensohn, *Malki Ba-Kodesh A* (St. Louise: Moinstel Printing, 1919), 10–13, 41–89 (in Hebrew).

13. Zeev Ivinsky, *Lechi: The First Pliers B* (Tel-Aviv: Avraham Stern Yair, 2003), 473–474 (in Hebrew).

14. Shaul Avishai, *Brit Hachashmonaim,* thesis in partial fulfillment of the requirements for a master's degree at the Hebrew University, Jerusalem, 1993 (in Hebrew).

15. Jacob Katz, "Orthodoxy in Historical Perspective," *Studies in Contemporary Jewry* 2 (1986): 9–10.

16. Aviezer Ravitzky, "'Forcing the End': Zionism and the State of Israel as Antimessianic Undertakings," *Studies in Contemporary Jewry* 7 (1991): 34–67.

17. Dov Schwartz, *Faith at the Crossroads: A Theological Profile of Religious Zionism* (Leiden: Brill, 2002); and *Religious Zionism between Reality and Messianism* (Tel-Aviv: Am Oved, 1999) (in Hebrew).

18. Gideon Aran, "A Mystic-Messianic Interpretation of Modern Israeli History: The Six Day War as a Key Event in the Development of the Original Religious Culture of Gush Emunim," *Studies in Contemporary Jewry* 4 (1988): 263-275.

19. David Berger, *The Rebbe, the Messiah and the Scandal of Orthodox Indifference* (London: Littman Library of Jewish Civilization, 2001).

20. Neri Horwitz, "Careful—Explosive!" *Meimad* 21 (2001): 15–18 (in Hebrew).

21. Neri Horwitz, *Jews!—The Shtetl is Burning: Torah Judaism between the 1991 Elections and the 2001 Elections* (Jerusalem: Floersheimer Public Research Institute, 2002) (in Hebrew).

22. Asher Cohen, *The Tallit and the Flag: Religious Zionism and the Vision of the Torah State in the Early Years of the State* (Jerusalem: Ben Zvi Institute, 1998), 48–55 (in Hebrew).

23. Gideon Aran, "From Pioneering to Torah Studying," in Avi Sagi and Dov Schwartz (eds.), *A Hundred Years of Religious Zionism: Ideological Concepts C* (Ramat Gan: Bar Ilan Press, 2003), 31–72 (in Hebrew).

24. Yoni Garb, "The Young Guard of the National Religious Party and the Ideological Roots of Gush Emunim," in Asher Cohen and Yisrael Harel (eds.),

Religious Zionism: The Era of Change (Jerusalem: Bialik Institute, 2005), 171–200 (in Hebrew); and Eliezer Don Yihya, "Stability and Change in the Camp Party: The National Religious Party and the Young Revolution," *State, Government and International Relations* 14 (5740 - 1980): 25-52 (in Hebrew).

25. Aran, "A Mystic-Messianic Interpretation of Modern Israeli History," *Studies in Contemporary Jewry* 4 (1988): 263–275.

26. Yoram Kirsh, "Woman Status at the Religious Zionist Society: Battles and Achievements," in Asher Cohen and Yisrael Harel (eds.), *Religious Zionism: The Era of Change* (Jerusalem: Bialik Institute, 2005), 386–421 (in Hebrew).

27. Shlomo Aviner (ed.), *Torat Eretz Yisrael: The Teachings of HaRav Tzvi Yehuda HaCohen Kook* (Jerusalem: Torat Eretz Yisrael, 1991).

28. Ibid.

29. Shlomo Kaniel, "Hill Dwellers: Are They the Biblical Pioneers?" in Asher Cohen and Yisrael Harel (eds.), *Religious Zionism: The Era of Change* (Jerusalem: Bialik Institute, 2005), 533–558 (in Hebrew).

30. Martin E. Marty and R. Scott Appleby, "Conclusion: An Interim Report on a Hypothetical Family," in Martin E. Marty and R. Scott Appleby (eds.), *Fundamentalism Observed* (Chicago: University of Chicago Press, 1991), 814–842.

31. Dov Schwartz, *The Messianic Idea in Jewish Medieval Literature* (Ramat Gan: Bar Ilan University Press, 1997), 9–12 (in Hebrew). Amos Funkenstein seeks to define apocalyptic messianism as "passive" messianism because the expectation is that it will begin through Divine intervention, whereas naturalistic messianism is defined as "active" and committed to human action. See his *Maimonides: Nature, History and Messianic Beliefs* (Tel-Aviv: Modesbooks, 1997), 74–75. In my opinion, the literature supports the conclusion that the active phenomena of current messianism often reflected quintessentially apocalyptic motives; accordingly, it is erroneous to refer to the latter approach as "passive."

32. Nancy T. Ammerman, "North American Protestant Fundamentalism," in Martin E. Marty and R. Scott Appleby (eds.), *Fundamentalism Observed* (Chicago: University of Chicago Press, 1991), 1–65.

33. Schwartz, *Faith at a Crossroads.*

34. Leon Festinger, Henry W. Riechen, and Stanley Schachter, *When Prophecy Fails* (Minneapolis: University of Minnesota Press, 1956).

35. John Stone has collected fourteen case studies of scholarly work on failed prophecies in his *Expecting Armageddon: Essential Readings in Failed Prophecy* (London: Routledge, 2000). Most of the case studies did not follow the cognitive dissonance theory.

36. Ibid., 1–29.

37. Nadav Shragai, *Mount of Dispute* (Jerusalem: Keter, 1995) (in Hebrew).

38. Gershom Gornberg, *The End of Days: Fundamentalism and the Struggle for the Temple Mount* (New York: Free Press, 2000).

39. Avi Dichter, paper presented at Herzliya College, December 16, 2003.

1. Religious Zionism and the Temple Mount Dilemma

1. *Ha'aretz*, May 17, 2007.

2. See Dov Schwartz, *Faith at a Crossroads: A Theological Profile of Religious Zionism* (Leiden: Brill, 2002), 156–192.

3. The pamphlet *Sefatei Cohen* (Lips of a Priest), dated 12 Heshvan 5681 (October 24, 1920), appears in Shlomo Zalman Shragai, "Rabbi Avraham Hacohen Kook, Zatsa"l, on the Restitution of the Place of Our Temple to the People of Israel," *Sinai* 85 (5739 - 1978): 193–198 (in Hebrew).

4. Ibid., 194.

5. Despite the importance of this thinker in consolidating the Orthodox approach, he has received limited research attention. Further biographical details on the Chafetz Chaim may be found in Eliezer Schweid, *Between Orthodoxy and Religious Humanism* (Jerusalem: Van Leer Institute, 1977), 12–14 (in Hebrew).

6. For example: Babylonian Talmud, Tractate Soteh, 49b.

7. See Robert Wistrich, "In the Footsteps of the Messiah," in Gideon Shimoni and Robert S. Wistrich (eds.), *Theodor Herzl, Visionary of the Jewish State* (Jerusalem: Hebrew University and Magnes Press, 1999), 231–238.

8. Israel Meir Hacohen, *Anticipation of Redemption* (Bnei Brak: Netzach, 5749 - 1989), 11 (in Hebrew).

9. Ibid., 17–24.

10. Shragai, "Rabbi Avraham Hacohen Kook," 197.

11. Avraham Yitzhak Kook, *Mishpat Cohen* (Jerusalem: Rav Kook Institute, 5745 - 1984), 183 (in Hebrew).

12. Hayyim Hirschenshon, *Malki Ba-Kodesh* A, St. Louise: Moinster Printing, 1919), 10–13, 41–89 (in Hebrew). Cf. Zalman Koren, "Memorandum concerning the Position of the Chief Rabbinate through the Generations on the Question of the Temple Mount," *Iturei Kohanim* 201 (5761 - 2000), 27–32 (in Hebrew).

13. Rabbi Kook's position differs from the position of Rabbi Avraham Ben David, who argued that since the destruction of the Temple the physical site where the Temple stood had lost its sanctity. According to Ben David's approach, the site can only regain its sanctity when the Temple is reconstructed; accordingly, the prohibition of *Karet* does not apply to those entering the Temple Mount area in this era. Rabbi Kook rejected this approach, preferring that of Maimonides, who

argued that the sanctity of the Temple Mount site is eternal because of the primeval sanctification of the site by God as the dwelling place of the Divine Presence. See Kook, *Mishpat Cohen*, 182–227.

14. Ibid., 203.

15. Koren, "Memorandum," 29–30.

16. Shlomo Aviner, *Lemikdashcha Tov* (Jerusalem: Hava Library, 5760 - 1999), 12–13 (in Hebrew).

17. For his detailed reasoning, see Bezalel Jolti, "The Prohibition on Entering the Temple Mount in These Times," *Oral Law* 10 (5728 – 1967), 39–45 (in Hebrew).

18. A summary of the meeting held on 1 Sivan 5727 (June 11, 1967) can be found in Yoel Cohen, "The Chief Rabbinate and the Temple Mount Question," in Itamar Warhaftig (ed.), *The Israel Chief Rabbinate: Seventy Years since Its Foundation* B (Jerusalem: Heikhal Shlomo, 5762 - 2003), 769 (in Hebrew).

19. Nadav Shragai, *Mount of Dispute* (Jerusalem: Keter, 1995), 29–35 (in Hebrew).

20. Cohen, "The Chief Rabbinate," 772–773.

21. The correspondence between Goren and Begin is quoted in Shlomo Goren, *The Temple Mount* (Tel-Aviv: Sifrei Hemed, 5752 - 1991), 32–33 (in Hebrew).

22. Ibid., 460–502.

23. Mordechai Eliyahu, "Torah Opinion," *Techumin C* (5752 - 1991): 432 (in Hebrew).

24. Cohen, "The Chief Rabbinate," 775–776.

25. See *Announcement of the Committee of Yesha Rabbis* (5752 - 1992).

26. "Halachic Ruling of the Union of Rabbis for the People of Israel and the Land of Israel," in *Organ of the Yesha Rabbis* 25 (5755 - 1994), 1 (in Hebrew).

27. *Organ of the Yesha Rabbis* 26 (5755 - 1994), 1.

28. *Yibaneh Hamikdash* 111–112 (5757 - 1996), 4.

29. *Decision of the Committee of Yesha Rabbis*, 18 Shevat 5766 (1996).

30. *Organ of the Yesha Rabbis*, Tevet 5755 (December 1994). The request was not signed by Rabbi Shlomo Aviner, a member of the secretariat. Rabbi Eliezer Melamed from the settlement Har Beracha signed the request, although in the same issue of the *Organ* he wrote that the time had not yet come to engage in warfare to fight for the right to build the Temple and reinstate the sacrifices. In national terms, however, he argued that it should be demanded that Israel control the site.

31. Aviner, *Lemikdashcha Tov*.

32. *Hatzofe*, September 12, 2003 (in Hebrew).

33. Ibid., September 19, 2003.

34. Ibid., October 10, 2003.

35. Ibid., September 19, 2003.

36. Ibid.

37. Ibid., October 10, 2003.

38. Ibid., February 2, 2004. This figure is based on information from the Israel Police.

39. See n. 3.

40. *Me'at Min Ha'or* 251 (5761 - 2001), 3 (in Hebrew).

2. Messianic Naturalism as the Product of Dissonance

1. *Yibaneh Hamikdash* 29 (5750 - 1990), 19–23 (in Hebrew).

2. From Ministry of Finance statistics quoted on their Web site: *www.mof.gov.il*.

3. Israel Ariel, "Two Thousand Years in One Instant: An Interview with Rabbi Israel Ariel," *Or Chozer* 7 (5751 - 1991). The interview was reprinted in full in *Yibaneh Hamikdash* 44 (5751 - 1991): 15–17, and *Yibaneh Hamikdash* 45 (5751 - 1991): 18–19 (in Hebrew).

4. Ibid.

5. Ibid.

6. *Lekhatchilah* 47 (5759 - 1999) (in Hebrew).

7. Israel Ariel, *Prayerbook for the Temple (Sefarad Ritual)* B (Jerusalem: Karta, 1996), 524–525 (in Hebrew). In a memorandum he prepared for the Chief Rabbinate, Rabbi Zalman Koren stated that Rabbis Zvi Yehuda Hacohen Kook and David Hacohen were taken to the Western Wall through the Lions' Gate and the Temple Mount without their knowledge. See Zalman Koren, "Memorandum concerning the Position of the Chief Rabbinate through the Generations on the Question of the Temple Mount," *Iturei Kohanim* 201 (5761 - 2000): 27–32 (in Hebrew).

8. Ariel, *Prayerbook for the Temple*, 525–526.

9. *Lekhatchilah* 47 (5759 - 1999).

10. Haggai Segal, *Yamit, The End: The Struggle to Stop the Withdrawal from Sinai* (Jerusalem: Beit El Library, 5759 - 1999), 249 (in Hebrew).

11. Ibid., 271–276.

12. Ehud Sprinzak, *The Ascendance of Israel's Radical Right* (New York: Oxford University Press, 1991), 261–274.

13. *Yibaneh Hamikdash* 29 (5750 - 1990): 19–23 (in Hebrew).

14. Ibid.

15. Ibid.

16. *Drishat Hamikdash* 3 (5763 - 2003) (in Hebrew).

17. Ariel, *Prayerbook of the Temple*, 527–528.

18. Ibid., 529.

19. *Yibaneh Hamikdash* 29 (5750 - 1990): 19–23.

20. Ibid.

21. Ariel's characterization of this particular aspect as political is presumably due to the presence of divergent positions regarding the location of the Kodesh Kodashim (the place where the Divine spirit resides). The generally accepted position is the Foundation Stone in the Dome of the Rock. However, the architect Tuvya Sagiv argues, based on his own examination, that the location of the Kodesh Kodashim is actually in the plaza between the Mosque of Omar and the Al-Aqsa Mosque (see Tuvya Sagiv, "The Place Is to the South," *Techumin* 14 (5754 - 1984): 437–472 [in Hebrew]). The importance of Sagiv's approach from the perspective of the Temple Mount activists is that there is no need to demolish the mosques on the Temple Mount to rebuild the Temple. It may be assumed that this is the "political question" to which Ariel alludes.

22. *Yibaneh Hamikdash* 29 (5750 - 1990): 19–23.

23. *What's New in the Temple Institute*, Rosh Hashanah 5754 - 1994 (in Hebrew).

24. *What's New in the Temple Institute*, Ellul 5752 - 1992 (in Hebrew).

25. *What's New in the Temple Institute*, Pessah 5753 - 1993. The Chief Rabbinate faced sharp criticism following its participation in these conferences. *Ha'aretz* journalist Uzzi Benziman wrote that the Chief Rabbis must recognize that their official status requires them to refrain from encouraging the conference, since they bear responsibility for maintaining the peaceful status quo on the Temple Mount: "Experience shows, as Rabbis Shapira and Eliahu are also aware, that there are enough people willing to translate academic conclusions into action" (*Ha'aretz*, October 16, 1989).

26. *What's New in the Temple Institute*, Ellul 5752 - 1992.

27. *What's New in the Temple Institute*, Pessah 5754 - 1994.

28. *What's New in the Temple Institute*, Nissan 5756 - 1996.

29. Gershom Gornberg, *The End of Days: Fundamentalism and the Struggle for the Temple Mount*, (New York: Free Press, 2000), 174.

30. *What's New in the Temple Institute*, Hanukkah 5752 - 1992.

31. *What's New in the Temple Institute*, High Holydays 5757 - 1997.

32. A comprehensive list is provided in *What's New in the Temple Institute,* Tishrei 5757 - 1997.

33. *What's New in the Temple Institute,* Pessah 5752 - 1992.

34. *What's New in the Temple Institute,* Rosh Hashanah 5754 - 1994.

35. *What's New in the Temple Institute,* High Holydays, 5757 - 1997.

36. *What's New in the Temple Institute,* Pessah 5754 - 1994.

37. See www.templeinstitute.org/red_heifer/red_heifer_contents.htm.

38. *What's New in the Temple Institute,* High Holydays 5755 - 1995.

39. Israel Ariel, *In the Footsteps of the Temple Candelabrum* (Jerusalem: Temple Institute, 1997) (in Hebrew).

40. *Besheva,* December 25, 2003 (in Hebrew). See also: *What's New in the Temple Institute,* Tishrei 5760 - 2000.

41. *Drishat Hamikdash* 4 (5763 - 2003) (in Hebrew).

42. From the conference program, 16 Nissan 5761 - 2001.

43. *Ha'aretz,* July 8, 2004.

44. This assertion is supported by Sarina Chen, whose master's thesis includes an extensive examination of the first conference of the movement. See her *Central Themes in the Rhetoric's and the Practice of the Temple Admirers,* master's thesis, Hebrew University, Jerusalem, 2001, 15, 32–37 (in Hebrew).

45. From the institute's Web site: *www.temple.org.il.*

46. The late Minister of Religious Affairs, Professor Avner Chai Shaki (who served in this position from 1990 to 1992) visited the institute several times. One occasion was during a conference of the heads of religious councils held at the institute. The director-general of the Ministry for Jerusalem Affairs, Yeshayahu Barzel, arranged a special grant for the institute. Two members of the National Religious Party faction on the Jerusalem city council, Shmuel Meir and Shmuel Shakedi, managed to secure municipal support. Yitzhak Kolitz participated in a conference organized by the institute. These visits were reported by the institute newsletter *What's New in the Temple Institute* during 5752 (1992) and 5753 (1993).

47. Karen Armstrong, *The Battle for God: Fundamentalism in Judaism, Christianity and Islam* (New York: Knopf, 2000), xii–xvi.

3. The Movement for Redemption and Yehuda Etzion

1. The comments were quoted in *Nekudah* 88 (1985), 25 (in Hebrew).

2. Yochai Rudik, *Land of Redemption* (Jerusalem: Institute for the Study of the Thought of Rabbi A. Y. H. Kook Zatza"l, 5749 - 1989), 168 (in Hebrew).

3. Dov Schwartz, *Challenge and Crisis in the Circle of Rabbi Kook* (Tel-Aviv: Am Oved, 2001), 85 (in Hebrew).

4. Ibid., 86.

5. For a more detailed examination of this aspect, see Dov Schwartz, *The Land of Reality and Imagination: The Status of the Land of Israel in Religious Zionist Thought* (Tel-Aviv: Am Oved, 1997), 101–127 (in Hebrew).

6. Shlomo Aviner, ed., *Conversations of Rabbi Zvi Yehuda: The Land of Israel* (Jerusalem: Hava Library, 5765 - 2005), 269 (in Hebrew).

7. For further details on the exiled underground activists, see Shlomit Eliash, *The Exiles of the Etzel and Lechi* (Ramat Gan: Bar Ilan University, 1996) (in Hebrew).

8. The biographical details about Ben Dov were taken from several sources. An autobiographical essay quoted in Nadav Shragai, *Mount of Dispute* (Jerusalem: Keter, 1995) 101–103 (in Hebrew); Haggai Segal, *Dear Brothers: The West Bank Jewish Underground* (New York: Beit-Shamai, 1988), 46–50; and illuminating comments by Israel Eldad relating to key milestones in the life of Ben Dov in his accompaniment to Ben Dov's book *Prophecy and Tradition in Redemption* (Tel-Aviv: Yair, 5739 - 1978) (in Hebrew).

9. Ben Dov, *Prophecy and Tradition*; and *Jewish Redemption in Political Crisis* (Jerusalem: Hamatmid, 5720 - 1959) (in Hebrew).

10. Gershom Scholem, "The Crisis of Tradition in Jewish Messianism," *The Messianic Idea in Judaism* (New York: Shocken Books, 1971), 49–77.

11. This hypothesis is presented by Amnon Raz Karkotzkin in his article "Between 'Brit Shalom' and the Temple: The Dialectics of Redemption and Messianism following Gershom Scholem," *Theory and Criticism* 20 (2002): 87—112 (in Hebrew).

12. Gerald Kromer, "Praying with a Gun: Religious Motifs in the Propaganda of Lechi," in Chaim Genizi (ed.), *Religion and Underground: The Land of Israel during the Mandate Period* (Bnai Brak: Moreshet, 5755 - 1995), 65–66 (in Hebrew).

13. For further details on Eldad, see David Ohana, "Nietzsche Left and Right: The National Existentialism of Israel Eldad," in Yaacov Golomb (ed.), *Nietzsche in Hebrew Culture* (Jerusalem: Magnes, 5762 - 2002), 251–277 (in Hebrew); and Yosef Heller, *Lechi: Ideology and Politics* (Jerusalem: Keter, 1989), 135–139 (in Hebrew).

14. Israel Eldad, "What Dictatorship Do We Require?" *Sulam* 27 (5712 - 1952): 5 (in Hebrew).

15. Ibid., 7.

16. Israel Eldad, "Some Simple Comments about Jewish Morality," *Sulam* 58 (5714 - 1954): 11–12 (in Hebrew).

17. Mordechai Shalev, "Beyond Humanism," *Sulam* 35 (5712 - 1952): 6–9 (in Hebrew).

18. Anita Shapira, "Zionism and Political Messianism," *Walking toward the Horizon* (Tel-Aviv: Am Oved, 1988), 11–13 (in Hebrew).

19. Ben Dov, *Jewish Redemption*, 29.

20. Ibid., 69–72.

21. Ibid., 171–180.

22. Ibid., 183.

23. Aviezer Ravitzky, *Messianism, Zionism, and Jewish Religious Radicalism* (Chicago: University of Chicago Press, 1993), 10–39.

24. Ben Dov, *Prophecy and Tradition*, 60–61.

25. Ben Dov, *Jewish Redemption*, 183–210.

26. Jacob L. Talmon, *The Myth of the Nation and the Vision of Revolution* (London: Secker and Warburg; and Berkeley and Los Angeles: University of California Press, 1981), 475–503.

27. Ze'ev Sternhal, Mario Sznajder, and Michal Asheri, *The Foundations of Fascism* (Tel-Aviv: Am Oved, 1992), 20–21, 328 (in Hebrew).

28. Ben Dov, *Jewish Redemption*, 239.

29. Ibid., 239.

30. For further discussion of this issue, see Gershon Weiler, *Jewish Theocracy* (Tel-Aviv: Am Oved, 1976), 13–87 (in Hebrew).

31. Ben Dov, *Jewish Redemption*, 37.

32. Ben Dov, *Prophecy and Tradition*, 53–55.

33. Ibid., 83–89.

34. Ibid., 128–158.

35. Ibid., 158–160.

36. Ibid., 167–168.

37. Ben Dov, *Jewish Redemption*, 241–242.

38. Ibid., 245–252.

39. Ibid., 262.

40. Ibid., 265–280.

41. Ibid., 288–318.

42. Gershon Gorenberg, *The End of Days: Fundamentalism and the Struggle for the Temple Mount* (New York: Free Press, 2000), 116–117.

43. Yehuda Etzion, "At Last to Raise the 'Flag of Jerusalem,'" *Nekudah* 93 (5745 - 1985), 22–24 (in Hebrew).

44. Yehuda Etzion, "Rabbi Feinstein Comes to Israel," *Nekudah* 98 (5746 - 1986), 14–15, 36.

45. Etzion, "At Last," 24.

46. Ibid., 22–23.

47. Ibid.

48. Yehuda Etzion, "From 'The Flag of Jerusalem' to 'The Movement for Redemption,'" *Nekudah* 94 (5746 - 1986), 29 (in Hebrew).

49. For further details, see Shragai, *Mount of Dispute*, 99–100.

50. Gideon Aran, *The Land of Israel between Religion and Politics: The Lessons of the Movement to Stop the Withdrawal from Sinai* (Jerusalem: Jerusalem Institute for Israel Studies, 1985), 1–8 (in Hebrew).

51. Yehuda Etzion, *The Temple Mount* (Jerusalem: Self-published, 5745 - 1985), 3 (in Hebrew).

52. Ibid.

53. Etzion, "At Last," 28.

54. Ehud Sprinzak, *Between Extra-Parliamentary Protest and Terror: Political Violence in Israel* (Jerusalem: Jerusalem Institute for Israel Studies, 1995), 108–110 (in Hebrew).

55. Yehuda Etzion, "And It Came to Pass after Yigal Sent His Hand against Isaac," *Labrit* 3 (5756 - 1996): 40–43.

56. The Jerusalem District Court convicted three residents of Bat Ayin of attempting to murder the girls; they received sentences of between twelve and fifteen years in prison. Other residents from the settlement were suspected of committing additional terrorist acts, including attacks on Arabs, plotting to attack Israeli politicians, and even planning to blow up mosques around the country, including the mosques on the Temple Mount. However, all the remaining suspects were released due to lack of evidence. See *Ma'ariv*, September 23, 2003 (in Hebrew).

57. The principles of the Movement for Redemption were presented at a members meeting in Bat Ayin and appear in *Labrit* 1 (5753 - 1993): 4–5, 19 (in Hebrew).

58. The document is quoted in Sprinzak, *Between Extra-Parliamentary Protest and Terror*, 110.

59. Yehuda Etzion, "More Strength to the Rabbis," *Nekudah* 188 (5756 - 1996): 50–54 (in Hebrew).

60. His action did not prevent his promotion in the IDF; while he was refusing to perform reserve duty, he was promoted to the rank of major.

61. *Ha'aretz*, December 11, 1997.

62. Amnon Ramon, *The Attitude of the State of Israel and the Different Sections of the Jewish Public to the Temple Mount (1967–1996)* (Jerusalem: Jerusalem Institute of Israel Studies, 1997), 17–20 (in Hebrew).

63. The minutes of the meeting appear in *Yibaneh Hamikdash* 18 (5749 - 1999): 27–28 (in Hebrew).

64. *Hatzofeh*, September 12, 1992; see also *Yibaneh Hamikdash* 53 (5752 - 2002): 13–17 (in Hebrew).

65. From a position paper distributed at the conference under the heading "The Second Annual Conference of Temple Supporters" (Tishrei 5760 - 2000) (in Hebrew).

66. According to the personal testimony of Baruch Ben-Yossef in a conversation with the author on May 24, 2001.

67. Yehuda Etzion, *See and Renew: For the Sanctification of Israel and the Times* (Jerusalem: Self-published, 5755 - 1985), 6–7 (in Hebrew).

68. Richard Landes, "Millennialism in the Western World," *Encyclopedia of Millennialism and Millennial Movements* (New York: Routledge, 2000), 257–265.

69. Yehuda Etzion, "'We Cannot Ascend and See?' We Can: Now Let's Get Moving!" *Nekudah* 134 (5750 - 1990), 34–37 (in Hebrew).

70. See Rudik, *Land of Redemption*, 186–188 (in Hebrew).

71. Michael Karpin, *Murder in the Name of God: The Conspiracy against Yitzhak Rabin* (Tel-Aviv: Zemora Beitan, 1999) (in Hebrew).

72. Indeed, he published an article in *Nekudah* under the title "This Is the Theory of Zealotry," in which he defined himself as part of the chain of zealots committed to "fulfilling God's word—as they best understand it and in their sacred responsibility." See *Nekudah* 179 (5754 - 1994), 26–30 (in Hebrew).

73. Thus, for example, the former leader of the National Religious Party, Effi Eitam, in an interview for *Ha'aretz* following his election to his position, was unable to conceal his admiration for Etzion's devotion to the struggle for the Temple Mount, admitting that Etzion's commitment to this issue is far greater than his own. *Ha'aretz*, Supplement, March 22, 2002, 20 (in Hebrew).

74. Sprinzak, *Between Extra-Parliamentary Protest and Terror*, 110.

4. Gershon Salomon and the Temple Mount Faithful

1. For further details on these riots, see Nadav Shragai, *Mount of Dispute* (Jerusalem: Keter, 1995) 340–363 (in Hebrew).

2. Although it seems probable that the ensuing riots were planned in advance.

3. From a movement publication.

4. With the exception of one occasion in April 1981.

5. Shmuel Berkovitz, *The Temple Mount and the Western Wall in Israel Law* (Jerusalem: Jerusalem Institute for Israel Studies, 2001).

6. Interview with Yoel Lerner, September 2, 2004.

7. *El Rosh Hahar* 2 (5745 - 1985), 1 (in Hebrew).

8. The journalist Nadav Shragai discussed the events in detail in *Mount of Dispute*, 340–363.

9. Interview with Yosef Elboim, September 2, 2004.

10. *Kol Ne'emanei Har Habayit* 3 (5748 - 1988), 3 (in Hebrew).

11. See n. 5.

12. The declaration was published on 1 Ellul 5748 (1988), and appears in *Yibaneh Hamikdash* 14 (5749 - 1989): 16 (in Hebrew).

13. *El Rosh Hahar* 1 (5744 - 1984), 2–3 (in Hebrew).

14. *El Rosh Hahar* 2 (5745 - 1985), 7.

15. *El Rosh Hahar* 3 (5745 - 1985), 2, 7.

16. Zeev Ivinsky, *Lechi: The First Pliers* B. (Tel-Aviv: Avraham Stern Yair, 2003), 473–474 (in Hebrew).

17. See *Yibaneh Hamikdash* 63 (5752 - 1992): 9–10 (in Hebrew). Articles in *Yibaneh Hamikdash*, the newsletter of the Movement for the Establishment of the Temple, have urged its members not to denigrate the Temple Mount Faithful, particularly in their comments to the media; this in itself reflects the tension between the two movements. See *Yibaneh Hamikdash* 11 (5749 - 1989): 8 (in Hebrew).

18. Stanley Goldfoot is a colorful and exceptional figure. As a young man during the British Mandate period in Palestine, he worked as a reporter for international English-language newspapers, while at the same time volunteering in the Lechi underground movement. Goldfoot was active in the Temple Mount Faithful, and his journalistic contacts helped him develop contacts with the fundamentalist Christian community, to whom he introduced Salomon. For more about Goldfoot's unique life and activities over five decades, see *Kol Ha'ir*, October 13, 1995, 44–49 (in Hebrew).

19. The address of the Web site is www.templemountfaithful.org.

20. Yaakov Ariel, *On Behalf of Israel: American Fundamentalist Attitudes toward Jews, Judaism, and Zionism 1865–1945* (New York: Carlson, 1991).

21. Catherine Wessinger, *How the Millennium Comes Violently: From Jonestown to Heaven's Gate* (New York: SevenBridge Press, 2000).

22. *The Voice of the Temple Mount*, 2001.

23. It is interesting to compare this ideology to the stages included in the dispensionalist perspective, which currently dominates fundamentalist evangelical thinking. This approach also believes that the redemption of the world comprises distinct stages, and the current reality constitutes the next-to-last stage before the return of Jesus.

24. *The Voice of the Temple Mount*, Spring 2000.

25. *The Voice of the Temple Mount*, 2000.

26. www.templemountfaithful.org/help.htm.

27. Yaakov Ariel, *Philosemites or Antisemites?* (Jerusalem: SICSA, 2002), 37.

28. Shragai, *Mount of Dispute*, 295–298.

5. Haredi Messianistic Activism

1. Lilly Weissbord, "Gush Emunim Ideology: from Religious Doctrine to Political Action," *Middle Eastern Studies* 18, no. 3 (1982): 265–275.

2. From a letter inviting readers to join the movement, dated 25 Kislev 5748. The letter was attached to *Yibaneh Hamikdash* 2 (5748 - 1987) (in Hebrew).

3. Yosef Elboim, *Yibaneh Hamikdash* 8 (5748 - 1988): 7–8 (in Hebrew).

4. With the exception of individual prayers, the only religious ritual the movement managed to hold on the Temple Mount was the "Pouring of Water"—an ancient ceremony relating to the duties of the High Priest during the pilgrimages at the Festival of Tabernacles while the Temple was standing. These activities were undertaken in a clandestine and secret manner. The movement also attempted to perform the Passover sacrifice on the Temple Mount, but without success. See Nadav Shragai, *Mount of Dispute* (Jerusalem: Keter, 1995), 149–155 (in Hebrew).

5. *Yibaneh Hamikdash* 1 (5748 - 1987), n.p. (in Hebrew).

6. Ibid.

7. Yosef Elboim, "Choosing a Name for Our Group," *Yibaneh Hamikdash* 2 (5748-1988): n.p. (in Hebrew).

8. *Yibaneh Hamikdash* 16 (5749 - 1989): 22–23.

9. *Yibaneh Hamikdash* 20 (5749 - 1989): 1.

10. Kach later split, and Benjamin Zeev Kahane became leader of a faction known as Kahane Chai. For further details on the split, see Ehud Sprinzak, *Between Extra-Parliamentary Protest and Terror: Political Violence in Israel* (Jerusalem: Jerusalem Institute for the Study of Israel, 1995), 124–126 (in Hebrew).

11. Thus, the "Desecration of God's Name" in Kahanist thought comes to be synonymous with the very presence of non-Jews in the Land of Israel. Those who deny the Jewish right to the Land of Israel effectively deny the exclusive author-

ity of God, and therefore desecrate His name. Accordingly, action to sanctify God's name means to remove non-Jews from Israel. For details on the ideology of Kach, see Aviezer Ravitzky, "The Roots of Kahanism: Consciousness and Political Reality," *Jerusalem Quarterly* 39 (1986): 90–108; and Ehud Sprinzak, *The Ascendance of Israel's Radical Right* (New York: Oxford University Press, 1991), 211–250.

12. Benjamin Zeev Kahane, "The Temple Mount: A Religious War," *Yibaneh Hamikdash* 45 (5751 - 1991): 7–10 (in Hebrew).

13. Pinchas Gil, "Down with the Occupation!" *Yibaneh Hamikdash* 48 (5752 - 1992): 7.

14. David Shafir, "Sanctifying the Name Is Greater than Desecrating the Name," *Yibaneh Hamikdash* 48 (5752 - 1992): 8–11 (in Hebrew).

15. Benjamin Zeev Kahane, "Lovers of God: Hate Evil," *Yibaneh Hamikdash* 51 (5752 - 1992): 27–29 (in Hebrew).

16. Elitzur Segal, "Looking for the Way," *Yibaneh Hamikdash* 51 (5752 - 1992): 30–31 (in Hebrew).

17. Yosef Elboim, "Understand This and We Shall Rejoice in His House," *Yibaneh Hamikdash* 51 (5752 - 1992): 31–35 (in Hebrew).

18. James Barr, *Fundamentalism* (London: SCM Press, 1981), 1–11; Hava Lazarus-Yafeh, "Contemporary Fundamentalism: Judaism, Christianity, Islam," in Laurence J. Silberstein (ed.), *Jewish Fundamentalism in Comparative Perspective* (New York: New York University Press, 1993), 49–50.

19. Israel Bartal, "True Knowledge and Wisdom: On Orthodox Historiography," *Studies in Contemporary Jewry* 10 (1994): 178–192.

20. See introduction.

21. A body enforcing moral norms within the Haredi society.

22. The details of this affair appear in *Yibaneh Hamikdash* 18 (5749 - 1989): 9–22 (in Hebrew).

23. Aviezer Ravitzky, *Messianism, Zionism, and Jewish Religious Radicalism* (Chicago: University of Chicago Press, 1993), 10–39.

24. Shir Hashirim Rabba 2:7.

25. Ravitzky, *Messianism*, 63–70.

26. Dov Elboim, "A Conversation with a Well-Known *Admor (Rebbe)* in Bnei Brak," *Yibaneh Hamikdash* 30 (5750 - 1990): 31 (in Hebrew). The author is the uncle of Yosef Elboim.

27. "Over the past century, Heaven has taught us that success smiles on those who take the initiative in our land, while those 'Sages' who sat still suffered a total failure. . . . Even ignoramuses know that in our world, the 'world of action,' mundane actions cause sublime actions. . . . Even after the sea miraculously parts,

passive observation is not enough—one must enter the sea thereby." Yosef Elboim, *Yibaneh Hamikdash* 22 (5750 - 1990): 33 (in Hebrew).

28. Yosef Elboim, "Renewing the Worship in This Time," *Yibaneh Hamikdash*
34 (5750 - 1990): 4 (in Hebrew).

29. Ariel Israel, "Two Thousand Years in One Instant: An Interview with
Rabbi Israel Ariel," *Or Chozer* 7 (5751 - 1991) (in Hebrew); repr. *Yibaneh Hamikdash*
45 (5751 - 1991): 18–19 (in Hebrew).

30. See introduction.

31. For example, Gershom Scholem, *Devarim Bego* (Tel-Aviv: Am Oved,
1976), 178–188 (in Hebrew).

32. An enlightening example of the use of the works of Maimonides to justify messianic activism may be found in David Berger's studies of the Chabad
movement: *The Rebbe, the Messiah and the Scandal of Orthodox Indifference* (London:
Littman Library of Jewish Civilization, 2001). A further example of activism appears in the thoughts of Rabbi Tsevi Hirsch Kalischer as presented in Jody Elizabeth Myers, *Seeking Zion: Modernity and Messianic Activism in the Writings of Tsevi
Hirsch Kalischer* (Oxford: Littman Library of Jewish Civilization, 2003).

33. David Hartman, *Crisis and Leadership: Epistles of Maimonides* (Philadelphia:
Jewish Publication Society of America, 1985), 179–186

34. Jacob Katz, "The Historical Figure of Rabbi Tsevi Hirsch Kalischer," in
Jewish Nationalism: Essays and Studies (Jerusalem: Zionist Library, 5739 - 1980),
285–307 (in Hebrew).

35. Michael Silber, "The Beating Jewish Heart in a Foreign Land," *Cathedra*
73 (1994): 84–105 (in Hebrew).

36. The journal of the Movement for the Establishment of the Temple
reprinted the third chapter of Kalischer's *Drishat Zion*, which addresses the proposal to reinstate the sacrifices; see *Gevinei Kruz: The Mouthpiece of the Movement for
the Establishment of the Temple* 4–5 (5761 - 2001) (in Hebrew).

37. Midrash Tanchuma, Pekudei.

38. Several articles examining this subject from a religious perspective have appeared in recent years, a fact that in itself emphasizes the topical nature of the debate. See, for example Mordechai Eliyahu, "The Third Temple: Of Man or of
Heaven?" *Conclave for Study of the Laws of Sanctity and the Temple* (5743 - 1983): 71–76
(in Hebrew); Shlomo Goren, "The Commandment to Build the Temple in the Present Time," *Iturei Kohanim* 31 (5748 - 1988): 13–21 (in Hebrew); Yitzhak Shapiro
and Yosef Peli, *To the Hill of the Levonah: In Favor of Ascending the Temple Mount and
Demanding the Temple* (Yizhar: Self-published, 5759 - 1999) (in Hebrew); and Shlomo
Aviner, *Lemikdashcha Tov* (Bet El: Hava Library, 5760 - 2000) (in Hebrew).

39. Elboim, "Renewing the Worship," 3–5.

40. Ariel, "Two Thousand Years in One Minute," 17.

41. For example, "We would remain silent in the face of the antics of these agitated youths [the laying of the cornerstone of the Temple by the Temple Mount Faithful movement] did they not carry a torch of flame that is liable to kindle the entire region as in a bonfire. . . . Of this it is written: Do not ascend, for the Lord is not among you, and be not like those thugs who are liable to bring disaster upon the people dwelling in Zion and elsewhere" (*Hamodi'a*, 21 Tishrei 5750- 1990) (in Hebrew).

42. Aviezer Ravitzky, "Models of Peace in Jewish Thought," *With God's Knowledge: Studies in the History of Jewish Thought* (Jerusalem: Keter, 1991), 13–33 (in Hebrew).

43. David Chazoni, "Your Plowshares into Swords: The Lost Biblical Peace," *Techelet* 3 (5758 - 1998): 78–101 (in Hebrew).

44. Editorial comment, *Yibaneh Hamikdash* 47 (5752 - 1992): 1–3 (in Hebrew).

45. Elitzur Segal, "The Temple and Pikuah Nefesh," *Yibaneh Hamikdash* 7 (5748 - 1988): 2–5 (in Hebrew).

46. The delicate balance between "innovation" and "reform" is discussed in the studies of Menachem Friedman, "The Chief Rabbinate: An Unsolvable Dilemma," *Medina, Mimshal Veyachasim Beinleumi'im* 3 (1972): 121–122 (in Hebrew); and *Society and Religion: Non-Zionist Orthodoxy in the Land of Israel* (Jerusalem: Yad Yitzhak Ben-Zvi, 5738 - 1978), 67–70 (in Hebrew).

47. Menachem Friedman, "Jewish Zealots: Conservative versus Innovative," in Laurence J. Silberstein (ed.), *Jewish Fundamentalism in Comparative Perspective: Religion, Ideology, and the Crisis of Modernity* (New York: New York University Press, 1993), 148–149.

48. For a detailed discussion of the traditional Jewish perceptions of redemption, see Amos Funkenstein, *Maimonides: Nature, History and Messianic Beliefs* (Tel-Aviv: Modesbooks, 1997), 74–75; and Jacob Katz, "Israel and the Messiah," *Commentary* 73 (1982): 34–41.

49. *Yated Hashavua*, 8 Av 5751 - 1991, 9 (in Hebrew).

50. Yonina Talmon, "Millenarian Movements," *Archives européennes de sociologie* (1966), 177–178.

51. David Bar Haim, "What Is the True Path?" *Yibaneh Hamkidash* 37 (5750 - 1990): 32–35 (in Hebrew).

52. Jacob Katz, "Orthodoxy as a Response to the Departure from the Ghetto and the Reform Movement," *Halacha Bametzar* (Jerusalem: Magnes, 5752 - 1992), 9–20 (in Hebrew).

53. David Shafir, "Guardians of the City or Destroyers of the City," *Yibaneh Hamikdash* 7 (5748 - 1988): 8 (in Hebrew).

54. One of the leaders of the Lithuanian section of the Haredi community. Rabbi Eliashiv was chosen to head the community after the death of Rabbi Eliezer Shach in 2002.

55. Dov Elboim, *"A Conversation."* This article was written in the form of the record of a discussion between Elboim and "a famous rabbi from Bnei Brak." It is interesting to note that Elboim presents a line of argument that is similar to that which emerged in the Mizrachi movement, with a distinction between religious-rabbinical leadership and political leadership, whereby the political leaders engaged in "limited consultation" with the rabbis. On this arrangement, see Asher Cohen, *The Tallit and the Flag: Religious Zionism and the Vision of the Torah State in the Early Years of the State* (Jerusalem: Ben Zvi Institute, 1998), 90 (in Hebrew).

56. Yehudah Shaviv, "The Double Destruction," *Nekudah* 173 (Kislev 5744 - 1984), 29 (in Hebrew); repr. *Yibaneh Hamikdash* 75 (5754): 9.

57. On the status of the "great leaders of the generation" (*gedolei hador*), see Menachem Friedman, *The Haredi Society: Sources, Trends and Processes* (Jerusalem: Jerusalem Institute for Israel Studies, 1991), 40–51, 104–114 (in Hebrew); and Binyamin Baron, *The Torah Opinion and Faith in the Sages in Haredi Thought*, master's thesis, Hebrew University, Jerusalem, 1996 (in Hebrew).

58. Elizur Segal, "The Path of the Movement for the Establishment of the Temple," *Yibaneh Hamikdash* 27 (5750 - 1990): 35 (in Hebrew).

59. Yechiel Etz-Shemen [Yosef Elboim], *Yibaneh Hamikdash* 73 (5754 - 1994): 9–10 (in Hebrew).

60. Avigdor Elboim (published in the name of Baruch Ben-Yossef), "If at Least They Dwelt in the Land of Israel and Shouted Messiah," *Yibaneh Hamikdash* 77 (5754 - 1994): 7–8 (in Hebrew).

61. Talmon, "Millenarian Movements," 167–168.

62. Lazarus-Yafeh, "Contemporary Fundamentalism," 45–51.

63. In 2005 a self-proclaimed "Sanhedrin" was established in Israel under the leadership of Rabbi Adin Steinsaltz. Behind the scene stood the leaders of the Temple Mount movements as Rabbi Israel Ariel and Yosef Elboim. See *Ha'aretz*, November 3, 2005.

64. *Yibaneh Hamikdash* 16 (5749 - 1989): 2.

65. *Yibaneh Hamikdash* 23 (5750 - 1990): 2.

66. *Yibaneh Hamikdash* 27 (5750 - 1990): 2–5.

67. *Yibaneh Hamikdash* 57 (5752 - 1992): 16. The argument here is based on a Talmudic saying that "occupation" implies a physical presence in a place and public familiarity with this presence. "How have you inherited? By presence" (Kiddushin 26).

68. Elitzur Segal, "Sovereignty on the Temple Mount", *Yibaneh Hamikdash* 5 (5748 - 1998): 5–6 (in Hebrew).

69. The position of Ben-Yossef was supported by Mordechai David Ackerman, an Orthodox rabbi from the Lithuanian stream and a member of the move-

ment. Yosef Rotstein of the Gur Hassidic sect completely rejected Ben-Yossef's arguments, which he believed were motivated by political considerations and intended solely for publicity. Eliezer Rokach, a Belzer Hassid, stated that "we must do things that lead to the goal, and not cross over every limit, since this might push us backwards." The entire debate was published in *Yibaneh Hamikdash* 59 (5753 - 1993): 8–16, 22 (in Hebrew).

70. *Yibaneh Hamikdash* 64 (5753 - 1993): 3–5 (in Hebrew).

71. The idea of allowing the Arabs to control the Temple Mount was first raised during the peace negotiations between Israel and Egypt. Menachem Begin, the Israeli prime minister at the time, proposed that a Vatican-type model be applied to the Temple Mount, providing a special legal status for functionaries on the site (the Waqf). At the Camp David conference (July 11–24, 2000), Israel suggested several models for Palestinian management of the site, including waiving Israeli sovereignty. All the proposals were rejected by the Palestinians. For details, see Menachem Klein, "The Temple Mount: A Challenge, Threat and Promise on the Path to a Political Agreement," in Yitzhak Ritter (ed.), *Sovereignty of God and Man: Sanctity and Political Centrality on the Temple Mount* (Jerusalem: Jerusalem Institute of Israel Studies, 2001), 269–296 (in Hebrew).

72. *Yibaneh Hamikdash* 71 (5754 - 1994): 2.

73. Further information about the Temple Feasts may be found in Amnon Ramon, "Beyond the Western Wall: The Attitude to the Temple Mount on the Part of the State of Israel and Sectors of the Jewish Public (1967–1999)," in Yitzhak Ritter (ed.), *Sovereignty of God and Man: Sanctity and Political Centrality on the Temple Mount* (Jerusalem: Jerusalem Institute of Israel Studies, 2001), 127–130 (in Hebrew).

74. *Decision of the Committee of Yesha Rabbis*, 18 Shvat 5756 (February 7, 1996) (in Hebrew).

75. See *Going Up in Sanctity: A Journal for Matters of the Temple and its Sanctities*, vols. 1–8 (5760–5763 - 2000–2003) (in Hebrew); Yehudah Shaviv and Israel Rosen, *Come and Let Us Ascend: A Collection of Articles and Manifestos on the Subject of the Temple Mount in Modern Times* (Gush Etzion: Zomet, 5763 - 2003) (in Hebrew); Shlomo Aviner, *Maimonides' Laws of Messiah* (Jerusalem: Hava Library, 5763 - 2003) (in Hebrew); *Nekudah* 242 (May 2001), 17–29; and Hillel Weiss, *The King's Path* (Tel-Aviv: Ariel Institute, 5763 - 2003) (in Hebrew).

76. The umbrella organization of settlements in Yesha—Judea, Samaria, and the Gaza Strip.

6. Yitzhak Ginzburg and "Od Yosef Chai" Yeshiva

1. See Shaul Avishai, *Brit Hachashmonaim*, thesis in partial fulfillment of the requirements for a master's degree at the Hebrew University, Jerusalem, 1993 (in Hebrew).

2. The biographical information about Ginzburg was taken from pnimi.org.il, the Web site of the Gal Eini association, which disseminates his philosophy, and from *Besheva*, 26 Sivan 5763 (2003), 32–33 (in Hebrew).

3. In July 2003, the State Attorney's Office decided to indict Ginzburg for racial incitement in his book *The Immediate Imperative: Root Treatment* (Rehovot: Gal Eini, 5761 - 2001) (in Hebrew). The indictment was canceled after Ginzburg issued a public apology.

4. Hava Lazarus-Yafeh, "Contemporary Fundamentalism: Judaism, Christianity, Islam," in Laurence J. Silberstein (ed.), *Jewish Fundamentalism in Comparative Perspective* (New York: New York University Press, 1993), 49.

5. See: Ephraim Auerbach, *The Sages: Their Concepts and Belifs* (Jerusalem: Magnes Press, 1979), 649–692; and Yaakov Blidstein, "The Political Dimension of the Concept of the Choice of the Jewish People in the Literature of the Sages," in Shmuel Almog and Michael Hed (eds.), *The Concept of Election among the Jews and Other Nations* (Jerusalem: Shazar Center, 2001), 99–120 (in Hebrew).

6. David Novak, *The Election of Israel* (Cambridge: Cambridge University Press, 1995), 215–218.

7. Moshe Halamish, "Some Aspects of the Question regarding the Kabbalists' Attitude toward the Non-Jews," in Moshe Halamish and Assa Kasher (eds.), *Israeli Philosophy,* (Tel-Aviv: Papyrus, 5743 - 1983), 49–71 (in Hebrew).

8. See Moshe Halamish, *The Theoretical Approach of R. Schneur Zalman of Ladi and Its Relationship to Kabbalism and Early Hassidism*, thesis in partial fulfillment of the requirements for the degree of doctor of philosophy at the Hebrew University, Jerusalem, 5736 - 1975, 165 (in Hebrew). See also Yoram Jacobson, "The Visceral Soul in the Thought of Rabbi Schneur Zalman of Ladi," in *Mesuot*, Michael Oron and Amos Goldreich (eds.), (Jerusalem: Bialik Institute, 5744 - 1984), 224–242 (in Hebrew).

9. Yitzhak Ginzburg, *The Dominion of Israel* A (Rehovot: Gal Eini, 5759 - 1999), 213–218 (in Hebrew).

10. Israel Ariel (Leibowitz), *His Pride Is in Israel* (Rehovot: Gal Eini, 5760 - 2000) (in Hebrew).

11. A fierce debate ensued after Ginzburg was quoted in the media as claiming that the commandment "You shall not murder" does not apply to the killing of Arabs. Yoel Bin-Nun, a leader of Gush Emunim, strongly attacked this statement. The journal *Nekudah* reported at length on the dispute between the two figures. See *Nekudah* 131 (1989), 14–15 (in Hebrew). The following issue continued the examination of the Halachic aspects of this debate.

12. *Jewish Week*, April 12, 1996, 12, 31.

13. Gershon Weiler, *Jewish Theocracy* (Tel-Aviv: Am Oved, 1976), 72–86 (in Hebrew).

14. A further example of this is the approach of the Maharal (Rabbi Judah Loew) of Prague. See Jacob Katz, *Between Jews and Gentiles: The Attitude of Jews to Their Neighbors during the Medieval and Early Modern Period* (Jerusalem: Bialik Institute, 5737 - 1977), 131–144 (in Hebrew).

15. This messianic principle was also embodied in the approach of Rabbi Kalischer and the perception of the "messianic ascents" among the students of the Gra. See Jody Myers, *Seeking Zion: Modernity and Messianic Activism in the Writings of Tsevi Hirsch Kalischer* (Oxford: Littman Library of Jewish Civilization, 2003).

16. This claim was raised, for example, in Michael Ben Horin (ed.), *Baruch Is the Man: A Memorial Book for the Holy Dr. Baruch Goldstein, May God Avenge His Blood* (Jerusalem: Medinat Yehuda, 5755 - 1995) (in Hebrew).

17. Ehud Sprinzak, *Brother against Brother: Violence and Extremism in Israeli Politics from Altalena to the Rabin Assassination* (New York: Free Press, 1999), 241–243.

18. *Ha'aretz*, December 25, 2001 (in Hebrew).

19. *Encyclopedia Judaica*, vol. 10 (1971), 977–986.

20. Yitzhak Ginzburg, "Baruch Is the Man," in Michael Ben Horin (ed.), *Baruch Is the Man: A Memorial Book for the Holy Dr. Baruch Goldstein, May God Avenge His Blood* (Jerusalem: Medinat Yehuda, 5755—1995), 25 (in Hebrew).

21. Ibid., 27–28.

22. Israel Yuval, "Revenge and Curse, Blood and Libel," *Zion* 58 (5753 - 1993): 63—70 (in Hebrew).

23. For more detailed discussion of the question of "holy terror," see Ehud Sprinzak, *Between Extra-Parliamentary Protest and Terror*, 124–126. It should be noted in this context that suicide is forbidden by the Halacha; only for the purpose of "sanctifying God's name" is permission granted to commit suicide.

24. Ginzburg, *Baruch Is the Man*, 32.

25. Ibid., 32–33.

26. The position of the Maharal has become the subject of a contemporary Halachic debate between those advocating collective punishment, such as Rabbi Yaacov Ariel, and those opposing this approach, such as Rabbi Shlomo Goren. See Yaakov Blidstein, "The Act of Nablus: Collective Punishment and Contemporary Halachic Thought," *'Et Hada'at* A (5757 - 1997): 48–55 (in Hebrew).

27. Ginzburg, *Baruch Is the Man*, 36.

28. "The House of Joseph," *Lehavah* 1, 5761 - 2001 (in Hebrew).

29. The perception of the zealot as simultaneously both a victim and an aggressor is one of the characteristics of religious zealotry as a sociological phenomenon. This aspect is discussed in detail in Gideon Aran, "Jewish Zealotry: Sociological Aspects," in Eyal Ynon (ed.), *The Rule of Law in a Polarized Society* (Jerusalem: Israel Democracy Institute, 1998), 63–75 (in Hebrew).

30. Ginzburg, *Baruch Is the Man*, 41.

31. This synagogue is considered the heart of the Religious Zionist establishment. The mere fact that Ginzburg gave a sermon in such an institution is further evidence of the status he has acquired among the religious population.

32. *Ha'aretz*, May 15, 2002 (in Hebrew).

33. Yonina Talmon, "Millenarian Movements," *Archives européennes de sociologie* (1966), 178.

34. Ginzburg, *The Dominion of Israel* A, 156.

35. This handwritten response was sent to me by Ginzburg's personal assistant, David Shirel, in June 2003.

36. Joseph Weiss, "A Late Jewish Utopia of Religious Freedom," *Studies in Eastern European Jewish Mysticism* (New York: Oxford University Press, 1985), 209–248.

37. The Halachic "rule of the persecutor" can be summed up by the principle "he who rises to kill you, kill him first." This rule applies in any case where a person's life is endangered; the "persecutor" may then be killed to avoid the danger. This law of self-defense applies whether or not the Sanhedrin is in existence. The obligation and right to save life applies at all times and to any person who realizes that their own life, or someone else's, is in danger. For a more detailed discussion, see Eliav Shochetman, "A Jewish Regime Cannot Be a 'Persecutor,'" *Techumin* 19 (5759 - 1999): 40–48 (in Hebrew).

38. For further discussion of the subject of religious zealotry, see Menachem Friedman, "Religious Zealotry in Israeli Society," in Salomon Poll and Ernest Krausz (eds.), *On Ethnic and Religious Diversity in Israel* (Ramat Gan: Bar Ilan University, 1975), 91–111.

39. *Lehavah* 15, 5761 - 2001 (unsigned) (in Hebrew).

40. Ibid., 9.

41. Ginzburg, *Baruch Is the Man*, 27–28.

42. Menachem Friedman, "Jewish Zealots: Conservative Versus Innovative," in Laurence J. Silberstein (ed.), *Jewish Fundamentalism in Comparative Perspective: Religion, Ideology, and the Crisis of Modernity* (New York: New York University Press, 1993), 148–163.

43. Ginzburg, *The Dominion of Israel* B, 268.

44. Ibid., 270–271.

45. Jacob Talmon, *The Origins of Totalitarian Democracy* (London: Secker and Warburg, 1955), 1–16.

46. Ginzburg, *The Dominion of Israel* B, 264.

47. Ginzburg, *The Immediate Imperative*, 29–30.

48. Ibid., 96–97.

49. Ibid., 99–100.

50. *Lehavah* 33,5762 - 2002 (in Hebrew).

51. Ginzburg, *The Dominion of Israel* B, 45–46.

52. Gabriel A. Almond, R. Scott Appleby, and Emmanuel Sivan, *Strong Religion: The Rise of Fundamentalism around the World* (Chicago: University of Chciago Press, 2003). Ginzburg and his students use the Internet quite extensively, and the Gal Eini Association uses the Web to disseminate the rabbi's writings and statements. "Od Yosef Chai" yeshiva even produced an image movie for screening on PCs.

53. Aviezer Ravitzky, *Messianism, Zionism, and Jewish Religious Radicalism* (Chicago: University of Chicago Press, 1993), 181–206.

54. Ginzburg, *The Dominion of Israel* A, 128–132.

55. *Lehavah* 5, 5761 - 2001 (in Hebrew).

56. Ginzburg, *The Immediate Imperative*, 104.

57. Ginzburg, *The Dominion of Israel* A, 267–280.

58. Ibid., 265–266.

59. Gideon Aran, "From Religious Zionism to Zionist Religion: The Roots of Gush Emunim," *Studies in Contemporary Jewry* 2 (1986): 116–143.

60. Ginzburg, *The Immediate Imperative*, 34.

61. Lazarus-Yafeh, "Contemporary Fundamentalism," 45–46.

62. Ginzburg, *The Immediate Imperative*, 143–166. For further discussion of the concept of the two messiahs, see Josef Heinemann, "The Messiah of Ephraim and the Premature Exodus of the Tribe of Ephraim," *Harvard Theological Review* 68 (1975): 1–15.

63. In 2000, the association received NIS 235,821 from the state; in 2002, NIS 238,570; and in 2003, NIS 149,952. The figures appear on the Web site of the Ministry of Finance (www.mof.gov.il). In November 2003, the support was discontinued after the Israel Movement for Progressive [Reform] Judaism wrote to the attorney-general demanding that funding be ceased in view of the association's encouragement of acts of incitement and hatred against the Arab population.

64. Ginzburg, *The Dominion of Israel* A, 129–131.

65. On the tension in Chabad regarding the identity of the Messiah, see David Berger, *The Rebbe, the Messiah and the Scandal of Orthodox Indifference* (London: Littman Library of Jewish Civilization, 2001).

66. From the Web site of the Gal Eini Association: www.pnimi.org.il/sheaelot/hakdama/mashiach.asp.

67. Yitzhak Ginzburg, "Who Holds the Key to Redemption?" *Yibaneh Hamik-dash* 8 (5749 - 1989): 14–16 (in Hebrew).

68. For further discussion of this aspect, see Moshe Idel, "Patterns of Redeeming Action in Medieval Times," in Zvi Bars (ed.), *Messianism-Mendel and Eschatology* (Jerusalem: Zalman Shazar Center, 5744 - 1984), 253–279 (in Hebrew).

69. *Lehavah* 44, 5762-2002 (in Hebrew).

70. Ibid.

71. Shlomo Aviner, *Lemikdashcha Tov* (Jerusalem: Hava Library, 5760 – 2000), 13 (in Hebrew).

72. Yitzhak Shapiro and Yosef Peli, *To the Hill of the Levonah: In Favor of Ascending the Temple Mount and Demanding the Temple* (Yitzhar: Self-published, 5759 - 1999), 157, 164 (in Hebrew).

73. Ginzburg, *Who Holds the Key?* 14.

74. *Lehavah* 7, 5763 - 2003.

75. Ginzburg, *The Dominion of Israel* A, 42.

76. Ginzburg, *The Immediate Imperative*, 95.

77. Summary of a discussion at "Od Yosef Chai" yeshiva, *Yibaneh Hamikdash*, 29 (5750 - 1990): 27–29 (in Hebrew).

78. The announcement appeared in *Yibaneh Hamikdash*, 38 (5751 - 1991): 20.

79. William Shafir, "Jewish Messianism Lubavitch-Style: An Interim Report," *Jewish Journal of Sociology* 35 (1993): 115–128; and Martin H. Katchen, "Who Wants Messiah Now? Pre-Millenialism and Post-Millenialism in Judaism," *Australian Journal of Jewish Studies* 5 (1991): 59–76.

80. "To the Mountain of Myrrh"—the name of the association is based on Song of Songs 4:6.

81. For example: Shapiro and Peli, *To the Hill of the Levonah*; and Yitzhak Shapiro and Yosef Peli, *To the Mount of Myrrh* (Yitzhar: El Har Hamor, 5757 - 1997) (in Hebrew).

82. The Chabad movement includes different factions, each of which has its own approach regarding the death of Menachem-Mendel Schneerson, the seventh leader of the dynasty. Some factions acknowledge his death; others refuse to do so; and others still admit that he died, but anticipate that he will return from the dead. See Berger, *The Rebbe*.

83. Ginzburg, *The Immediate Imperative*, 93. Under the leadership of the late Rebbe, Chabad emissaries were often referred to as "soldiers in the Lord's army." Presumably this explains the choice of this epithet for the activists in the Temple Guard.

84. Sources gathered by Yehuda Shaviv, "The Commandments of Guarding the Temple," *Zefiyah* 4 (5754 - 1994): 11–28 (in Hebrew).

85. *Hatzofeh*, May 26, 1995 (in Hebrew).

86. *Lehavah* 9, 5761-2001.

87. *Prophecy for His Dwelling-Places* 1, 5763 - 2003 (in Hebrew).

88. This discourse is typical of the approach of Gush Emunim, which seeks to manifest physical ownership of the holy sites. See Michael Feiga, *Two Maps of the West Bank* (Jerusalem: Magnes Library, 5763 - 2003), 105–107 (in Hebrew).

89. *Guide for the Guard*, on a Web site that is not currently accessible: www.3rd-temple-builders.com/guard.html.

90. *Prophecy for His Dwelling-Places* 3, 5763 - 2003.

91. This was the explanation given by Shuki Hess, the director of the association, in an interview with the newspaper *Besheva*, February 6, 2003 (in Hebrew).

92. The content of the declaration appeared in *Lehavah* 15, 5761 - 2001. The signatories included Dov Lior, Shabbtai Rappoport, Eliezer Waldman, Zefaniyah Drori, Menachem Felix, Yehuda Shaviv, Yuval Sherlo, and Israel Rosen, as well as others.

93. *Besheva*, February 6, 2003 (in Hebrew).

94. *Toar* 13, 2002, 24 (in Hebrew).

95. See n. 11.

96. For a more detailed discussion of the efforts by the legal system to address Ginzburg, see Raphael Cohen-Almagor, "Why Incitement Should be Excluded from the Principle of Freedom of Expression," *State and Society* 3, no. 1 (2003): 561–584 (in Hebrew).

Concluding Remarks

1. From the Passover Haggadah.

2. Yaakov Levinger, *Between Routine and Renewal: Trends in Contemporary Jewish Philosophy* (Jerusalem: Deot, 1973), 137 (in Hebrew).

3. Gabriel A. Almond, Scott R. Appleby, and Emmanuel Sivan, *Strong Religion: The Rise of Fundamentalism around the World* (Chicago: University of Chicago Press, 2003), 145–190.

4. Samuel Heilman and Menachem Freidman, "Religious Fundamentalism and Religious Jews: The Case of the Haredim," in Martin E. Marty and R. Scott Appleby (eds.), *Fundamentalisms Observed* (Chicago: University of Chicago Press, 1984), 197–264.

5. Shlomo Deshen, "The Emergence of the Israeli Sephardi Ultra-Orthodox Movement," *Jewish Social Studies* 11, no. 2 (2005): 77–101.

6. Laurence Davidson, *Islamic Fundamentalism* (Westport: Greenwood Press, 1998), 19–30.

7. Ibid., 31–48.

8. For a more detailed discussion of the divisions that were created among the Gush Emunim rabbis over the Disengagement, see Motti Inbari, "Fundamentalism in Crisis: The Response of the Gush Emunim Rabbinical Authorities to the Theological Dilemmas Raised by Israel's Disengagement Plan," *Journal of Church and State* 49, no. 4 (2007): 697–718.

9. A list of all the signatories appeared on the Web site of Arutz 7 on November 24, 2004 (in Hebrew). www.inn.co.il/news.php?id=92045.

10. *Kim'ah-kim'ah*, referring to the need to move toward redemption through mundane, gradual steps.

11. This is a reference to a saying in the Babylonian Talmud (Sanhedrin 98a): if the Jews have merits justifying their redemption then "I shall expedite" this, and redemption will come speedily; and if not, redemption will still come, but only "in its time" as appointed.

12. *Ma'ayanei Hayeshu'ah* 211, 22 Av 5765 - 2005 (in Hebrew).

13. *Me'at Min Ha'or* 311, 5 Ellul 5765 - 2005 (in Hebrew).

14. The Yesha Council did not promote active resistance against the evacuation, such as blocking roads. It also claimed that those acts are disturbing to the struggle. On the other hand, the council did not condemn those acts. See "Yesha Council Confesses: The Embracing Was a Mistake," www.inn.co.il, November, 14, 2005 (in Hebrew). www.inn.co.il/News/News.aspx/126462.

15. Jacob Katz, "Orthodoxy in Historical Perspective," *Studies in Contemporary Jewry* 2 (1986): 17.

Bibliography

Almond, Gabriel A., Appleby, R. Scott, and Sivan, Emmanuel. *Strong Religion: The Rise of Fundamentalisms around the World.* Chicago: Chicago University Press, 2003.

Ammerman, Nancy T. "North American Protestant Fundamentalism." In Martin E. Marty and R. Scott Appleby (eds.), *Fundamentalism Observed.* Chicago: University of Chicago Press, 1991, 1–65.

Aran, Gideon. "From Pioneering to Torah Studying." In Avi Sagi and Dov Schwartz (eds.), *A Hundred Years of Religious Zionism: Ideological Concepts C.* Ramat Gan: Bar Ilan Press, 2003, 31–72 (in Hebrew).

———. "From Religious Zionism to Zionist Religion: The Roots of Gush Emunim." *Studies in Contemporary Jewry* 2 (1986): 116–143.

———. "Jewish Zealotry: Sociological Aspects." In Eyal Ynon (ed.), *The Rule of Law in a Polarized Society.* Jerusalem: Israel Democracy Institute, 1998, 63–75 (in Hebrew).

———. *The Land of Israel between Religion and Politics: The Lessons of the Movement to Stop the Withdrawal from Sinai.* Jerusalem: Jerusalem Institute for Israel Studies, 1985 (in Hebrew).

———. "A Mystic-Messianic Interpretation of Modern Israeli History: The Six Day War as a Key Event in the Development of the Original Religious Culture of Gush Emunim." *Studies in Contemporary Jewry* 4 (1988): 263–275.

Ariel, Israel. *In the Footsteps of the Temple Candelabrum.* Jerusalem: Temple Institute, 1997 (in Hebrew).

———. *Prayerbook for the Temple (Sefarad Ritual)* B. Jerusalem: Karta, 1996.

———. "Two Thousand Years in One Instant: An Interview with Rabbi Israel Ariel." *Or Chozer* 7 (5751 - 1991). Repr. *Yibaneh Hamikdash* 44 (5751 - 1991), 15–17, and *Yibaneh Hamikdash* 45 (5751 - 1991), 18–19 (in Hebrew).

Ariel (Leibowitz), Israel. *His Pride Is in Israel.* Rehovot: Gal Eini, 5760 - 2000 (in Hebrew).

Ariel, Yaakov. *On Behalf of Israel: American Fundamentalist Attitudes toward Jews, Judaism, and Zionism 1865–1945.* New York: Carlson, 1991.

———. *Philosemites or Antisemites?* Jerusalem: SICSA, 2002.

Armstrong, Karen. *The Battle for God: Fundamentalism in Judaism, Christianity and Islam.* New York: Knopf, 2000

Auerbach, Ephraim. *The Sages: Their Concepts and Beliefs.* Jerusalem: Magnes Press, 1979.

Avi-Yonah, Michael. *Jerusalem the Holy City.* New York: Schoken Books, 1976.

Aviner, Shlomo. *Lemikdashcha Tov.* Jerusalem: Hava Library, 5760 - 2000 (in Hebrew).

————. *Maimonides' Laws of Messiah.* Jerusalem: Hava Library, 5763 - 2003 (in Hebrew).

———— (ed.). *Conversations of Rabbi Zvi Yehuda: The Land of Israel.* Jerusalem: Hava Library, 5765 - 2005 (in Hebrew).

———— (ed.). *Torat Eretz Yisrael: The Teachings of HaRav Tzvi Yehuda HaCohen Kook.* Jerusalem: Torat Eretz Yisrael Publications, 1991.

Avishai, Shaul. *Brit Hachashmonaim.* Thesis in partial fulfillment of the requirements for a master's degree at the Hebrew University, Jerusalem, 1993 (in Hebrew).

Bar Haim, David. "What Is the True Path?" *Yibaneh Hamkidash* 37 (5750 - 1990): 32–35 (in Hebrew).

Baron, Binyamin. *The Torah Opinion and Faith in the Sages in Haredi Thought.* Master's thesis, Hebrew University, Jerusalem, 1996 (in Hebrew).

Barr, James. *Fundamentalism.* London: SCM Press, 1981.

Bartal, Israel. "True Knowledge and Wisdom: On Orthodox Historiography." *Studies in Contemporary Jewry* 10 (1994): 178–192.

Ben Dov, Shabbtai. *Jewish Redemption in Political Crisis.* Jerusalem: Hamatmid, 5720 - 1959 (in Hebrew).

————. *Prophecy and Tradition in Redemption.* Tel-Aviv: Yair, 5739 - 1978 (in Hebrew).

Ben Horin, Michael (ed.). *Baruch Is the Man: A Memorial Book for the Holy Dr. Baruch Goldstein, May God Avenge His Blood.* Jerusalem: Medinat Yehuda, 5755 - 1995 (in Hebrew).

Berger, David. *The Rebbe, the Messiah and the Scandal of Orthodox Indifference,* London: Littman Library of Jewish Civilization, 2001.

Berkovitz, Shmuel. *The Temple Mount and the Western Wall in Israel Law.* Jerusalem: Jerusalem Institute for Israel Studies, 2001.

Blidstein, Yaakov. "The Act of Nablus: Collective Punishment and Contemporary Halachic Thought." *'Et Hada'at* A (5757 - 1997): 48–55 (in Hebrew).

————. "The Political Dimension of the Concept of the Choice of the Jewish People in the Literature of the Sages." In Shmuel Almog and Michael Hed (eds.), *The Concept of Election among the Jews and Other Nations.* Jerusalem: Shazar Center, 2001, 99–120. (in Hebrew).

Chazoni, David. "Your Plowshares into Swords: The Lost Biblical Peace." *Techelet* 3 (5758 - 1998): 78–101 (in Hebrew).

Chen, Sarina. *Central Themes in the Rhetoric's and the Practice of the Temple Admirers.* Thesis in partial fulfillment of the requirements for a master's degree at the Hebrew University, Jerusalem, 2001.

Cohen, Asher. *The Tallit and the Flag: Religious Zionism and the Vision of the Torah State in the Early Years of the State.* Jerusalem: Ben Zvi Institute, 1998 (in Hebrew).

Cohen, Yoel. "The Chief Rabbinate and the Temple Mount Question." In Itamar Warhaftig (ed.), *The Israel Chief Rabbinate—Seventy Years since Its Foundation* B. Jerusalem: Heikhal Shlomo, 5762 - 2003 (in Hebrew).

Cohen-Almagor, Raphael. "Why Incitement Should be Excluded from the Principle of Freedom of Expression." *State and Society* 3, no. 1 (2003): 561–584 (in Hebrew).

Davidson, Laurence. *Islamic Fundamentalism.* Westport: Greenwood Press, 1998.

Decision of the Committee of Yesha Rabbis, 18 Shevat 5756 (February 7, 1996) (in Hebrew).

Deshen, Shlomo. "The Emergence of the Israeli Sephardi Ultra-Orthodox Movement." *Jewish Social Studies* 11, no. 2 (2005): 77–101.

Don Yihya, Eliezer. "Stability and Change in the Camp Party: The National Religious Party and the Young Revolution." *State, Government and International Relations* 14 (5740 - 1980): 25–52 (in Hebrew).

Elboim, Avigdor [Baruch Ben Yosef]. "If at Least They Dwelt in the Land of Israel and Shouted Messiah." *Yibaneh Hamikdash* 77 (5754 - 1994): 7–8 (in Hebrew).

Elboim, Dov. "A Conversation with a Well-Known *Admor* in Bnei Brak." *Yibaneh Hamikdash* 30 (5750 - 1990): 31 (in Hebrew).

Elboim, Yosef. "Choosing a Name for Our Group." *Yibaneh Hamikdash* 2 (5748 - 1988): n.p. (in Hebrew).

———. "Renewing the Worship in This Time." *Yibaneh Hamikdash* 34 (5750 - 1990): 3–5 (in Hebrew).

———. "Understand This and We Shall Rejoice in His House." *Yibaneh Hamikdash* 51 (5752 - 1992): 31–35 (in Hebrew).

Eldad, Israel. "Some Simple Comments about Jewish Morality." *Sulam* 58 (5714 - 1954): 11–12 (in Hebrew).

———. "What Dictatorship Do We Require?" *Sulam* 27 (5712 - 1952): 5, 7 (in Hebrew).

Eliash, Shlomit. *The Exiles of the Etzel and Lechi.* Ramat Gan: Bar Ilan University, 1996 (in Hebrew).

Eliyahu, Mordechai. "The Third Temple: Of Man or of Heaven?" *Conclave for Study of the Laws of Sanctity and the Temple* (5743 - 1983): 71–76 (in Hebrew).

———. "Torah Opinion." *Techumin* 3 (5742 - 1982): 423.

Etzion, Yehuda. "And It Came to Pass after Yigal Sent His Hand against Isaac." *Labrit* 3 (5756 - 1996): 40–43 (in Hebrew).

———. "At Last to Raise the 'Flag of Jerusalem.'" *Nekudah* 93 (5745 - 1985): 22–24 (in Hebrew).

———. "From 'The Flag of Jerusalem' to 'The Movement for Redemption.'" *Nekudah* 94 (5746 - 1986): 29 (in Hebrew).

———. "More Strength to the Rabbis." *Nekudah* 188 (5756 - 1996): 50–54 (in Hebrew).

————. "Rabbi Feinstein Comes to Israel." *Nekudah* 98 (5746 - 1986): 14–15, 36 (in Hebrew).

————. *See and Renew: For the Sanctification of Israel and the Times.* Jerusalem: Self-published, 5755 - 1985. (in Hebrew).

————. *The Temple Mount.* Israel: Self-published, 5745 - 1985 (in Hebrew).

————. "This Is the Theory of Zealotry." *Nekudah* 179 (5754 - 1994): 26–30 (in Hebrew).

————. "'We Cannot Ascend and See?' We Can: Now Let's Get Moving!" *Nekudah* 134 (5750 - 1990): 34–37 (in Hebrew).

Encyclopedia Judaica, vol. 10 (1971): 977–986.

Feiga, Michael. *Two Maps of the West Bank.* Jerusalem: Magnes Library, 5763 - 2003 (in Hebrew).

Festinger, Leon, Riechen, Henry W., and Schachter, Stanley. *When Prophecy Fails.* Minneapolis: University of Minnesota Press, 1956.

Friedman, Menachem. "The Chief Rabbinate: An Unsolvable Dilemma." *Medina, Mimshal Veyachasim Beinleumi'im* 3 (1972): 118–128 (in Hebrew).

————. *The Haredi Society: Sources, Trends and Processes.* Jerusalem: Jerusalem Institute for Israel Studies, 1991 (in Hebrew).

————. "Jewish Zealots: Conservative Versus Innovative." In Laurence J. Silberstein (ed.), *Jewish Fundamentalism in Comparative Perspective: Religion, Ideology, and the Crisis of Modernity* New York: New York University Press, 1993, 148–163.

————. "Religious Zealotry in Israeli Society." In Salomon Poll and Ernest Krausz (eds.), *On Ethnic and Religious Diversity in Israel.* Ramat Gan: Bar Ilan University, 1975, 91–111.

————. *Society and Religion: Non-Zionist Orthodoxy in the Land of Israel.* Jerusalem: Yad Yitzhak Ben-Zvi, 5738 - 1978 (in Hebrew).

Funkenstein, Amos. *Maimonides: Nature, History and Messianic Beliefs.* Tel-Aviv: Modesbooks, 1997.

Garb, Yoni. "The Young Guard of the National Religious Party and the Ideological Roots of Gush Emunim." In Asher Cohen and Yisrael Harel (eds.), *Religious Zionism: The Era of Change.* Jerusalem: Bialik Institute, 2005, 171–200 (in Hebrew).

Gil, Pinchas. "Down with the Occupation!" *Yibaneh Hamikdash* 48 (5752 - 1992): 7 (in Hebrew).

Ginzburg, Yitzhak. "Baruch Is the Man." In Michael Ben Horin (ed.), *Baruch Is the Man: A Memorial Book for the Holy Dr. Baruch Goldstein, May God Avenge His Blood.* Jerusalem: Medinat Yehuda, 5755 - 1995, 19–47 (in Hebrew).

————. *The Dominion of Israel* A. Rehovot: Gal Eini, 5759 - 1999, (in Hebrew).

————. A handwritten response from June 2003.

————. *The Immediate Imperative: Root Treatment.* Rehovot: Gal Eini, 5761 - 2001 (in Hebrew).

————. "Who Holds the Key to Redemption?" *Yibaneh Hamikdash* 8 (5749 - 1989): 14–16 (in Hebrew).

Goren, Shlomo. "The Commandment to Build the Temple in the Present Time." *Iturei Kohanim* 31 (5748 - 1988): 13–21 (in Hebrew).

————. *The Temple Mount.* Tel-Aviv: Sifrei Hemed, 5752 - 1991 (in Hebrew).

Gornberg, Gershom. *The End of Days: Fundamentalism and the Struggle for the Temple Mount.* New York: Free Press, 2000.

Hacohen, Israel Meir. *Anticipation of Redemption.* Bnei Brak: Netzach, 5749 - 1989 (in Hebrew).

Halamish, Moshe. "Some Aspects of the Question regarding the Kabbalists' Attitude toward the Non-Jews." In Moshe Halamish and Assa Kasher (eds.), *Israeli Philosophy.* Tel-Aviv: Papyrus, 5743 - 1983 (in Hebrew).

————. *The Theoretical Approach of R. Schneur Zalman of Ladi and Its Relationship to Kabbalism and Early Hassidism.* Thesis in partial fulfillment of the requirements for the degree of doctor of philosophy at the Hebrew University, Jerusalem, 5736 - 1975 (in Hebrew).

Hartman, David. *Crisis and Leadership: Epistles of Maimonides.* Philadelphia: Jewish Publication Society of America 1985.

Heilman, Samuel, and Freidman, Menachem. "Religious Fundamentalism and Religious Jews: The Case of the Haredim." In Martin E. Marty and R. Scott Appleby (eds.), *Fundamentalisms Observed.* Chicago: University of Chicago Press, 1984, 197–264.

Heinemann, Josef. "The Messiah of Ephraim and the Premature Exodus of the Tribe of Ephraim." *Harvard Theological Review* 68 (1975): 1–15.

Heller, Yosef. *Lechi: Ideology and Politics.* Jerusalem: Keter, 1989 (in Hebrew).

Hirschensohn, Hayyim. *Malki Ba-Kodesh* A. St. Louise: Moinster Printing, 1919 (in Hebrew).

Horwitz, Neri, "Careful—Explosive!" *Meimad* 21 (2001): 15–18 (in Hebrew).

————. *Jews!—The Shtetl Is Burning: Torah Judaism between the 1991 Elections and the 2001 Elections.* Jerusalem: Floersheimer Public Research Institute, 2002 (in Hebrew).

"The House of Joseph." *Lehavah* 1 (5761 - 2001) (in Hebrew).

Idel, Moshe, "Patterns of Redeeming Action in Medieval Times." In Zvi Bars (ed.), *Messianism and Eschatology.* Jerusalem: Zalman Shazar Center (5744 - 1984), 253–279 (in Hebrew).

Inbari, Motti, "Fundamentalism in Crisis: The Response of the Gush Emunim Rabbinical Authorities to the Theological Dilemmas Raised by Israel's Disengagement Plan." *Journal of Church and State* 49, no. 4 (2007): 697-718.

Ivinsky, Zeev. *Lechi: The First Pliers* B. Tel-Aviv: Avraham Stern Yair, 2003 (in Hebrew)

Jacobson, Yoram. "The Visceral Soul in the Thought of Rabbi Schneur Zalman of Ladi." In Michael Oron and Amos Goldreich (eds.), *Mesuot.* Jerusalem: Bialik Institute, 5744 - 1984, 224–242 (in Hebrew).

Jolti, Bezalel. "The Prohibition on Entering the Temple Mount in These Times."
    Oral Law 10 (5728 - 1967): 39–45 (in Hebrew).

Kahane, Benjamin Zeev. "Lovers of God: Hate Evil." *Yibaneh Hamikdash* 51 (5752 -
    1992): 27–29 (in Hebrew).

——. "The Temple Mount: A Religious War." *Yibaneh Hamikdash* 45 (5751 - 1991):
    7–10 (in Hebrew).

Kaniel, Shlomo. "Hill Dwellers: Are They the Biblical Pioneers?" In Asher Cohen
    and Yisrael Harel (eds.), *Religious Zionism: The Era of Change.* Jerusalem:
    Bialik Institute, 2005, 533–558 (in Hebrew).

Karpin, Michael. *Murder in the Name of God: The Conspiracy against Yitzhak Rabin.*
    Tel-Aviv: Zemora Beitan, 1999 (in Hebrew).

Katchen, Martin H. "Who Wants Messiah Now? Pre-Millenialism and Post-
    Millenialism in Judaism." *Australian Journal of Jewish Studies* 5 (1991): 59–76.

Katz, Jacob. *Between Jews and Gentiles: The Attitude of Jews to Their Neighbors during the
    Medieval and Early Modern Period.* Jerusalem: Bialik Institute, 5737 - 1977.

——. "The Historical Figure of Rabbi Tsevi Hirsch Kalischer." *Jewish National-
    ism: Essays and Studies.* Jerusalem: Zionist Library, 5739 - 1980, 285–307
    (in Hebrew).

——. "Israel and the Messiah." *Commentary* 73 (1982): 34–41.

——. "Orthodoxy as a Response to the Departure from the Ghetto and the Re-
    form Movement." *Halacha Bametzar.* Jerusalem: Magnes, 5752 - 1992, 9–20
    (in Hebrew).

——. "Orthodoxy in Historical Perspective." *Studies in Contemporary Jewry* 2
    (1986): 3–17.

Kirsh, Yoram. "Woman Status at the Religious Zionist Society: Battles and Achieve-
    ments." In Asher Cohen and Yisrael Harekl (eds.), *Religious Zionism: The
    Era of Change.* Jerusalem: Bialik Institute, 2005, 386–421 (in Hebrew).

Klein, Menachem, "The Temple Mount: A Challenge, Threat and Promise on the
    Path to a Political Agreement." In Yitzhak Ritter (ed.). *Sovereignty of God
    and Man: Sanctity and Political Centrality on the Temple Mount.* Jerusalem:
    Jerusalem Institute of Israel Studies, 2001, 269–296. (in Hebrew).

Kook, Avraham Yitzhak. *Mishpat Cohen.* Jerusalem: Rav Kook Institute, 5745 - 1984
    (in Hebrew).

Koren, Zalman. "Memorandum concerning the Position of the Chief Rabbinate
    through the Generations on the Question of the Temple Mount." *Iturei
    Kohanim* 201 (5761 - 2000): 27–32 (in Hebrew).

Kromer, Gerald. "Praying with a Gun: Religious Motifs in the Propaganda
    of Lechi." In Chaim Genizi (ed.), *Religion and Underground: The Land of
    Israel during the Mandate Period.* Bnai Brak: Moreshet, 5755 - 1995, 65–66
    (in Hebrew).

Landes, Richard. "Millennialism in the Western World." *Encyclopedia of Millenni-
    alism and Millennial Movements.* New York: Routledge, 2000, 257–265.

Lazarus-Yafeh, Hava. "Contemporary Fundamentalism: Judaism, Christianity, Islam." In Laurence J. Silberstein (ed.), *Jewish Fundamentalism in Comparative Perspective.* New York: New York University Press, 1993, 42–55.

Levinger, Yaakov. *Between Routine and Renewal: Trends in Contemporary Jewish Philosophy.* Jerusalem: Deot, 1973 (in Hebrew).

Marty, Martin E., and Appleby, R. Scott. "Conclusion: An Interim Report on a Hypothetical Family." In Martin E. Marty and R. Scott Appleby (eds.), *Fundamentalism Observed.* Chicago: University of Chicago Press, 1991, 814–842.

Myers, Jody. *Seeking Zion: Modernity and Messianic Activism in the Writings of Tsevi Hirsch Kalischer.* Oxford: Littman Library of Jewish Civilization, 2003.

Novak, David. *The Election of Israel.* Cambridge: Cambridge University Press, 1995

Ohana, David. "Nietzsche Left and Right: The National Existentialism of Israel Eldad." In Yaacov Golomb (ed.), *Nietzsche in Hebrew Culture.* Jerusalem: Magnes Press, 5762 - 2002, 251–277 (in Hebrew).

Ramon, Amnon. *The Attitude of the State of Israel and the Different Sections of the Jewish Public to the Temple Mount (1967–1996).* Jerusalem: Jerusalem Institute of Israel Studies, 1997 (in Hebrew).

———. "Beyond the Western Wall: The Attitude to the Temple Mount on the Part of the State of Israel and Sectors of the Jewish Public (1967–1999)." In Yitzhak Ritter (ed.), *Sovereignty of God and Man: Sanctity and Political Centrality on the Temple Mount.* Jerusalem: Jerusalem Institute of Israel Studies, 2001, 113–142 (in Hebrew).

Ravitzky, Aviezer. "'Forcing the End': Zionism and the State of Israel as Antimessianic Undertakings." *Studies in Contemporary Jewry* 7 (1991): 34–67.

———. *Messianism, Zionism, and Jewish Religious Radicalism.* Chicago: University of Chicago Press, 1993.

———. "Models of Peace in Jewish Thought." *With God's Knowledge: Studies in the History of Jewish Thought.* Jerusalem: Keter, 1991, 13–33 (in Hebrew).

———. "The Roots of Kahanism: Consciousness and Political Reality." *Jerusalem Quarterly* 39 (1986): 90–108

Raz Karkotzkin, Amnon, "Between 'Brit Shalom' and the Temple: The Dialectics of Redemption and Messianism following Gershom Scholem." *Theory and Criticism* 20 (2002): 87–112 (in Hebrew).

Rudik, Yochai. *Land of Redemption.* Jerusalem: The Institute for the Study of the Thought of Rabbi A. Y. H. Kook Zatza"l, 5749 - 1989 (in Hebrew).

Sagiv, Tuvya. "The Place Is in the South." *Techumin* 14 (5754 - 1984): 437–472 (in Hebrew).

Scholem, Gershom. "The Crisis of Tradition in Jewish Messianism." *The Messianic Idea in Judaism.* New York: Shocken Books, 1971, 49–77.

———. *Devarim Bego.* Tel-Aviv: Am Oved, 1976 (in Hebrew).

Schwartz, Dov. *Challenge and Crisis in the Circle of Rabbi Kook.* Tel-Aviv: Am Oved, 2001.

———. *Faith at a Crossroads: A Theological Profile of Religious Zionism.* Leiden: Brill, 2002.

———. *The Land of Reality and Imagination: The Status of the Land of Israel in Religious Zionist Thought.* Tel-Aviv: Am Oved, 1997 (in Hebrew).

———. *The Messianic Idea in Jewish Medieval Literature.* Ramat Gan: Bar Ilan University Press, 1997 (in Hebrew).

———.. *Religious Zionism between Reality and Messianism.* Tel-Aviv: Am Oved, 1999 (in Hebrew).

Schweid, Eliezer. *Between Orthodoxy and Religious Humanism.* Jerusalem: Van Leer Institute Publications, 1977 (in Hebrew).

"The Second Annual Conference of Temple Supporters." Tishrei 5760 - 2000 (in Hebrew).

Segal, Elitzur. "Looking for the Way." *Yibaneh Hamikdash* 51 (5752 - 1992): 30–31 (in Hebrew).

———. "The Path of the Movement for the Establishment of the Temple." *Yibaneh Hamikdash* 27 (5750 - 1990): 35 (in Hebrew).

———. "Sovereignty on the Temple Mount." *Yibaneh Hamikdash* 5 (5748 - 1998): 5–6 (in Hebrew).

———. "The Temple and Pikuah Nefesh." *Yibaneh Hamikdash* 7 (5748 - 1988): 2–5 (in Hebrew).

Segal, Haggai. *Dear Brothers: The West Bank Jewish Underground.* New York: Beit-Shamai Publications, 1988.

———. *Yamit, The End: The Struggle to Stop the Withdrawal from Sinai.* Jerusalem: Beit El Library, 5759 - 1999 (in Hebrew).

Shafir, David. "Guardians of the City or Destroyers of the City." *Yibaneh Hamikdash* 7 (5748 - 1988): 8 (in Hebrew).

———. "Sanctifying the Name Is Greater than Desecrating the Name." *Yibaneh Hamikdash* 48 (5752 - 1992): 8–11 (in Hebrew).

Shafir, William. "Jewish Messianism Lubavitch-Style: An Interim Report." *Jewish Journal of Sociology* 35 (1993): 115–128.

Shalev, Mordechai. "Beyond Humanism." *Sulam* 35 (5712 - 1952): 6–9 (in Hebrew).

Shapira, Anita. "Zionism and Political Messianism." *Walking toward the Horizon.* Tel-Aviv: Am Oved, 1988, 11–22 (in Hebrew).

Shapiro, Yitzhak, and Peli, Yosef. *To the Hill of the Levonah: In Favor of Ascending the Temple Mount and Demanding the Temple.* Yitzhar: Self-published, 5759 - 1999 (in Hebrew).

———. *To the Mount of Myrrh.* Yitzhar: El Har Hamor, 5757 - 1997 (in Hebrew).

Shaviv, Yehuda. "The Commandments of Guarding the Temple." *Zefiyah* 4 (5754 - 1994): 11–28 (in Hebrew).

———. "The Double Destruction." *Nekudah* 173 (5744 - 1984): 29 (in Hebrew).

Shaviv, Yehuda, and Israel Rosen, (eds.). *Come and Let Us Ascend: A Collection of Articles and Manifestos on the Subject of the Temple Mount in Modern Times.* Gush Etzion: Zomet, 5763 - 2003 (in Hebrew).

Sheffer, Shaul. *The Temple Mount: Crown of Our Glory.* Jerusalem: Yefe Nof, 5729 - 1968 (in Hebrew).

Shochetman, Eliav. "A Jewish Regime Cannot Be a 'Persecutor.'" *Techumin* 19 (5759 - 1999): 40–48 (in Hebrew).

Shragai, Nadav. *Mount of Dispute.* Jerusalem: Keter, 1995 (in Hebrew).

Shragai, Shlomo Zalman. "Rabbi Avraham Hacohen Kook, Zatsa"l, on the Restitution of the Place of Our Temple to the People of Israel." *Sinai* 85 (5739 - 1978): 193–198 (in Hebrew).

Silber, Michael. "The Beating Jewish Heart in a Foreign Land." *Cathedra* 73 (1994): 84–105 (in Hebrew).

Sprinzak, Ehud. *The Ascendance of Israel's Radical Right.* New York: Oxford University Press, 1991.

———. *Between Extra-Parliamentary Protest and Terror: Political Violence in Israel.* Jerusalem: Jerusalem Institute for Israel Studies, 1995 (in Hebrew).

———. *Brother against Brother: Violence and Extremism in Israeli Politics from Altalena to the Rabin Assassination.* New York: Free Press, 1999

Sternhal, Ze'ev, Sznajder, Mario, and Asheri, Michal. *The Foundations of Fascism.* Tel-Aviv: Am Oved, 1992 (in Hebrew).

Stone, John. *Expecting Armageddon: Essential Readings in Failed Prophecy.* London: Routledge, 2000.

Talmon, Jacob L. *The Myth of the Nation and the Vision of Revolution.* London: Secker and Warburg; and Berkeley and Los Angeles: University of California Press, 1981.

———. *The Origins of Totalitarian Democracy.* London: Secker and Warburg, 1955.

Talmon, Yonina. "Millenarian Movements." *Archives européennes de sociologie* (1966), 156–200.

Weiler, Gershon. *Jewish Theocracy.* Tel-Aviv: Am Oved, 1976 (in Hebrew).

Weiss, Hillel. *The King's Path.* Tel-Aviv: Ariel Institute, 5763 - 2003 (in Hebrew).

Weiss, Joseph. "A Late Jewish Utopia of Religious Freedom." *Studies in Eastern European Jewish Mysticism.* New York: Oxford University Press, 1985, 209–248.

Weissbord, Lilly. "Gush Emunim Ideology: From Religious Doctrine to Political Action." *Middle Eastern Studies* 18, no. 3 (1982): 265–275.

Wessinger, Catherine. *How the Millennium Comes Violently: From Jonestown to Heaven's Gate.* New York: SevenBridge Press, 2000.

Wistrich, Robert. "In the Footsteps of the Messiah." In Gideon Shimoni and Robert Wistrich (ed.), *Theodor Herzl, Visionary of the Jewish State.* Jerusalem: Hebrew University and Magnes Press, 1999, 231–238.

Yuval, Israel. "Revenge and Curse, Blood and Libel." *Zion* 58 (5753 - 1993): 33–90 (in Hebrew).

Zohar, David. *Jewish Commitment in a Modern World: R. Hayyim Hirschensohn and His Attitude towards Modernity.* Jerusalem: Shalom Hartman Institute, 2003 (in Hebrew).

Newspapers

Basheva

Ha'aretz

Hamodia

Hatzofe

Iated Hashavua

Kol Hair

Nekudah

Jewish Week

Newsletters

Beit Yosef Lehava 2001

Drishat Hamikdash 2003–2004

El Rosh Hahar 1984–1985

Gevinei Kruz: The Mouthpiece of the Movement for the Establishment of the Temple 2001–2004

Kol Ne'emanei Har Habayit 1987–1998

Lechatchilah 1997–2005

Lehavah 2001–2002

Ma'ayanei Hayeshu'ah 2005

Me'at Min Ha'or 2001, 2005

Prophecy for His Dwelling-Places 2003–2004

Organ of the Yesha Rabbis 1994, 2002–2005

The Voice of the Temple Mount 2000–2004

What's New in the Temple Institute 1992–2000

Rabbinical Journals

Going Up in Sanctity: A Journal for Matters of the Temple and Its Sanctities, vols. 1–8 2000–2003

Iturei Kohanim 1984–2004

Labrit 1993, 1996

Techumin 1980–2004

Yibaneh Hamikdash 1987–2005

Leaflets

Announcement of the Committee of Yesha Rabbis 1992.
Decision of the Committee of Yesha Rabbis 1996.
The Second Annual Conference of Temple Supporters 2000.
The Temple Mount Faithful
Woman of the Temple 2001.

Web Sites

www.hahmakom.org.il
www.inn.co.il
www.ittn.org
www.manhigut.org.il
www.mof.gov.il
www.moriya.org.il
www.pnimi.org.il
www.templeinstitute.org
www.templemountfaithful.org
www.tkuma.org.il/hhb.html222.3rd-temple-builders.com

Interviews

Baruch Ben-Yossef, May 24, 2001.
Joel Lerner, September 2, 2004
Yossef Elboim, September 2, 2004

Index

207